Heading outdoors eventually leads within.

The first people on Earth were hikers and campers. So today, when we walk the land and bed down on it, we're living in the most primitive, elemental way known to our species. We're returning to a way of life intrinsic to the human experience. We're shedding the burden of millennia of civilization. We're seeking catharsis. We're inviting enlightenment.

hikingcamping.com publishes unique guidebooks – literate, entertaining, opinionated – that ensure you make the most of your precious time outdoors. Our titles cover spectacular wildlands in western North America.

nomads@hikingcamping.com   hiking camping.com

Copyright © 2013 by Kathy and Craig Copeland
All Rights Reserved
1st edition June 2002, 2nd edition August 2005
3rd edition May 2008, 4th edition July 2013

Photographs by the authors
Production and maps by C.J. Poznansky,
  giddyupgraphics@mac.com
Cover and interior design by Matthew Clark,
  www.subplot.com
Printed in China by Asia Pacific Offset

Published in Canada by hikingcamping.com, inc.
P.O. Box 8563, Canmore, Alberta T1W 2V3 Canada
fax: 1.866.431.3894 email: nomads@hikingcamping.com

Library and Archives Canada Cataloguing in Publication

Copeland, Kathy, 1959-
  Where locals hike in the Canadian Rockies: the premier trails in
Kananaskis Country, near Canmore & Calgary / boot-tested and written
by Kathy & Craig Copeland. — 4th ed., July 2013

Includes index.   ISBN 978-1-927462-01-0

  1. Hiking—Alberta—Kananaskis Country—Guidebooks. 2. Trails—
Alberta—Kananaskis Country—Guidebooks. 3. Kananaskis Country
(Alta.)—Guidebooks. I. Copeland, Craig, 1955- II. Title.

GV199.44.C22K36 2013   796.522097123'32   C2013-901000-9

Front cover photo: The Royal Group, from Northover Ridge (Trip 24)

Back cover photos, from top to bottom: Three Isle Lake (Trip 23), Ascending above
Guinn's Pass (Trip 18), Bighorn sheep, Glacier lily, Elbow River meadows (Trip 27)

Contents

Introduction
North America's Preeminent Alps 3

Map Kananaskis Country. 5

Trips at a Glance 6

Kananaskis 4 / Land of Many Uses 4 / Canadian Rockies Weather 4 / Frontcountry Camping 8 / Backcountry Camping 9 / Leave Your Itinerary 9 / Physical Capability 11 / Distances and Elevations 11 / Maps 11 / Carry a Compass 12 / Wildflower Hikes 13 / Children's Hikes 14 / Rainy-Day Hikes 14 / Wilderness Ethics 15 / Hiking with Your Dog 18 / Wildlife 19 / Bears 20 / Know Before You Go 22

Dayhikes & Backpack Trips 23

Shoulder-Season Trips 207

Information Sources 287

Your Guides 288

Other Titles from hikingcamping.com. 290

Your Trip. 295

Index 298

Northover Ridge (Trip 24)

Mount Kidd, above Kananaskis River, from Highway 40

North America's Preeminent Alps

The Brewster tour buses go to Banff National Park. The ten-year-old Subarus go to Kananaskis Country. But the mountains themselves, regardless of geopolitical distinctions, are all part of the same range. Welcome to the Canadian Rockies, North America's preeminent alps.

Hikers and climbers in Calgary and Canmore cherish their big backyard. They call it *K-Country*. Those living elsewhere remain unaware of it. Confession: we were among them.

We first hiked in the Canadian Rocky Mountain national parks while travelling from the U.S. during the late 1980s. We were astounded. Though we'd previously hiked much of the world's vertical topography, here we felt like pious peasants stumbling upon Chartre Cathedral. We were compelled to immigrate.

The first several years we lived in Calgary, however, our intent to explore the national parks was so fundamentalist that we largely ignored K-Country. Friends said we were crazy to spend every weekend driving to Banff, Kootenay, Yoho and Jasper national parks. We thought they were lazy, settling for K-Country because it was close.

Not until after the publication of *Don't Waste Your Time®️ in the Canadian Rockies*, our hiking guidebook on the national parks, did we turn our attention to K-Country. Again we were astounded. And this time, chagrined as well.

Like the rest of the Canadian Rockies, the mountains of K-Country are among our planet's most scenically captivating. Its foothills afford splendid shoulder-season hiking as early as May and as late as November. On summer weekends, locals flock to a few popular K-Country trails, but elsewhere you won't encounter hordes like those that unceasingly throng Banff's Lake Louise and Moraine Lake.

Every trail in this book leads to sensational scenery. The rapture you'll experience on these hikes trivializes the effort you'll expend. The drama usually unfolds soon: the rewards generously dispensed well before arrival at the destination. You'll be inspired by immense forests, piercing peaks, tumbling glaciers, sheer cliffs, rowdy creeks, sprawling meadows, psychedelic wildflowers. Awaiting you are climactic vistas with startling impact.

You now hold in your hands the key to K-Country's superlative dayhikes and backpack trips. We never intended this to be an encyclopedically exhaustive volume. Books that detail every wretched, obscure scratch in the dirt overburden and confuse the vast majority of hikers, therefore failing to guide them. By definition, a *guide*book should winnow and recommend, sparing the reader unnecessary, tedious decision-making. It should also be eloquent. Guidebooks have languished too long as a knuckle-dragging subspecies of literature. So our goal was to write a superior primer—accurate of course, but also lucid, as well as entertaining—that most local or visiting hikers would find helpful and enjoyable.

What's not in this book? Punishing, dreary, sketchy trips, mostly. Their appeal is limited to inveterate explorers and intrepid mountaineers. The average hiker would find these journeys frustrating, disappointing, or overwhelming. We've also omitted several trails in southern K-Country that are lacklustre compared to those we did include. Presenting inferior options would be to advocate hiking exclusively in K-Country, which is ridiculous when just up the highway are dozens more premier trails in the same mountain range, albeit in the national parks.

Now you can quickly, easily choose a K-Country hike, confident each one in this book offers a fulfilling experience. Most of the trails are well constructed and maintained. A few are rougher—unmaintained routes, bootbeaten paths—but lead to especially gratifying destinations. Our precise *By Vehicle* and *On Foot* directions, and the maps accompanying each trip, ensure you'll find your way without difficulty.

We hope *Where Locals Hike* compels you to get outdoors more often and stay out longer. Do it to cultivate your wild self. It will give you perspective. Do it because the backcountry teaches simplicity and self-reliance—qualities that make life more fulfilling. Do it to remind yourself why wilderness needs and deserves your protection. A deeper conservation ethic develops naturally in the mountains. And do it to escape the cacophony that muffles the quiet, pure voice within.

Kananaskis

Kin-e-ah-kis was a legendary Indian who survived an axe-blow to the head. The name *Kin-e-ah-kis* was anglicized to *Kananaskis*. Captain John Palliser, leader of a British scientific expedition in the mid-1800s, bestowed the name on a river and two passes in the heart of this region: the Kananaskis River, as well as North and South Kananaskis passes. Later, the name was given to Upper and Lower Kananaskis lakes.

Land of Many Uses

K-Country is not one big park. It's a recreation area comprising several provincial parks and protected areas. It has a multiple-use policy that extends far beyond hiking. Restricted but permissible activities include mountain biking, horseback riding, fishing, hunting, snowmobiling, power boating, OHV driving, logging, oil and gas exploration, hydro-electric power generation, free-range cattle grazing, and the operation of a golf resort. Most of these activities are severely limited. Some are confined to specific, small, remote areas.

Canadian Rockies Weather

Start building your shrine to placate the weather gods. Summer in the Canadian Rockies is woefully short.

Mid-July through mid-October is prime hiking season here. That's when alpine trails are likely to be snow-free. But don't count on more than two-and-a-half months of pleasant, high-country conditions. Passes can be snow-covered into July. Snowfall is possible on any day, and likely at higher elevations after August.

Our 19 shoulder-season trips enable you to hike as early as May, as late as November. These trails are snow-free sooner and longer than others, because they're at lower elevations and have ample sun exposure. (see page 8)

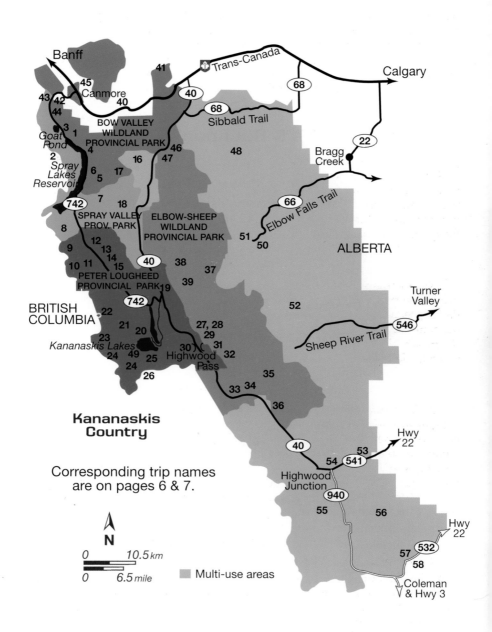

Banff

45
Canmore
43 42
44
40
Goat 3 1
Pond
4
2
Spray
Lakes
Reservoir
6 5
17

742
7 18
SPRAY VALLEY
PROV. PARK
8

9
12
13
10 11 14
15
PETER LOUGHEED
PROVINCIAL PARK 19

742

BRITISH
COLUMBIA 22
21 20
23
Kananaskis Lakes
24 49 25
24
26

41

Trans-Canada

40

68

68

Sibbald Trail

BOW VALLEY
WILDLAND
PROVINCIAL PARK
46
16 47
48

ELBOW-SHEEP
WILDLAND
PROVINCIAL PARK

40 38
39

37

51
50

Calgary

22

Bragg
Creek

66

Elbow Falls Trail

ALBERTA

Turner
Valley

52

546

Sheep River Trail

27, 28
29
30 31
Highwood 32
Pass

35
33 34
36

**Kananaskis
Country**

Corresponding trip names
are on pages 6 & 7.

N

0   10.5 km

0   6.5 mile

Multi-use areas

Hwy
22

40
54 541
Highwood
Junction

940

55

56

53

57 532
58

Hwy
22

Coleman
& Hwy 3

> ## Trips at a Glance
> *Trips in each category are listed according to geographic location: starting in the north and moving roughly from west to east, then south. After the trip name, the round-trip distance is listed, followed by the elevation gain.*

Dayhikes & Backpack Trips

#	Name	Distance			Elevation gain	
1	Middle Sister	19 km	(11.8 mi)	/	1419 m	(4654 ft)
2	Old Goat Glacier	10.5 km	(6.5 mi)	/	620 m	(2034 ft)
3	Three Sisters Pass	6 km	(3.7 mi)	/	595 m	(1952 ft)
4	West Wind Pass	4.2 km	(2.6 mi)	/	378 m	(1240 ft)
5	Sparrowhawk Tarns	10 km	(6.2 mi)	/	680 m	(2230 ft)
6	Read's Tower	9.1 km	(5.6 mi)	/	1125 m	(3590 ft)
7	Buller Passes	13.2 km	(8.2 mi)	/	670 m	(2198 ft)
8	Tent Ridge	10.6 km	(6.6 mi)	/	780 m	(2560 ft)
9	Birdwood Traverse	17.5 km	(10.9 mi)	/	710 m	(2330 ft)
10	Burstall Pass	15 km	(9.3 mi)	/	480 m	(1574 ft)
11	French & Robertson Glaciers	14 km	(8.7 mi)	/	740 m	(2427 ft)
12	Rummel Lake	8.6 km	(5.3 mi)	/	355 m	(1164 ft)
13	Chester Lake	9 km	(5.6 mi)	/	315 m	(1030 ft)
	Three Lakes Valley	13.5 km	(7.4 mi)	/	555 m	(1820 ft)
14	Headwall Lakes	14 km	(8.7 mi)	/	430 m	(1410 ft)
15	James Walker Basins	15.8 km	(9.8 mi)	/	600 m	(1968 ft)
16	Mt. Allan	14.6 km	(9 mi)	/	1313 m	(4307 ft)
17	Memorial Lakes	16 km	(10 mi)	/	759 m	(2490 ft)
18	Galatea Lakes	17 km	(10.5 mi)	/	670 m	(2198 ft)
	Guinn's Pass	16 km	(10 mi)	/	870 m	(2854 ft)
19	King Creek Ridge	7 km	(4.3 mi)	/	729 m	(2390 ft)
20	Mt. Indefatigable	7.6 km	(4.7 mi)	/	920 m	(3018 ft)
21	Invincible Lake	14 km	(8.7 mi)	/	635 m	(2082 ft)
22	North Kananaskis Pass	34.4 km	(21.3 mi)	/	660 m	(2165 ft)
23	South Kananaskis Pass	24.8 km	(15.4 mi)	/	610 m	(2000 ft)
24	Northover Ridge	33.7 km	(20.9 mi)	/	1180 m	(3870 ft)
25	Rawson Lake	7.8 km	(4.8 mi)	/	300 m	(984 ft)
26	Elk Lakes / Petain Basin	29.4 km	(18.2 mi)	/	846 m	(2775 ft)
27	Elbow Lake / Piper Pass	19.2 km	(11.9 mi)	/	617 m	(2024 ft)
28	Tombstone Lakes	22.1 km	(13.7 mi)	/	545 m	(1988 ft)
29	Rae Lake	17.2 km	(10.7 mi)	/	432 m	(1417 ft)
30	Pocaterra Ridge	9.3 km	(5.8 mi)	/	550 m	(1804 ft)

31	Ptarmigan Cirque	4.5 km	(2.8 mi)	/	214 m	(702 ft)
32	Little Arethusa	5.4 km	(3.3 mi)	/	559 m	(1832 ft)
33	Mt. Lipsett	12 km	(7.4 mi)	/	705 m	(2312 ft)
34	Mist Mountain	11 km	(6.8 mi)	/	1263 m	(4143 ft)
35	Mist Ridge	23 km	(14.3 mi)	/	1058 m	(3470 ft)
36	Picklejar Lakes	9 km	(5.6 mi)	/	474 m	(1555 ft)
37	Talus Lake	30.8 km	(19.1 mi)	/	612 m	(2008 ft)
38	Paradise Pass	38.2 km	(23.8 mi)	/	994 m	(3260 ft)
39	West Fork Little Elbow R.	42.8 km	(26.5 mi)	/	1197 m	(3927 ft)

Shoulder-Season Dayhikes

40	Grotto Canyon	6 km	(3.7 mi)	/	235 m	(771 ft)
41	Mt. Yamnuska	9.8 km	(6.1 mi)	/	875 m	(2870 ft)
42	Grassi Lakes	3.8 km	(2.4 mi)	/	155 m	(508 ft)
43	Mt. Rundle, South Summit	5.2 km	(3.2 mi)	/	852 m	(2795 ft)
44	Ha Ling Peak	5.4 km	(3.3 mi)	/	741 m	(2476 ft)
45	Mt. Lady Macdonald	6.6 km	(4.1 mi)	/	917 m	(3008 ft)
46	Wasootch Ridge	11 km	(6.8 mi)	/	1010 m	(3315 ft)
47	Old Baldy Ridge	16 km	(10 mi)	/	854 m	(2802 ft)
48	Jumpingpound Ridge	17 km	(10.5 mi)	/	640 m	(2100 ft)
49	Upper Kananaskis Lake	14.9 km	(9.2 mi)	/	negligible	
50	Forgetmenot Ridge	14 km	(8.7 mi)	/	715 m	(2345 ft)
51	Nihahi Ridge	10 km	(6.2 mi)	/	735 m	(2410 ft)
52	Mt. Ware	17.4 km	(10.8 mi)	/	524 m	(1719 ft)
53	Bull Creek Hills	15 km	(9.3 mi)	/	719 m	(2358 ft)
54	Junction Hill	8.5 km	(5.3 mi)	/	797 m	(2614 ft)
55	Raspberry Ridge	9 km	(5.6 mi)	/	653 m	(2142 ft)
56	Mt. Burke	16 km	(10 mi)	/	935 m	(3067 ft)
57	Hailstone Butte	4 km	(2.5 mi)	/	327 m	(1073 ft)
58	Windy Peak Hills	9 km	(5.6 mi)	/	500 m	(1640 ft)

3155-m (10,350-ft) Mt. Smith-Dorrien,
from Sawmill trailhead

For weather forecasts and trail-condition reports, contact the Barrier Lake, Peter Lougheed Provincial Park, or Elbow Valley visitor information centres. They're listed in the back of this book, under *Info Sources*.

Regardless of the forecast, always be prepared for heavy rain, harsh wind, plummeting temperatures, sleet, hail: the whole miserable gamut. Likewise, allow for the possibility of searing sun and soaring temperatures. The weather can change dramatically, with alarming speed. Though the sky is clear at dawn, it might be filled with ominous black clouds by afternoon. Storms can dissipate equally fast.

Statistics indicate that, throughout the Canadian Rockies, you can expect a third of summer days to be rainy. The average monthly maximum and minimum temperatures reveal the following. In June, highs along the Front Range (the eastern edge of the Rockies) reach about 20° C (67° F), and the lows stay just above freezing. July is usually the hottest month. August can be almost as hot as July but generally isn't. September tends to be slightly warmer than May. Summer highs in the Rockies average 24° C (75° F), lows average 7° C (45° F). By September, highs in the Rockies are about 17° C (65° F), while the lows hover just above freezing.

Many hikers say fall is their favourite time in the Rockies. Bugs are absent, crowds diminish, larch trees are golden. But the shorter days restrict dayhiking, and the colder nights make backpacking less comfortable. We prefer the long days and warm nights of mid-summer.

Frontcountry Camping

K-Country has numerous, vehicle-accessible campgrounds. Visit www.albertaparks.ca for details. Find out when and how to reserve campsites by visiting www.reserve.albertaparks.ca or phoning 1-877-537-2757. Visit www.mountkiddrv.com or phone (403) 591-7700 for information about the privately-owned Mt. Kidd RV Park near Ribbon Creek.

Backcountry Camping

To stay overnight in a provincial-park backcountry campground, you need a permit. The per-person, per-night permit fee applies to anyone age 16 or older. You'll also have to pay a reservation fee if you book in advance. If you plan your entire summer's backpack trips and book them all at the same time, you'll pay the reservation fee only once. You can reserve up to a year in advance. All the sites at provincial-park backcountry campgrounds are reservable. So think of reservations as a necessary form of trip insurance.

To purchase your permit via phone and credit card, and receive it via email or fax, call (403) 678-3136. (You can reach this number toll-free by first dialing 310-0000, if calling from within Alberta.) Need to change or cancel your reservation? They'll ding you for another reservation fee, but they'll refund your permit fee. You can also obtain a permit in person at the Barrier Lake, Peter Lougheed Provincial Park, and Elbow Valley visitor information centres.

Random camping ("free" or "wild" camping) is prohibited in provincial parks. But it is permitted in most wildland provincial parks and public land-use zones, provided you adhere to leave-no-trace practices, pitch your tent at least 50 m (55 yd) off trail, and at least 1 km (0.6 mi) from any road, any provincial-park boundary, or any provincial-recreation-area boundary. Before undertaking a backpack trip that involves random camping, phone one of the visitor information centres, explain your plans, and ask their advice.

Leave Your Itinerary

Even if you're hiking in a group, and especially if you're going solo, it's prudent to leave your itinerary in writing with someone reliable. Agree on precisely when they should alert the authorities if you have not returned or called. Be sure to follow through. Forgetting to tell your contact person that you've safely completed your trip would result in an unnecessary, possibly expensive search. You might be billed for it. And a rescue team could risk their lives trying to find you.

James Walker Creek Basins (Trip 13)

Petain Basin (Trip 26)

Physical Capability

Until you gain experience judging your physical capability and that of your companions, these guidelines might be helpful.

Anything longer than an 11-km (7-mi) round-trip dayhike can be very taxing for someone who doesn't hike regularly. A 425-m (1400-ft) elevation gain in that distance is challenging but possible for anyone in average physical condition. Very fit hikers are comfortable hiking 18 km (11 mi) or more and gaining 1200-plus meters (3936-plus feet) in a single day.

Backpacking 18 km (11 mi) in two days is a reasonable goal for most beginners. Hikers who backpack a couple times a season can enjoyably manage 27 km (17 mi) in two days. Avid backpackers should find 38 km (24 mi) in two days no problem. On three- to five-day trips, a typical backpacker prefers not to push beyond 16 km (10 mi) a day. Remember: it's always safer to underestimate your limits.

Distances and Elevations

There is no definitive source for accurate trail distances and elevations in K-Country. Maps, brochures, and trail signs sometimes state conflicting figures. But the discrepancies are usually small. And most hikers don't care whether a trail is 8.7 km (5.4 mi) or 9 km (5.6 mi), or an ascent is 715 m (2345 ft) or 720 m (2362 ft). Still, we made a supreme effort to be accurate when calculating distances and elevations for this book.

Maps

The maps in this book are for general orientation only. Our *On Foot* directions, however, are detailed and precise, written in a way that should help you visualize the terrain. Yet we do recommend topographical maps, for several reasons:

(1) On a long, rough hike, a topo map makes it even easier to follow our directions. (2) A topo map is safety equipment, because it can help ensure you don't get lost. (3) If the terrain through which you're hiking intrigues you, a topo map can contribute to a more fulfilling experience. (4) After reaching a high vantage, a topo map enables you to interpret the scenery.

The Surveys & Mapping Branch of the Department of Energy, Mines and Resources (DEMR) publishes 1:50 000 topo maps covering the province. They're sold at outdoor shops and bookstores. These maps can be frustrating, however, because DEMR doesn't update all the information, such as trail locations. Narrower, less popular trails are not always indicated, though the trails themselves are distinct on the ground. DEMR maps are also expensive, and you might need more than one for a long trip. Yet DEMR maps provide excellent topographic detail. A few trips in this book are covered only on DEMR maps, in which case we've listed the applicable DEMR map in the stats box.

Gem Trek publishes several K-Country topo maps. Most of the trips in this book are covered on Gem Trek maps. The title of the applicable Gem Trek map is listed in the stats box for each trip. These maps have contour

Basin beneath Mt. Bogart (Trip 5)

intervals of 25 or 40 meters. They indicate trails, state distances, and are thoroughly updated regularly. They're the most helpful maps for hikers. Buying one Gem Trek map saves you the expense of several DEMR maps. They're sold at www.gemtrek.com, outdoor shops, and bookstores.

Carry a Compass

Left and *right* are relative. Any hiking guidebook relying solely on these inadequate and potentially misleading terms should be shredded and dropped into a recycling bin. You'll find all the *On Foot* descriptions in this book include frequent compass directions. That's the simplest, reliable means of guiding hikers.

What about GPS? It might be invaluable if you're trekking cross-country (off trail), long distance. But most hikers generally find a map and compass totally adequate for navigation. Following our detailed directions while hiking the trails in this book, you won't need a GPS unit.

Keep in mind, the compass directions provided in this book are of use only if you're carrying a compass. Granted, our route descriptions are so detailed, you'll rarely have to check your compass. But bring one anyway, just in case. A compass is required hiking equipment—anytime, anywhere, regardless of your level of experience, or your familiarity with the terrain.

Clip your compass to the shoulder strap of your pack, so you can glance at it quickly and easily. Even if you never have to rely on your compass, occasionally checking it will strengthen your sense of direction—an enjoyable, helpful, and conceivably life-saving asset.

Remember that our stated compass directions are always in reference to true north, which slowly changes. (Visit http://geomag.nrcan.gc.ca/calc/mdcal-eng.php to calculate the current declination). In K-Country, as of the summer of 2013, true north is approximately 15° left of (counterclockwise from) magnetic north. If that puzzles you, read your compass owner's manual.

Wildflower Hikes

You might see wildflowers as early as mid-May in lower elevation, front-range meadows, such as on Jumpingpound Ridge (Trip 48) and the Windy Peak Hills (Trip 58).

In higher, front-range meadows, such as on Old Baldy Ridge (Trip 47), wildflowers usually blossom by mid-June.

Between early July and early August, you'll likely see more wildflowers on these hikes than you will elsewhere:

- Sparrowhawk Tarns (Trip 5)
- Burstall Pass (Trip 10)
- Galatea Lakes / Guinn's Pass (Trip 18)
- Ptarmigan Cirque (Trip 31)
- Mist Ridge (Trip 35)
- Paradise Pass (Trip 38)
- Forgetmenot Ridge (Trip 50)
- Windy Peak Hills (Trip 58)

photos: *1 Forgetmenot 2 Orchid 3 False dandelion 4 Moss campion*

Elbow Lake (Trip 27)

Children's Hikes

Your hikers-in-training should find these trails, or initial sections of trails, manageable and enjoyable:

- **Old Goat Glacier (Trip 2)** Let the little ones lead you to where the trail crosses the creek. Turn around there, before the steep ascent.

- **French & Robertson Glaciers (Trip 11)** Push the kids in a sturdy stroller to 3 km (1.9 mi). Walk with them from there, ascending left, soon reaching a stream and rock wall.

- **Galatea Lakes (Trip 18)** Between the trailhead and 2.6 km (1.6 mi), the trail crosses the creek seven times on stout bridges.

- **Elbow Lake (Trip 27)** The ascent to the lake is steep but short enough that many parents manage to herd kids. The lakeside campground makes this the easiest, K-Country option for backpacking with children. After wandering around the pretty lake, venture into meadows beyond.

- **Ptarmigan Cirque (Trip 31)** Starting near Highwood Pass—the highest point in Canada accessible by public road—this short trail launches into the alpine zone where, in season, wildflowers are rife.

- **Grotto Canyon (Trip 40)** A short, seemingly level, very kid-friendly outing into an intriguing, narrow defile.

- **Grassi Lakes (Trip 42)** Creeklets, streams, cascades, teal lakes, and Bow Valley views, all within a short distance. But only tough tykes will vanquish the ascent without hitching a ride on dad's shoulders.

- **Upper Kananaskis Lake (Trip 49)** Reverse our directions. Start at the Upper Lake day-use area and hike generally NW to the North Interlakes day-use area. This section of the trail hugs the shore, granting opportunities for water's edge play. It seems the kids will complete the 2.8 km (1.7 mi) between parking lots? One parent can dash back, drive the car around, and pick up the tribe at trail's end.

- **Windy Peak Hills (Trip 58)** Even those with attention spans as short as their legs should be able to reach the second bump. The challenge might be the 1 ¼ -hour drive from SW Calgary to the trailhead.

Rainy-Day Hikes

Though it's possible to hike most trails in a rainstorm, the peaks you came to see will likely be shrouded. Above treeline, you risk death by thunderbolt. But with the right attitude, on certain trails, a rainy-day hike is a revelation.

Mist cloaking mountains creates a mysterious atmosphere. New waterfalls appear, ever-present ones swell. Forest understory brightens, and the fragrance is headier. When sunlight bursts through tattered clouds, or a rainbow arches suddenly overhead, it's rousing.

So don't sit out the storm: hike it out. The lake trails below are good choices for a little wet-weather exercise. You'll be sheltered by forest most of the way. Even when the peaks above are invisible, the lakes themselves are beautiful.

- Chester Lake (Trip 13)
- Galatea Lakes (Trip 18)
- Rawson Lake (Trip 25)
- Elbow Lake (Trip 27)
- Grassi Lakes (Trip 42)
- Upper Kananaskis Lake (Trip 49)

Wilderness Ethics

We hope you're already conscientious about respecting nature and other people. If not, here's how to pay off some of your karmic debt load:

Let wildflowers live. They blossom for only a few fleeting weeks. Uprooting them doesn't enhance your enjoyment, and it prevents others from seeing them at all. We once heard parents urge a string of children to pick as many different-coloured flowers as they could find. Great. Teach kids to entertain themselves by destroying nature, so the world continues marching toward environmental collapse.

Three Isle Lake (Trip 23)

Give the critters a break. The wilderness isn't a zoo. The animals are wild. Recognize that this is their home, and you are an uninvited guest. Behave accordingly. Allow all of them plenty of space. Most are remarkably tolerant of people, but approaching them to take a photograph is harassment and can be dangerous. Some elk, for example, appear docile but can severely injure you. Approaching any bear is suicidal. Read our *Bears* section.

Stay on the trail. Shortcutting causes erosion. It doesn't save time on steep ascents, because you'll soon be slowing to catch your breath. On a steep descent, it increases the likelihood of injury. When hiking cross-country in a group, soften your impact by spreading out.

Roam meadows with your eyes, not your boots. Again, stay on the trail. If it's braided, follow the main path. When you're compelled to take a photo among wildflowers, try to walk on rocks.

Leave no trace. Be aware of your impact. Travel lightly on the land. At campgrounds, limit your activity to areas already denuded. After a rest stop, and especially after camping, take a few minutes to look for and obscure any evidence of your stay. Restore the area to its natural state.

When you think *camp*, don't assume *fire*. Campfires at backcountry campgrounds are a luxury, not a necessity. Down jackets and fleece pants trump campfires. If you indulge in a campfire, build it only in the fire pit provided, and keep the fire small. Don't plan to cook over a fire; it's inefficient and wasteful. If you pack food that requires cooking, bring a stove. Garbage with metal or plastic content will not burn; pack it all out. Limit your wood gathering to deadfall about the size of your forearm. Wood that requires effort (breaking, chopping, dragging) is part of the scenery; let it be. Before leaving your fire, douse it with water until there are no glowing embers. Remember that untended, unextinguished campfires are the prime cause of forest fires.

Be quiet at backcountry campgrounds. Noise is pollution. Silence is a key reward most of us expect in return for the time and effort we invest in backpacking. If you're loud—shouting, guffawing—you're polluting the wilderness and denying others the reward they've earned. Talk in the hushed tone appropriate for a cathedral, because that's where you are.

Pack out everything you bring. Don't drop a scrap of trash anywhere. None of us should ever have to see tissues, candy wrappers, nut shells, or cigarette butts in the backcountry. Are fruit peels trash? Yes. They take years to decompose, and wild animals won't eat them. If you bring fruit on your hike, you're responsible for the peels. And don't just pack out *your* trash. Leave nothing behind, whether you brought it or not. Keep a small, plastic bag handy, so cleaning up after yourself and others is easy.

Poop without impact. Use the outhouses at trailheads and backcountry campgrounds whenever possible. Don't count on them being stocked with toilet paper; always pack your own in a plastic bag. If you know there's a campground ahead, try to wait until you get there.

In the wilds, choose a site at least 60 m (66 yd) from trails and water sources. Ground that receives sunlight part of the day is best. Use a trowel to dig a small cat hole—10 to 20 cm (4 to 8 in) deep, 10 to 15 cm (4 to 6 in) wide—in soft, dark, biologically active soil. Afterward, throw a handful of

Ribbon Lake, from Guinn's Pass (Trip 18)

dirt into the hole, stir with a stick to speed decomposition, replace your diggings, then camouflage the site. Pack out used toilet paper in a plastic bag. You can drop the paper (not the plastic) in the next outhouse you pass. Always clean your hands with a sanitizer, like *Purell*. Sold in pharmacies, it comes in small bottles ideal for hikers.

Urinate off trail, well away from water sources and tentsites. The salt in urine attracts animals. They'll defoliate urine-soaked vegetation, so aim for dirt or pine needles.

Keep streams and lakes pristine. When brushing your teeth or washing dishes, do it well away from water sources and tentsites. Use only biodegradable soap. Carry water far enough so the wastewater will percolate through soil and break down without directly polluting the wilderness water. Scatter waste water widely. Even biodegradable soap is a pollutant; keep it out of streams and lakes. On short backpack trips, you shouldn't need to wash clothes or yourself. If necessary, rinse your clothes or splash yourself off—without soap.

Respect the reverie of other hikers. On busy trails, it's not necessary to communicate with everyone you pass. Most of us are seeking solitude, not a soiree. A simple greeting is sufficient to convey goodwill. Obviously, only you can judge what's appropriate at the time. But it's usually presumptuous and annoying to blurt out advice without being asked. "Boy, have you got a long way to go." "The views are much better up there." "Be careful, it gets rougher." If anyone wants to know, they'll ask. Some people are sly. They start by asking where you're going, so they can tell you all about it. Offer unsolicited information only to warn other hikers about conditions ahead that could seriously affect their trip.

Hiking With Your Dog

"Can I bring Max, my Pomeranian?"

Yes. Dogs are currently allowed throughout K-Country—in day-use areas, frontcountry campgrounds, backcountry campgrounds, and on backcountry trails—but must be leashed at all times. Please confirm this, however, at any of the visitor information centres. They're listed in the back of this book, under *Info Sources*.

Bringing your dog, however, isn't simply a matter of "Can I?" Ask yourself, "Should I?"

Consider safety. Dogs infuriate bears and are thus a danger to themselves, their owners and other hikers. If a dog runs off, it might reel a bear back with it.

Consider the environment. Many dog owners blithely allow their pets to foul trails and campgrounds. Are you certain Maxie's not infected with, thus spreading, giardia? Every time he poops, will you dispose of it properly?

Consider the rest of us. Most dog owners believe their pets are angelic, but other hikers rarely agree. A curious dog, even if friendly, can be a nuisance. A barking dog is irksome. A person continually yelling unheeded commands at a disobedient dog is infuriating, because it amounts to *two* annoying animals, not just one. An untrained dog, despite the owner's hearty reassurance that "he won't hurt you," can be frightening.

This isn't a request to leave your dog at home. We've backpacked with friends whose dogs we enjoyed immensely. This is a plea to see your dog objectively.

Wildlife

It's possible to see all kinds of animals—big and small—throughout the Canadian Rockies. Deer, chipmunks, squirrels, raccoons, skunks, bats and owls, you might expect. But also be on the lookout for eagles, elk, mountain goats, bighorn sheep, moose, coyotes, black bears and grizzlies. In the evening, watch for porcupines waddling out of the forest and beavers cruising ponds. Pikas and marmots are a common sight in alpine scree and talus. It's a rare and fortunate hiker who glimpses a wolf, wolverine, or cougar.

photos: *1 Elk 2 Mountain goat 3 Moose*

Bears

Bears are rarely a problem in the Canadian Rockies. But oblivious hikers can endanger themselves, other people, and the bears. If you're prepared for a bear encounter and know how to prevent one, you can hike confidently, secure in the understanding that bears pose little threat.

Grizzly bear

Only about 50 grizzly bears roam K-Country. There are many more black bears here, but no study has accurately estimated the number. You're more likely to see a bear while driving Hwy 40 than while hiking most backcountry trails. The visitor information centres (listed in the back of this book, under *Info Sources*) post trail reports that include bear warnings and closures. Check these before your trip; adjust your plans accordingly.

Black Bear

Grizzlies bears and black bears can be difficult to tell apart—even for an experienced observer. Both species range in colour from nearly white to cinnamon to black. Full-grown grizzlies are much bigger, but a young grizzly can resemble an adult black bear, so size is not a good indicator.

The most obvious differences are that grizzlies have a dished face; a big, muscular shoulder hump; and long, curved front claws. Blacks have a Roman nose; no hump; and shorter, less visible front claws. Grizzlies are potentially more dangerous than black bears, although a black bear sow with cubs can be just as aggressive. Be wary of all bears.

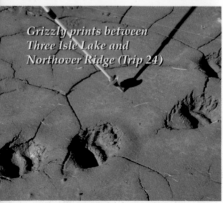

Grizzly prints between Three Isle Lake and Northover Ridge (Trip 24)

Any bear might attack when surprised. If you're hiking, and forest or brush limits your visibility, you can prevent surprising a bear by making noise. Bears hear about as well as humans. Most are as anxious to avoid an encounter as you are. If you warn them of your presence before they see you, they'll usually clear out. So use the most effective noisemaker: your voice. Shout loudly. Keep it up. Don't be embarrassed. Be safe. Yell louder near streams, so your voice carries over the competing noise. Sound off more frequently when hiking into the wind. That's when bears are least able to hear or smell you coming. To learn more, visit hikingcamping.com and download the *Bears Beware!* MP3.

Bears' strongest sense is smell. They can detect an animal carcass several kilometers (miles) away. So keep your pack, tent and campsite odor-free. Double or triple-wrap all your food in plastic bags. Avoid smelly foods, especially meat and fish. On short backpack trips, consider eating only fresh foods that require no cooking or cleanup. If you cook, do it as far as possible from where you'll be sleeping. Never cook in or near your tent; the fabric might retain odor. Use as few pots and dishes as you can get by with. Be fastidious when you wash them.

At night, store all your food, trash, and anything else that smells (cooking gear, sunscreen, bug repellent, toothpaste) out of bears' reach. Use the bear-proof food storage (metal lockers, or poles with cables) provided at backcountry campgrounds. Failure to properly store your food at night is to invite bears into your campsite, greatly increasing the chance of a dangerous encounter. And bears are smart. They quickly learn to associate a particular place, or people in general, with an easy meal. They become habituated and lose their fear of humans. A habituated bear is a menace to any hiker within its range.

If you see a bear, don't look it in the eyes; it might think you're challenging it. Never run. Initially be still. If you must move, do it in slow motion. Bears are more likely to attack if you flee, and they're fast, much faster than humans. A grizzly can outsprint a racehorse. And it's a myth that bears can't run downhill. They're also strong swimmers. Despite their ungainly appearance, they're excellent climbers too.

Climbing a tree, however, can be an option for escaping an aggressive bear. Some people have saved their lives this way. Others have been caught in the process. To be out of reach of an adult bear, you must climb at least 10 meters (33 feet) very quickly, something few people are capable of. It's generally best to avoid provoking an attack by staying calm, initially standing your ground, making soothing sounds to convey a nonthreatening presence, then retreating slowly.

What should you do when a bear charges? If you're certain it's a lone black bear—not a sow with cubs, not a grizzly—fighting back might be effective. If it's a grizzly, and contact seems imminent, lie face down, with your legs apart and your hands clasped behind your neck. This is safer than the fetal position, which used to be recommended, because it makes it harder for the bear to flip you over. If you play dead, a grizzly is likely to break off the attack once it feels you're no longer a threat. Don't move until you're sure the bear has left the area, then slowly, quietly, get up and walk away. Keep moving, but don't run.

Arm yourself with pepper spray as a last line of defense. It's sold at outdoor stores. Keep it in a holster—on your hip belt or shoulder strap—where you can grab it fast. Cayenne pepper, highly irritating to a bear's sensitive nose, is the active ingredient. Without causing permanent injury, it disables the bear long enough to let you escape. Many people have successfully used it to turn back charging bears.

Research presented to more than 300 bear experts at the 4th International Human-Bear Conflict Workshop, in Missoula, Montana, suggests pepper spray is more effective than firearms at stopping a bear attack. The combined results from two studies are convincing: 98% of people who used pepper spray to stop charging bears walked away from their encounters unharmed, and none of the people or bears died. 56% of people who used firearms to stop charging bears were injured, and 61% of the bears died.

Vigilance and noise making, however, should ensure you never encounter a bear at close range, thus never have to so much as unholster your pepper spray. Do so only if you really think your life is at risk, at which point the bear is at risk as well. A bear confronted by a human being is at one of the most precarious, dangerous moments of its life.

Any time bears act aggressively, they're following their natural instinct for self preservation. Often they're protecting their cubs or a food source. Yet if they maul a hiker, they're likely to be killed, or captured and moved, by wildlife management officers. So when you go hiking in the Canadian Rockies, you're accepting responsibility for the protection of these magnificent creatures.

Merrily disregarding bears is foolish and unsafe. Worrying about them is miserable and unnecessary. Everyone occasionally feels afraid when venturing deep into the mountains, but knowledge and awareness can quell fear of bears. Just take the necessary precautions and remain guardedly alert. Experiencing the grandeur of mountain wilderness is certainly worth risking the remote possibility of a bear encounter.

Know Before You Go

Bearanoia is pandemic, hence the detailed, at-your-fingertips, bear-safety suggestions above. The other threats to your well-being in the backcountry aren't necessarily less serious, but you're probably less concerned about them. So we've addressed them on our website rather than here in the book. For helpful information about cougars, ticks, lightning, and hypothermia, visit hikingcamping.com. In the home-page menu, click on "Free." Under "Free Articles," click on "Know Before You Go."

photos: **1** *Below James Walker Creek basins (Trip 15)* **2** *On Mt. Yamnuska (Trip 41)* **3** *Guinn's Pass (Trip 18)* **4** *Elbow River Valley (Trip 27)* **5** *Tombstone Lake (Trip 28)*

Dayhikes and Backpack Trips

TRIP 1
Middle Sister

LOCATION	Bow Valley Wildland Provincial Park immediately SE of Canmore
ROUND TRIP	19 km (11.8 mi)
ELEVATION GAIN	1419 m (4654 ft)
KEY ELEVATIONS	trailhead 1350 m (4428 ft), summit 2769 m (9085 ft)
HIKING TIME	6 to 8 hours
DIFFICULTY	challenging
MAPS	Gem Trek *Best of Canmore* Gem Trek *Canmore and Kananaskis Village*

Opinion

Like satellite dishes precisely positioned for optimal reception, Canmore's posh chalets are aimed at the Three Sisters, so the image of this striking trinity comes beaming in through their cathedral windows. And all the outdoor athletes in this mountain-mad town have clambered atop the sisters. Little Sis is a climb. Big Sis is a moderate scramble. Middle Sis is a hike.

But "hike" doesn't mean easy. You'll trudge the length of a violently-gouged canyon, boulder-hop through a bleak basin, then slog across talus and scree to the summit, which lacks a full panorama because the dominant sibling obscures the western horizon. You'll ascend a cartilage-crunching 1419 m (4654 ft) in the process—mostly on a route, mind you, not a trail. You'll probably be chipping away at this chore, up and back, for at least six hours. And the exploit begins and ends with a half-hour road-walk.

So it's not a premier trip. It's a worthwhile trip to a Bow Valley icon. We've included it in this book, despite the poor effort/reward ratio, because the central sister is a magnetic destination. Her popularity, however, is due only to her membership in the celebrated sorority, her showy visage, and her convenient location on the edge of Canmore.

You're going anyway? Then go for the going's sake. Challenging workouts can be fun if challenge itself is the prize. You can earn a powerful sense of athletic accomplishment here. The terrain you'll traverse—Stewart Creek canyon and basin—is not classically beautiful, but it is feral, gnarly, turbulent, which can stimulate an active mind. It's like picking your way through the debris of a recent cataclysm: neither soothing nor boring.

Because this is a route, be more attentive than you would on a trail. Watch for the sporadic cairns, so you'll stay oriented. Guard against ankle injury by using trekking poles. Stay hydrated by carrying at least three litres

photos: **1** *Canmore and the Bow Valley, from summit of Middle Sister* **2** *Summit of Middle Sister is upper right* **3** *Summiting Middle Sister* **4** *Upper reaches of Stewart Creek basin* **5** *Middle Sister left, Big Sister right, above Cougar Creek neighbourhood*

of water per person. Stewart Creek is feeble and unreliable up-canyon. You'll find no water in the basin above.

Fact

By Vehicle

In **Canmore**, drive W on Main (8th) Street. Turn left (S) onto 8th Avenue. Follow it over the Bow River bridge. At the T-junction, turn left onto Three Sisters Drive. Ascend, bearing left (S) where Smith-Dorrien / Spray Trail (Hwy 742) forks right. At the four-way intersection turn left (E) onto Three Sisters Parkway. Reach a stop sign at the next four-way intersection. Reset your trip odometer to 0 here and proceed straight (SE).

From the Three Sisters Parkway overpass spanning the **Trans-Canada** (Hwy 1), drive uphill (SW) to a stop sign at a four-way intersection. Reset your trip odometer to 0 here, turn left and proceed SE.

From **either approach**, enter a roundabout at 0.6 km (0.4 mi). Right leads to the golf course, left leads to condos. Proceed straight (SE) through the roundabout. The road is currently blocked at 1.1 km (0.7 mi). Turn around here and park well off the road (either side), at 1350 m (4428 ft).

Because the location of the vehicle barrier has shifted, and might again, the starting point for our *On Foot* distances is where pavement ends.

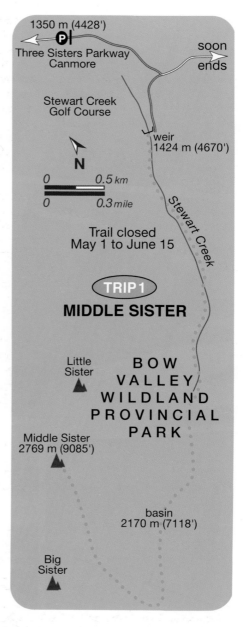

1350 m (4428')

Three Sisters Parkway
Canmore

soon
ends

Stewart Creek
Golf Course

weir
1424 m (4670')

N

0   0.5 km

0   0.3 mile

Trail closed
May 1 to June 15

TRIP 1

MIDDLE SISTER

Little
Sister

**BOW
VALLEY
WILDLAND
PROVINCIAL
PARK**

Middle Sister
2769 m (9085')

basin
2170 m (7118')

Big
Sister

Stewart Creek

On Foot

Follow the **unpaved road** ESE. Little Sister is visible right (SW). Your immediate goal, the mouth of Stewart Creek canyon, is visible right (SSE). Ignore any spurs. Stay on the main road, curving right (SSE).

Reach a **fork** at 1.7 km (1.1 mi). The main road continues left (ESE). Turn right (W) onto the smaller road (chained to prevent vehicle traffic). Just beyond the chain, ignore a right (N) spur. Continue the gentle ascent W.

After passing right and left spurs, the road curves left (SSW). You're entering **Stewart Creek canyon**. Reach **road's end** at 2.3 km (1.4 mi), 1424 m (4670 ft), on the E bank of **Stewart Creek**. If you cycled here, stash and lock your bike, because the terrain ahead resembles what you see upstream: a jumbled chaos of boulders and trees.

Continue by crossing to the creek's far (W) bank. It's easy if the two planks are still in place atop the weir that partially obstructs the creek. Once across, follow a bootbeaten path NW up to a **former road**, then turn left (S) and follow the road SSW.

In about ten minutes, re-cross to the creek's left (E) bank, rejoin the former road, and continue upstream (S). About 15 minutes farther, reach a fork. Right (SW) descends to the creek. Go left (S) and ascend.

Up-canyon, follow sections of bootbeaten route and the occasional cairn. Your mission: head generally SW by keeping to Stewart Creek's **main ravine**. Most of the year, the creek is dry in its upper reaches, so it poses no obstacle. Ignore a tributary drainage (left / S) and later a talus-filled gully (right / NW).

Where the main ravine deepens, the hike becomes more challenging. Steep, narrow paths skirt the roughest, rockiest sections. But it's also possible to scramble directly through the **bedrock dryfalls**. Whichever feels most comfortable for you is the way forward. If you're unable to either negotiate or bypass the dryfalls… checkmate. Game over. Thanks for coming out to play. Time to the return to the trailhead.

Eventually the gap between Little and Middle sisters is visible right (NW). Be aware that's not your goal. Your ascent route is farther: between Middle and Big Sister.

Above the bedrock dryfalls, follow the obvious, comfortable route bootbeaten into scree on the ravine's left (SE) bank. It soon switchbacks, vaulting you above the ravine near where it pinches out at 2170 m (7118 ft). You've entered a broad, desolate **basin**, brimming with industrial-size talus.

Middle Sister is right (N) above you, about one hour distant. You'll reach it from left (S) to right (N) via the escarpment ahead (W). Ascend the talus. Aim for where you can easily surmount the **escarpment**. You'll soon see a distinct, bootbeaten route funneling hikers upward. Follow it.

Tan scree is visible on the summit ridge (NNE). The route climbs to that scree. A rapidly improving view of the peaky horizon is your motivation. Step onto the 2769-m (9085-ft) summit of **Middle Sister** at 9.5 km (5.9 mi). Moderately strong hikers will arrive within 3½ hours of departing the trailhead and will need about 2½ hours for the return trip.

Little Sister is nearby (NE). Beyond it, across the Bow Valley, is the Fairholme Range. Big Sister is also nearby (SW). Mount Lawrence Grassi is NW. Mt. Lougheed is SE. Numerous other peaks are visible and, with map in hand, easy to identify.

TRIP 2
Old Goat Glacier

LOCATION	Spray Valley Provincial Park
	Hwy 742, near N end Spray Lakes Reservoir
ROUND TRIP	10.5 km (6.5 mi)
ELEVATION GAIN	620 m (2034 ft)
KEY ELEVATIONS	trailhead 1720 m (5640 ft)
	end of moraine 2340 m (7675 ft)
HIKING TIME	3 to 3½ hours
DIFFICULTY	moderate
MAP	Gem Trek *Canmore and Kananaskis Village*

Opinion

Glaciers are like dull, rusty knives. They don't merely slice the earth's skin. They rip it, tear it, hack it, leaving a gash as appalling as any flesh wound. Exploring these gaping lacerations is fascinating. This one, the hanging canyon gouged by Old Goat Glacier, is little known and seldom visited. Yet you can hike there and back in just three hours. And the trailhead is only a 20-minute drive from Canmore.

The climactic sight on this gratifying excursion is the canyon's southwest wall, which is also the northeast face of 3110-m (10,200-ft) Old Goat Mtn, highest peak in the Goat Range. The lengthy, soaring, vertical wall is much more impressive than Old Goat Glacier, which is now a tiny remnant of the implacable force that long ago slashed open the canyon.

The hike, entirely on an adequate trail, is rewarding from the start. The short, forested approach is mostly creekside. You'll soon burst into a basin beneath an imposing headwall. Then you'll ascend a steep talus slope, enjoying rapidly expanding views of Spray Lakes Reservoir and the Three Sisters massif (Trip 1). Once you surpass the trees and enter the canyon, the crest of a moraine offers a gentle ascent probing the realm of rock and ancient ice.

Before scampering up Mount Rundle's south summit (Trip 43), Ha Ling Peak (Trip 44), or Mt. Lady Macdonald (Trip 45), Canmore's three most popular hiking destinations, ask yourself: "Would I prefer solitude today?" If your answer is "yes," you're much more likely to find it in Old Goat Glacier canyon.

Fact

By Vehicle

In Canmore, drive W on Main (8th) Street. Turn left onto 8th Avenue. Follow it over the Bow River bridge. At the T-junction, turn left onto Three Sisters Drive. Ascend, soon forking right onto Smith-Dorrien / Spray Trail

(Hwy 742). Pass the Canmore Nordic Centre and reset your trip odometer to 0. Pavement ends at 1.2 km (0.7 mi). The road levels in Whiteman's Gap then descends S. At 10.2 km (6.3 mi) cross the bridge over the Goat Pond outlet canal. At 13.6 km (8.4 mi) pass the ranger station. Slow down. At 13.8 km (8.6 mi) pass a sign for Spray Lake West. Turn right 100 m (110 yd) farther and proceed across the dam. At 14.5 km (9 mi) turn left and follow the west-shore road past numerous campsites. At 15.8 km (9.9 mi)—just before a culvert and directly across the road from campsites 16 and 17—turn right (W) into a small clearing. At the entrance is a sign indicating that fires and camping are prohibited. There's room for two vehicles in the clearing. A third vehicle could park just past the entrance, on the right, before the culvert. The elevation here is 1720 m (5640 ft).

On Foot

Follow the trail into the forest, along the creek's right (NW) bank. Head upstream, SSW. In two minutes, ignore a right fork; bear left on the main trail beside the creek. Within ten minutes, the striking wall of Old Goat Mtn is visible ahead.

About 20 minutes from the trailhead, the ascent route is in view SSW. It's between the prow of a cliff (left), and the forested headwall (right). You'll ascend the talus slope just left of the forest, ultimately gaining the canyon now hidden by the prow.

The grade is negligible for about 35 to 40 minutes, until a moderate ascent begins at 1845 m (6052 ft). Soon reach a creek and **avalanche run-out** beneath the headwall. The run-out might be snow-covered through July, but that shouldn't impede your progress. Angle left (S) and hop the creek. A path bootbeaten through the alders will be evident if enough snow has melted. Cairns and bits of flagging might also mark the way.

Beyond the run-out, look for a cairn at the base of the **steep slope** ahead. Close inspection will reveal that a discernible, bootbeaten, cairned path continues upward—just left of the forest, just right of the giant boulders. It initially climbs SE. Thanks to this path, the ascent is surprisingly merciful.

At 2060 m (6757 ft), about an hour from the trailhead, a big, **solitary spruce tree** with draping branches offers a respite from sun or rain. The path continues on the grass-and-dirt margin between rock and trees. Behind you, Spray Lakes Reservoir is visible. Beyond and above it looms the Three Sisters massif (Trip 1). Another ten minutes of anti-gravity effort will bring you to the edge of the glacier-gouged hanging **canyon** bound by 700-m (2296-ft) walls.

The path, ascending gently now, continues SSE beside a cordon of trees on a grassy ramp. Here you can begin to appreciate

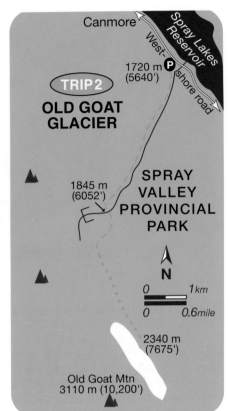

the long, towering, sheer face of **Old Goat Mtn**, on the far side of the canyon. A rainstorm will set off a dozen cascades in the mountain's natural spillways. Old Goat's 3110-m (10,200-ft) summit, however, is never visible from within the canyon. To see it all, ascend Read's Tower (Trip 6), on the east side of Spray Lakes Reservoir.

The ramp ends within eight minutes, at 4.8 km (3 mi), 2300 m (7544 ft). But the path resumes atop the nearby **moraine**. Angle right, drop into the shallow gully (snow filled into July), then gain the crest of the moraine. Proceed SSE.

About seven minutes farther, the moraine widens and is nearly level. It's a good place to lounge while you survey the surrounding desolation and try to fathom how the diminutive **Old Goat Glacier** once had the crushing mass to grind this canyon into existence. Beyond, the moraine crest narrows again but affords another 15 minutes of easy hiking deeper into the canyon.

TRIP 3
Three Sisters Pass

LOCATION	Bow Valley Wildland Provincial Park
	Hwy 742, N of Spray Valley Reservoir
ROUND TRIP	6 km (3.7 mi)
ELEVATION GAIN	595 m (1952 ft)
KEY ELEVATIONS	trailhead 1670 m (5478 ft), pass 2265 m (7429 ft)
HIKING TIME	2½ to 3½ hours
DIFFICULTY	moderate
MAP	Gem Trek *Canmore and Kananaskis Village*

Opinion

Any sunny weekend, spring through fall, it's possible to arrive at the Goat Creek trailhead (launch pad for Ha Ling Peak, Trip 44) and find the parking lot so full you can only squeeze in a motorcycle. There might be 100 hikers on the peak, giving it an irksome, ant-farm atmosphere.

It was precisely such a day that we drove a few minutes farther down the road to the Three Sisters Pass trailhead and discovered… nobody. We hiked in solitude.

Triple Sis Pass lacks Ha Ling's popularity not because it's scenically inferior or markedly more difficult, but simply because it's not a peak.

Ha Ling is to Canmore what the Grouse Grind is to Vancouver: de rigueur. The pass near the three siblings? Obscure.

That's the first of this trip's many shining attractions: You might have it all to yourself. You almost certainly will not feel oppressed by a crowd.

Shining attraction #2: The bootbeaten route climbs through a relatively narrow drainage that briefly constricts to a sharp-walled gorge then continues up a canyon. In early summer, a snowmelt stream careens down the canyon, then cascades through the gorge. You'll hike beside this stream most of the way. The sight and sound of it are refreshing.

Shining attraction #3: The straight-shot ascent through the gorge and canyon is beautiful. It's rough for only about ten minutes, when bypassing the gorge. Otherwise the grade is merely steep, and the rocky terrain is exciting. Above the gorge, you're out of the trees most of the way, so you'll see it all.

Shining attraction #4: The pass is an impressive vantage. The far (east) side is nearly vertical, so it grants an aerial perspective of Canmore, the Bow Valley, and the Fairholme Range beyond. The iconic Three Sisters peaks are nearby. Big Sister looms directly above the pass.

Just one caution: Don't hike here in summer. The stream diminishes by then and can vanish in fall. It's a waste to devote a full summer day to such a short hike. And all that rock creates a natural oven that, on a hot day, will

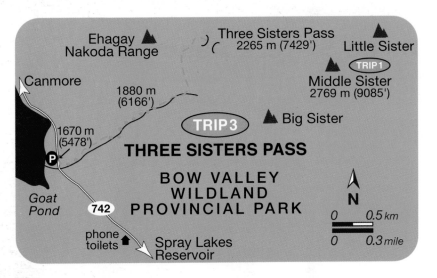

Ehagay
Nakoda Range

Three Sisters Pass
2265 m (7429')

Little Sister

TRIP 1

Middle Sister
2769 m (9085')

Canmore

1880 m
(6166')

TRIP 3

Big Sister

1670 m
(5478')

THREE SISTERS PASS

P

BOW VALLEY
WILDLAND
PROVINCIAL PARK

N

Goat
Pond

742

0   0.5 km
0   0.3 mile

phone
toilets

Spray Lakes
Reservoir

bake your enchilada. So schedule Three Sisters Pass for late spring or early summer, when the stream is rollicking.

Fact

Before your trip

Three Sisters Pass is on a helicopter flight path. Flights are always possible. But the regular shuttles between Canmore and Mt. Assiniboine Lodge are on Wednesdays, Fridays, and Sundays. If you avoid hiking here on those days, uninterrupted silence is likely.

By Vehicle

In **Canmore**, drive W on Main (8th) Street. Turn left onto 8th Avenue. Follow it over the Bow River bridge. At the T-junction, turn left onto Three Sisters Drive. Ascend, soon forking right onto Smith-Dorrien / Spray Trail (Hwy 742). Pass the Canmore Nordic Centre and reset your trip odometer to 0. Pavement ends at 1.2 km (0.7 mi). After crossing Whiteman's Gap, proceed generally SE to 11.8 km (7.3 mi).

From the **junction of Hwy 40 and Kananaskis Lakes** Trail (50 km / 31 mi S of Trans-Canada Hwy 1, or 17 km / 10.5 mi N of Highwood Pass), turn SW onto Kananaskis Lakes Trail. Reset your trip odometer to 0. At 2.2 km (1.4 mi) turn right (NW) onto unpaved Smith-Dorrien / Spray Trail (Hwy 742). Continue to 51.4 km (31.9 mi).

For **either approach**, park in the small pullout on the W side of the road, at 1670 m (5478 ft). It's 1.5 km (0.9 mi) N of the toilets and telephone near the N end of Spray Lakes Reservoir.

photos: *1 Approaching Big Sister, from Three Sisters Pass 2 Canmore and Fairholme Range, from Three Sisters Pass*

1

2

The gorge above the bypass route

On Foot

From the pullout, walk the road S about 90 m (98 yd). Turn left into the broad, dry, rocky **drainage**. Follow it NE about 120 m (130 yd) to where a cairn (left / NW) indicates a narrow **path**. It exits the drainage, rises onto the dryas-covered bank, and enters forest. Paralleling the drainage, the path leads generally NE.

At 1773 m (5815 ft), about 15 minutes from the trailhead, begin ascending. Two minutes farther, drop 1.5 m (5 ft) to continue on the path. At 1828 m (5996 ft), about 30 minutes along, pass a slabby, **tributary drainage** (right / SE).

The main drainage soon narrows into a sharp, bedrock **gorge**. In early summer, a cascade fills the gorge, but by fall it might be dry. At the bottom of this gorge, rockhop across the stream, then bypass the gorge via the narrow, rough, bootbeaten route ascending steeply on the right (SE) wall.

The **bypass route** climbs among tight trees. In about ten minutes, it drops left, onto bedrock at the **top of the gorge**, at 1880 m (6166 ft). Proceed up-canyon by re-crossing to the left (N) side of the stream.

A cairned path—bootbeaten into talus, scree and dirt—makes the rest of the ascent straightforward. Ahead, the path briefly crosses to the right (S) side of the stream, then resumes on the left (N) side.

At 2135 m (7003 ft), about 1¼ hours from the trailhead, the path veers left (N) into **forest** and steepens. It exits the trees just shy of your destination. Crest **Three Sisters Pass** at 3 km (1.9 mi), 2265 m (7429 ft).

Big Sister soars to 2936 m (9630 ft) from the right (SE) edge of the pass. Middle Sister (Trip 1) is directly E. Little Sister is ENE. Canmore is NNE. Beyond the town, the Fairholme Range creates the Bow Valley's far wall. Above you, NNW, is the Ehagay Nakoda Range—the massif comprising

Up-canyon, en route to the pass

2545-m (8348-ft) Mt. Lawrence Grassi, and Ha Ling Peak (Trip 44). SW is the Spray Valley, from which you ascended.

Returning from the pass, sure-footed hikers reach the top of the gorge in 30 minutes. Look left for the cairn indicated where the bypass route ascends into the trees on the SE wall. It takes about ten minutes to descend the bypass route. Maintain a swift pace and you'll intersect the road, near the trailhead, about one hour after departing the pass.

TRIP 4
West Wind Pass / Windtower

LOCATION	Spray Valley Provincial Park
	Hwy 742, NE shore Spray Lakes Reservoir
ROUND TRIP	4.2 km (2.6 mi) to pass, plus 5.6 km (3.4 mi) to tower
ELEVATION GAIN	378 m (1240 ft) to pass, plus 610 m (2000 ft) to tower
KEY ELEVATIONS	trailhead 1707 m (5600 ft), pass 2085 m (6841 ft)
	tower 2695 m (8842 ft)
HIKING TIME	1¼ to 1¾ hours for pass
	plus 2¾ to 3¾ hours for tower
DIFFICULTY	easy to pass, moderate to tower
MAP	Gem Trek *Canmore and Kananaskis Village*

Opinion

Most of us have no idea where the heck we are. If we walked beyond sight of familiar features, we'd become disoriented and would soon be lost.

We don't know where nearby rivers come from, or where they flow to. What's over the next hill? Well, uh, hmmm, we're really not quite sure. If asked to describe what's visible from the nearest mountaintop, we'd be flummoxed.

We're ignorant of geography because it seems irrelevant. Who cares about geography when 99% of our travel is in automobiles, perhaps GPS equipped, on paved roads bristling with directional signs? Getting lost is unlikely, a momentary frustration at worst.

For most of human history, however, we either walked or rode horses, and to do either without meeting our demise required us to be keenly aware of our location, our destination, and what lay between. Geographic knowledge was mission critical.

Prior to books and maps, that knowledge was sometimes passed along in conversation, but often we had to earn it by climbing high, peering in all directions, and memorizing what we saw as if our lives depended on it—because they did.

Mountain passes and peaks afforded opportunities to gain invaluable insight. Today, the value of that insight has diminished, but gaining it can still be intriguing, challenging, gratifying, and just plain fun.

Plus it acquaints you with some astounding people: relatives of yours. The strongest and bravest of your ancestors. The ones who sought vantage points so their genes might live on in you.

The Canadian Rockies offer countless places to ascend in their footsteps. One of the most convenient and scenically rewarding is also among the easiest: the trail to West Wind Pass and the route continuing up Windtower.

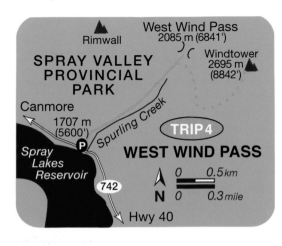

West Wind Pass
2085 m (6841')

Rimwall

Windtower
2695 m
(8842')

SPRAY VALLEY PROVINCIAL PARK

Canmore
1707 m
(5600')

Spray Lakes Reservoir

Spurling Creek

TRIP 4

WEST WIND PASS

0   0.5 km

N   0   0.3 mile

742

Hwy 40

Swift hikers can reach the pass, fully appreciate the expansive view, and return to the trailhead within two hours. The trail climbs aggressively but rewards quickly and generously.

Broad, grassy, West Wind Pass invites you to lie about, gazing at sights near and far, below and above. The northeast side of the pass is sheer, granting an aerial view of Wind Ridge, Wind Valley, and the Bow Valley. Turn around, and you'll see most of the Spray Valley. Look up and there's Rimwall and Windtower.

Many hikers imagine themselves quickly dispatching the remaining ascent to the tower. Then they roll over and resume their idle reverie at the pass. But if you're fit and capable, jump up and press on, because you will dispatch it quickly. You'll be in open, subalpine terrain, clambering over

Descending from West Wind Pass to Spray Lakes Reservoir

ledges, striding along benches, admiring distant peaks. After surmounting treeline, you'll tweak the nose of mighty Mt. Lougheed, then—ta da!—step onto the summit of Windtower.

The panorama includes Canmore, the Bow Valley beyond, and all the mountains on both sides. And if the wind isn't molesting you, it's possible to linger long up here, because the descent can take as little as 1½ hours: one hour back to West Wind Pass, then 30 minutes down to the trailhead.

Fact

Before your trip

Though the trail to West Wind Pass is usually snow-free by mid-April, it's closed when bighorn sheep are lambing: April 1 through June 15. This closure also helps prevent hikers from encountering the grizzlies that frequent the area during the birthing season.

If you intend to summit Windtower, pause before departing the trailhead. You'll save time and energy later by orienting yourself now. West Wind Pass is left (NE), hidden in forest. Mt. Lougheed is right (E). Windtower is between them. Beneath the tower and the mountain, notice how the upper edge of the treeline appears to form an arc.

At the apex of that arc—right of the rockbands, beneath Lougheed's left shoulder—you can see the bootbeaten route ascending into the scree. If you prefer to hike rather than scramble, *that's* how far right (S) you must traverse from the pass before making any significant elevation gain to Windtower.

By Vehicle

In Canmore, drive W on Main (8th) Street. Turn left onto 8th Avenue. Follow it over the Bow River bridge. At the T-junction, turn left onto Three Sisters Drive. Ascend, soon forking right onto Smith-Dorrien / Spray Trail (Hwy 742). Pass the Canmore Nordic Centre and reset your trip odometer to 0. Pavement ends at 1.2 km (0.7 mi). After crossing Whiteman's Gap, proceed generally SE. Park in the pullout (right / W) just before Spurling Creek, at 18.5 km (11.5 mi), 1707 m (5600 ft).

On Foot

The trail starts on the E side of the road, across from the N edge of the pullout. It ascends steeply above Spurling Creek. Your general direction of travel will be NE all the way to the pass.

Soon attain views. The Goat Range is SW, beyond Spray Lakes Reservoir. Break out of the trees to enter **West Wind Pass** at 2.1 km (1.3 mi), 2085 m (6841 ft). Swift hikers will be here in less than an hour.

The NE edge of the pass plunges into Wind Valley. Wind Ridge forms the valley's NW wall. The pass is between the vertical faces of Rimwall (left / NW) and Windtower (right / E).

Just below the W edge of West Wind Pass, where the trail levels in grass, look right. You'll see a right (E) fork curving and ascending right (SE); that's the route to Windtower. A few paces farther, ignore another right fork descending S into forest.

Rimwall, from West Wind Pass

The Windtower route is evident most of the way to the summit. Where the path fades, watch for cairns. If the route is unapparent, carry on as long as the going is reasonably easy. If you feel the hike is becoming a continuous scramble, you're off course. Back up and find a more inviting way forward. The correct route poses no serious obstacles.

The first leg is a long southward traverse, well below and far past the Windtower summit. Your elevation gain will remain gradual except where you must surmount low, rocky outcrops. Be patient. Keep hiking generally S.

At 2260 m (7415 ft), about 50 minutes after departing West Wind Pass, angle left (E) and temporarily aim for Mt. Lougheed. Begin a more aggressive ascent now, because you can do so without your feet needing assistance from your hands.

Soon reach the section of route, bootbeaten into scree, that you saw from the trailhead. After a steep pitch, the route turns N, directly toward Windtower. It's a scree slope the rest of the way, but the grade eases and remains consistently efficient. Arrive at the 2695-m (8842-ft) **summit** about 1¾ hours after departing West Wind Pass.

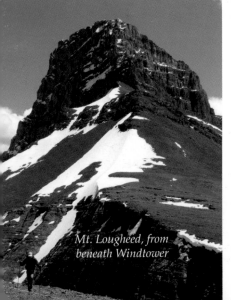

Mt. Lougheed, from beneath Windtower

TRIP 5
Sparrowhawk Tarns

LOCATION	Bow Valley Wildland Provincial Park
	Hwy 742, E of Spray Lakes Reservoir
ROUND TRIP	10 km (6.2 mi)
ELEVATION GAIN	680 m (2230 ft)
KEY ELEVATIONS	trailhead 1720 m (5642 ft)
	upper tarns 2400 m (7872 ft)
HIKING TIME	5 to 6 hours
DIFFICULTY	moderate
MAP	Gem Trek *Canmore and Kananaskis Village*

Opinion

Wandering is to hiking what scat singing is to music.

When you wander, you're improvising a jazz solo with your feet instead of your voice: *Bippity-bippity-doo-wop-razzamatazz-skoobie-doobie-bee-bop-a-lula-shabazz*. And a beautiful place to do it is the alpine cirque harbouring the Sparrowhawk Tarns.

Though it starts at an official day-use area, the Sparrowhawk trail dwindles about halfway. A discernible route continues only briefly, but that's enough. From there, you can wander all afternoon in a secretive, tarn-dappled enclave ringed by lofty peaks.

A *tarn* is a small, water-retaining depression left behind by a retreating glacier. Think of it as a high-elevation mountain pond. The half-dozen or so here punctuate a cirque that can be as vividly green as Ireland.

The tarns diminish, however, by the end of a hot, dry summer. Some years they evaporate entirely. The cirque is still beautiful in autumn; it just lacks exclamation marks. A sprinkling of golden larches will do their best to compensate.

The tarns are at the back of the cirque, 720 m (2362 ft) directly beneath towering Mt. Bogart. Mt. Sparrowhawk is linked to Mt. Bogart and is within view of the tarns, but it's 3 km (1.9 mi) distant. So why weren't these named the *Bogart Tarns*? Or better yet, the *Casablanca Tarns*? Call them what you will, just don't leave without seeing them.

Upon surpassing treeline, it might appear the entire area is visible. Not true. Proceed—on rock and grass, over slabs and ledges, along miniature waterways, past dainty wildflowers—into the cirque's deepest corners. Only by wandering can you appreciate the oddly harmonious mixture of the delicate and awesome that makes this such a compelling destination.

About halfway to Sparrowhawk tarns, you'll gaze up at the alplands between Read's Tower and Mt. Sparrowhawk. Sporting an S on your chest and a cape billowing from your shoulders, you might have energy to venture in that direction after visiting the tarns. If not, make mental note to return, next time following the directions for Read's Tower (Trip 6).

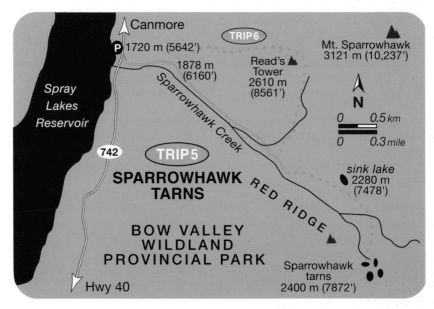

Fact

By Vehicle

In **Canmore**, drive W on Main (8th) Street. Turn left onto 8th Avenue. Follow it over the Bow River bridge. At the T-junction, turn left onto Three Sisters Drive. Ascend, soon forking right onto Smith-Dorrien / Spray Trail (Hwy 742). Pass the Canmore Nordic Centre and reset your trip odometer to 0. Pavement ends at 1.2 km (0.7 mi). After crossing Whiteman's Gap, proceed 22.7 km (14.1 mi) generally SE.

From the **junction of Hwy 40 and Kananaskis Lakes Trail** (50 km / 31 mi S of Trans-Canada Hwy 1, or 17 km / 10.5 mi N of Highwood Pass), turn SW onto Kananaskis Lakes Trail. Reset your trip odometer to 0. At 2.2 km (1.4 mi) turn right (NW) onto unpaved Smith-Dorrien / Spray Trail (Hwy 742). Continue to 40.7 km (25.2 mi).

From **either approach**, turn W into the trailhead parking lot at Sparrowhawk day-use area. Elevation: 1720 m (5642 ft).

On Foot

From the parking lot, head E and cross the road. N of Sparrowhawk Creek, the trail angles up the denuded roadside slope, enters forest, and begins a moderate ascent generally E. Gradually curve SE.

Within twelve minutes the ascent eases. A couple minutes farther, at 0.7 km (0.4 mi), 1878 m (6160 ft), bear right where a cairned left **fork** begins ascending NE to Read's Tower (Trip 6). Ahead, the Sparrowhawk trail skirts left of a chaotic jumble of deadfall.

photos: **1** *Ascending above Sparrowhawk tarns* **2** *Looking NW from the mouth of Sparrowhawk tarns cirque* **3** *The sink lake at the mouth of Sparrowhawk tarns cirque. Mt. Bogart beyond.*

At 2027 m (6650 ft), about 40 minutes from the trailhead, break into the **subalpine zone**. Cliffs are now visible on both sides of the canyon. You can also glimpse Spray Lakes Reservoir NW.

The trail fades among scattered, young trees atop an open, rocky, gentle knoll. Proceed up-canyon, generally SE, into sparse forest. The sketchy trail soon drops to intersect a **draw** at the base of a steep, bouldery, trail-less slope.

Cairns suggest a route upward, among the boulders. It's easier to turn right, briefly follow the draw, then turn left and ascend SW where the slope is greener, thus avoiding the rougher terrain. On the stone-and-dryas covered slope above, pass between a big boulder on a knob (left) and a talus slope (right).

Continue toiling upward among larches, on dirt and dryas. At 2280 m (7478 ft), about 1¾ hours from the trailhead, crest a **rib** overlooking a **sink lake** (E). You've entered the **cirque** beneath Bogart Tower (E), Mt. Bogart (ESE), and Red Ridge (SSW). South, below Red Ridge, is the creek that drains the uppermost tarns. They're still above you, out of sight.

To ramble deeper into the cirque, initially head SE. The terrain is convoluted, necessitating frequent ups and downs. But navigation is easy because you're well into the alpine zone, with no trees to obstruct your view. Follow your bliss. The **Sparrowhawk tarns** are numerous, scattered throughout the farthest reaches of the cirque. Their namesake, Mt. Sparrowhawk, is N, linked to Mt. Bogart by a long, SE-trending ridge.

After gaining more elevation, try curving ESE, to the tarns near the cirque's SE wall, beneath Mt. Bogart. After that, turn around. Head E, then ascend generally SW over slabs and ledges to the uppermost tarns. They're terraced at about 2400 m (7872 ft), below the cirque's SW wall. Finally, descend to the creek draining the uppermost tarns. Turn S in this lush, grassy basin. Work your way back to the rib above the sink lake. You're now on familiar ground. Return the way you came.

Fringed grass-of-parnassus

When you reach the open, flat area where defined trail resumes, pause. Study the slopes rising NE toward 3121-m (10,237-ft) Mt. Sparrowhawk. Left of it, directly N, is 2610-m (8561-ft) **Read's Tower** (Trip 6). Ascending between them offers an arduous but enjoyable day of exploration.

TRIP 6
Read's Tower

LOCATION	Bow Valley Wildland Provincial Park
	Hwy 742, E of Spray Lakes Reservoir
CIRCUIT	7.8 km (4.8 mi), plus 1.3 km (0.8 mi) detour on tower
ELEVATION GAIN	1125 m (3590 ft) up and around tower
KEY ELEVATIONS	trailhead 1720 m (5642 ft), tower 2610 m (8561 ft)
	col behind tower 2565 m (8413 ft)
	Sparrowhawk ridge 3000 m (9840 ft)
HIKING TIME	5 to 7 hours
DIFFICULTY	challenging
MAPS	page 41; Gem Trek *Canmore & Kananaskis Lakes*

Opinion

Comfort is a narcotic. Partake sparingly. It's sweetest not when you wallow in it, by relaxing all weekend, but when it washes over you after a challenging achievement like the completion of this circuit on the largely untracked west flank of Mt. Sparrowhawk.

Actually, Read's Tower—the centerpiece of the circuit—poses only a minor challenge compared to the other, increasingly demanding (and commensurately rewarding) options available here. After setting out on the Sparrowhawk tarns trail (Trip 5), you'll veer onto a steep route on a broad ridge leading to the base of the tower. Rapidly expanding views of the Spray Valley will fuel your motivation as you surge above treeline into trailless terrain. Then it's up the tower—an even steeper grunt culminating in a terrific view from the tiny, airy summit. The panorama includes the Goat Range, Mt. Assiniboine, Sparrowhawk tarns basin, and Mt. Sparrowhawk.

After a quick descent back to the tower's base, your next challenge is to reach the alpine col behind the tower. This too requires a taxing, off-trail ascent, but it's a necessary leg of the journey if you want to enjoy a full day's adventure. Attaining the col allows you to circle back to the trailhead via Sparrowhawk Creek canyon, marveling at new terrain rather than retracing your steps. The col also serves as launch pad for those with the verve to march all the way up 3121-m (10,237-ft) Mt. Sparrowhawk. Scramblers think it's easy, but the 1401-m (4595-ft) elevation gain and loss (bypassing Read's Tower) is formidable.

Departing the col, you'll careen cross-country into Sparrowhawk Creek canyon to intersect the Sparrowhawk tarns trail. The challenging option here is to lengthen the day and boost your fulfillment by ascending to the tarns and roaming the virginal basin beneath Mt. Bogart. Daylight permitting, do it. Read Trip 5 for a pep talk. Or simply cruise the trail down-canyon toward whatever small but prized comforts (a bag of chips? a cold beer?) you left in your vehicle to enjoy upon returning.

Spray Lakes Reservoir and Old Goat Mtn (Trip 2), from Read's Tower

Fact

By Vehicle

Follow the directions for Sparrowhawk tarns (Trip 5). Read's Tower and Sparrowhawk tarns share the same trailhead, at 1720 m (5642 ft).

On Foot

From the parking lot, head E and cross the road. N of Sparrowhawk Creek, the trail angles up the denuded roadside slope, enters forest, and begins a moderate ascent generally E.

Within twelve minutes the ascent eases. A couple minutes farther, at 0.7 km (0.4 mi), 1878 m (6160 ft), look for a **cairned left fork**. A distinctive, **white rock** is imbedded in the trail immediately before the fork. The rock's exposed surface is about the size of two boots. Abandon the Sparrowhawk tarns trail here. Go left (NE) onto the cairned path and begin a steep, rough ascent.

Though merely a boot-trodden route, the path is discernible. It's also sporadically cairned and flagged. Follow it generally ENE. About 22 minutes up, attain a grand view W and SW across Spray Lakes Reservoir. Five minutes farther, the path fades. Look right (S). See the talus just beyond the trees? The path resumes above it, turning left (NE) and ascending steeply.

Emerge from forest at 2080 m (6822 ft), about 40 minutes from the trailhead. You're now ascending on scree, dryas, and tufts of grass. Though still evident, the path is now unnecessary. The way forward is simply up.

At 2207 m (7240 ft), about 50 minutes from the trailhead, reach the first **level reprieve**, behind a couple stunted trees. Read's Tower is visible ahead (ESE). Mt. Sparrowhawk, the blocky summit on the far, rounded ridge, is ENE. The Goat Range is W. Spray Lakes Reservoir stretches from Mt. Shark in the S, to the Three Sisters in the N.

Continue ascending the ridge. Proceed through a stand of trees. Keep following the crest SE. Reach a **big cairn** where the ridge climaxes at 2.3 km (1.4 mi), 2341 m (7680 ft), immediately below Read's Tower. About one hour from the trailhead, this is a comfortable place to shed packs, relax, appreciate your accomplishment, and survey the terrain ahead. All while you savour a nip of that dark chocolate you remembered to bring.

Aiming for Read's Tower? The summit is only .65 km (0.4 mi) distant, requiring a mere 30-minute surge of energy. Drop into the **saddle**, curve left, and ascend E on the talus-strewn SW face. The grade is steep, relentless, but strong hikers will find it simply spurs them to maintain an efficient assault. Step onto the 2610-m (8561-ft) apex of **Read's Tower** about 1½ hours after departing the trailhead. You're surrounded by mountains near and far. Prominent among them are Mt. Assiniboine (W) and, slightly left of it, Eon Mtn.

After descending back to the **saddle** immediately below Read's Tower, you can of course retrace your steps: up to the cairn, then down the ridge to the trailhead. But you're within 0.7 km (0.4 mi) of the col behind Read's Tower. To complete a circuit through the col, don't return to the cairn on the ridge. Instead, from the lowpoint in the saddle, turn right (NE). Descend into the **basin** below the tower's NW face, then curve E and ascend out of it.

The col is obvious: left of and directly below Read's Tower, right of the steep slope rising to Mt. Sparrowhawk. A route bootbeaten into the talus should be evident. But because the route is in a **gully** shaded by the tower, it can remain snow-covered well into July. The slope is precipitous. A long, sliding fall on icy snow could leave you in a battered heap. Assess snow conditions before proceeding.

About 30 minutes after departing the saddle, crest the 2565-m (8413-ft) **col behind Read's Tower**. From here, you can continue ascending 1.8 km (1.1 mi) ENE to 3121-m (10,237-ft) **Mt. Sparrowhawk**. It's a long, tiring, but straight-forward slog. Beneath the summit block, round the right (S) side. The final ascent is from the E. The new view comprises 3107-m (10,191-ft) Mt. Lougheed (N, across Spencer Creek basin).

Back at the col behind Read's Tower, resume the circuit by descending S, cross-country, on the steep, dryas- and scree-covered slope. For an aerial view of the scoured, terraced basin on Mt. Sparrowhawk's lower reaches, detour left (SE). But return to the right (W) side of the stream that courses through the drainage you're descending, so you'll avoid a very steep thrash through krummholz below.

After dropping into the mouth of the **scoured basin**, bear right (SW). The gentle grade allows easy striding to the basin lip, where you'll peer SW down the final, untracked, steep slope. Below is Sparrowhawk Creek canyon. Your immediate goal: intersect the Sparrowhawk tarns trail (Trip 5).

See the lightly treed area? On its far side is a nearly naked berm. You'll find the trail on the crest of that berm. Now, over the lip you go, SW. Aim for the berm but favour the left (SE) side of the slope.

It takes about 30 minutes to hike the 2.1 km (1.3 mi) from the col to where you'll intersect the **Sparrowhawk tarns trail** at 2010 m (6593 ft). Left ascends SW to the tarns. Turn right to descend Sparrowhawk Creek canyon NW. The grade is gentle the rest of the way.

Within 30 minutes, having hiked another 2 km (1.2 mi), pass the cairn marking the Read's Tower route. You're now on familiar ground. Proceed straight. The **trailhead** is just 0.7 km (0.4 mi) farther W. You'll arrive there in about twelve minutes.

Read's Tower, from Sparrowhawk tarns basin (Trip 5)

TRIP 7
Buller Passes

LOCATION	Spray Valley Provincial Park
	Hwy 742, E of Spray Lakes Reservoir
ROUND TRIP	13.2 km (8.2 mi) to Buller Pass
CIRCUIT	14.7 km (9.1 mi) Buller & N Buller passes
	18.4 km (11.4 mi) including unnamed summit
ELEVATION GAIN	670 m (2198 ft) to Buller Pass
	845 m (2272 ft) to Buller & N Buller passes
	1152 m (3780 ft) to unnamed summit
	(includes regaining losses)
KEY ELEVATIONS	trailhead 1800 m (5905 ft), Buller Pass 2470 m (8102 ft)
	N Buller Pass 2470 m (8102 ft)
	unnamed summit 2737 m (8977 ft)
HIKING TIME	4 to 5 hours for Buller Pass
	7 to 8 hours for unnamed summit
DIFFICULTY	easy to Buller Pass, challenging to unnamed summit
MAP	Gem Trek *Canmore and Kananaskis Village*

Opinion

Real estate agencies, in their marketing, proclaim that "Purchasing a home is the most important thing people will do in their lives." Wow. What small, narrow lives they assume we're living. Surely, becoming capable, creative, wise and compassionate, by pursuing imaginative, challenging, fulfilling, meaningful endeavours, is what's most important in life. And along the way developing the confidence and flexibility to feel at home wherever we are. Judged by this loftier definition, going hiking is far more important than buying a home. So, off you go. On an adventurous, rewarding dayhike through the Buller passes, and up to an unnamed summit with a walloping view of Rocky Mountain wilderness.

You have several options here. Whichever you choose, only the first and last hour of the day will be in heavy timber. You'll mostly be above treeline, with the surrounding mountains in view. To make this a shorter, easier round trip, turn back at Buller Pass. The view from the pass—across Ribbon Lake basin to Guinn's Pass (Trip 18)—is outstanding, but the hike itself is merely worthwhile. The longer circuit, looping back via North Buller Pass, is preferable, adding a little more scenery and a lot more excitement—routefinding and cross-country travel. But if you want a panoramic vista that will blow open your doors and windows, detour about 40 minutes beyond North Buller Pass to an airy, unnamed summit high above the Sparrowhawk tarns (Trip 5). Given one of Alberta's famous blue skies, you'll see much of the Great Divide between Mt. Assiniboine and Mt. Rundle, including most of Spray Lakes Reservoir.

Buller Pass (left) and North Buller Pass (center), from Guinn's Pass (Trip 18)

Wait until late July before attempting the circuit. A snow cornice tends to linger long on the east side of North Buller Pass. Keep in mind, you'll be hiking a defined trail only as far as Buller Pass. Shortly beyond, you'll navigate trail-less, alpine terrain. The unnamed peak demands a short, steep ascent on talus and scree. But it's not a scramble, and it poses no exposure. North Buller Pass is also steep and rocky. Descending its west side is an exercise in slide-control. You'll quickly drop to walkable terrain, however, where navigation is simple: just head down-valley. A path soon develops. You'll re-join the main trail within 45 minutes of departing North Buller Pass.

Might North Buller or the unnamed summit outstrip your desire or ability? No worries. Examine them both after crossing Buller Pass and beginning the circuit. If they look too formidable, you can about face and head home via Buller Pass. So start early intending to do it all.

Fact

By Vehicle

In **Canmore**, drive W on Main (8th) Street. Turn left onto 8th Avenue. Follow it over the Bow River bridge. At the T-junction, turn left onto Three Sisters Drive. Ascend, soon forking right onto Smith-Dorrien / Spray Trail (Hwy 742). Pass the Canmore Nordic Centre and reset your trip odometer to 0. Pavement ends at 1.2 km (0.7 mi). After crossing Whiteman's Gap, proceed generally SE. At 31.4 km (19.5 mi) turn right (W) into Buller Mtn day-use parking lot. Elevation: 1800 m (5905 ft).

From the **junction of Hwy 40 and Kananaskis Lakes Trail** (50 km / 31 mi S of Trans-Canada Hwy 1, or 17 km / 10.5 mi N of Highwood Pass), turn SW onto Kananaskis Lakes Trail. Reset your trip odometer to 0. At 2.2 km (1.4 mi) turn right (NW) onto unpaved Smith-Dorrien / Spray Trail (Hwy 742) and drive generally NW. At 32.2 km (20 mi) turn left (W) into Buller Mtn day-use parking lot. Elevation: 1800 m (5905 ft).

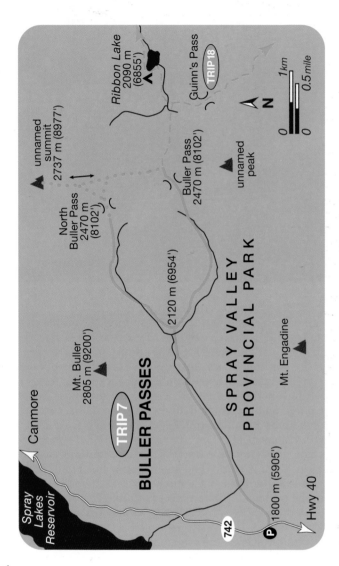

On Foot

Return to the highway and cross it. The trail begins on the E side. Immediately cross a small bridge, enter forest, and curve NE. This will remain your general direction of travel for the first hour.

Within 15 minutes, cross a bridge to Buller Creek's N bank. The trail ascends moderately then contours for nearly 1 km (0.6 mi) through pleasant Engelmann spruce forest. At 2.8 km (1.7 mi), 1995 m (6544 ft), cross a bridge to the creek's S bank. Ascend more steeply, then enjoy a level reprieve. Where the forest opens, you can look up both valleys: right (ESE) leads to Buller Pass; left (NE) leads to North Buller Pass. Mt. Buller is farther left (directly N).

Above Buller Pass. Mt. Kidd beyond

About an hour from the trailhead, pass a turquoise pool where the creek cascades into a rock bowl. Then cross a footlog over the creek's S fork. One minute beyond, watch closely for a **fork** near a tree blazed N-S. Here, at 3.7 km (2.3 mi), 2120 m (6954 ft), the narrow trail to North Buller Pass veers left (NE). For Buller Pass, bear right (SE) on the main trail. If you opt for the circuit linking both passes, you'll loop back to this fork.

Proceeding on the main trail, within 15 minutes ascend past an interesting gorge on the right and attain a view of cliffs. Larches appear in the upper subalpine zone. The trail begins curving NE. At 2240 m (7347 ft) Buller Pass is visible ahead.

Ascending gently into the upper basin, the trail grazes a creeklet and small cascade. Then it climbs the steep, rocky headwall, gaining 160 m (525 ft), to crest **Buller Pass** at 6.6 km (4.1 mi), 2470 m (8102 ft), about two hours from the trailhead. Ribbon Lake is visible E, in the basin far below the pass. Behind it is 2958-m (9702-ft) Mt. Kidd. North of the lake is 3144-m (10,315-ft) Mt. Bogart.

A rough trail descends the E side of the pass. It reaches a junction in 1.4 km (0.9 mi). From there, right climbs S to Guinn's Pass. Left goes N then W to arrive at Ribbon Lake in 1.2 km (0.75 mi). For details about Ribbon Lake, and the trail descending NE along Ribbon Creek to Hwy 40 near Kananaskis Village, read *Beyond Guinn's Pass* in Trip 18.

North Buller Pass

To complete a 14.7-km (9.1-mi) circuit via North Buller Pass, or to ascend the unnamed summit beyond it, descend the rocky trail ENE from Buller Pass. In about 15 minutes, near 2295 m (7528 ft), turn left (N) at the bottom of the chunky rocks, just above krummholz. Proceed onto smooth, leafy dryas. Dip into a depression, then ascend the dryas-covered slope. At 2420 m (7940 ft), hike N between **grassy knobs**.

To attain a panoramic vista atop the unnamed summit on the ridge N of North Buller Pass, continue reading the next section *Unnamed Summit*.

For **North Buller Pas**s, curve left (NW) before losing significant elevation. Ascend steep talus to crest the 2470-m (8102-ft) pass. You've hiked 1.7 km (1.1 mi) from Buller Pass. Skip below to *Circuit via North Buller Pass* for directions down-valley to the trailhead.

Unnamed Summit

From the **grassy knobs** between Buller and North Buller passes, it's another 40 minutes to the panoramic vista atop the unnamed summit on the ridge N of North Buller Pass.

Drop into the **draw** below the E side of North Buller Pass. Then ascend N on the **grassy rib** right of the dry, rocky gully. When grass and dryas end, keep toiling upward on steep scree until you surmount the ridge. Bear right and follow the crest generally N to the 2737-m (8977-ft) **unnamed summit** at the N end of the ridge N of North Buller Pass. You've hiked 10 km (6.2 mi) from the Buller Mtn trailhead. You're 1027 m (3370 ft) above Spray Lakes Reservoir. Spectacles are near and far in every direction.

Mt. Bogart is nearby NE. The Sparrowhawk tarns (Trip 5) are NNE, 330 m (1082 ft) below you. N, past the tarns, is 3121-m (10,237-ft) Mt. Sparrowhawk, and beyond it is 3108-m (10,194-ft) Mt. Lougheed. Red Ridge is N, immediately below you. NW, past Spray Lakes Reservoir and Goat Pond, is Mt. Rundle. Below Rundle's NE side, the Banff Springs Hotel is discernible. Mt. Assiniboine and her satellite peaks, Eon Mtn and Mt. Aye, are WSW. The beginning of Bryant Creek valley is SW. The Tower is SSW. Guinn's Pass is SSE. Mt. Kidd is SE. The Opal Range is farther SE, beyond Hwy 40.

Spray Lakes Reservoir and the Goat Range,
from the unnamed summit beyond North Buller Pass

Returning from Buller Pass

Departing the unnamed summit, after retracing your steps generally S along the ridgecrest, you have two choices. It's easier and more pleasant but longer to simply continue reversing your ascent route, dropping into the draw below the E side of North Buller Pass. From there, ascend W on steep talus to the 2470-m (8102-ft) pass. The other option is shorter and entails no elevation loss but is more challenging: traverse directly from the ridgecrest down to the pass, across an excruciatingly steep slope. Traction is awkward in the loose talus and negligible on the cement-like dirt. But it's doable if you're a mountain goat.

Circuit via North Buller Pass

From North Buller Pass, you'll hike 2.4 km (1.5 mi)—about 45 minutes—to intersect the main trail to Buller Pass.

Carefully work your way down the chunky scree littering the steep, W side of North Buller Pass. Reach flatter ground at 2325 m (7626 ft). Continue cross-country, generally W, occasionally on scraps of route beaten into the rocky, shrubby terrain. The cliffs in this valley are less dramatic than those en route to Buller Pass.

Curve SW, staying N of the **creek**. A snippet of trail in the creek gully leads up and out, skirting a waterfall in a small **box canyon**. A divided trail begins on the right, above the waterfall. It leads through trees to creekside willow flats. Proceed SW, briefly through willows. At 2205 m (7232 ft) cross to the creek's SE bank. In another 1 km (0.6 mi) intersect the **main trail to Buller Pass**, just above the turquoise pool where the creek cascades into a rock bowl. You're now on familiar ground. If you detoured to the unnamed summit, your total mileage here is 14.4 km (8.9 mi). Turn right. In a minute, cross a footlog over the creek's S fork. Follow the trail 3.9 km (2.4 mi), generally SW, back to the trailhead.

TRIP 8
Tent Ridge

LOCATION	Spray Valley Provincial Park
	Hwy 742, S of Spray Lakes Reservoir
LOOP	10.6 km (6.6 mi)
ELEVATION GAIN	780 m (2560 ft)
KEY ELEVATIONS	trailhead 1900 m (6232 ft)
	E-arm summit 2480 m (8136 ft)
	saddle 2386 m (7828 ft)
	W-arm summit 2540 m (8333 ft)
HIKING TIME	5 to 6 hours
DIFFICULTY	challenging due to light scrambling and brief route-finding
MAPS	Gem Trek *Canmore and Kananaskis Village*
	Gem Trek *Kananaskis Lakes*

Opinion

Imagine the earth's topography is a physical manifestation of sound. Hills would be yawns. Bigger mountains would be yells. And the peaks you'll see from Tent Ridge would be screams, howls, shrieks, screeches and roars.

This is the K-Country climax. Horseshoe-shaped Tent Ridge appears to have been tossed up against it: clang! The highpoint of the ridge bellows back in the fearsome north face of Mt. Smuts. Just beyond, numerous, massive, lofty summits—including Mounts Birdwood and Sir Douglas—riot for your attention. To oblige, bring a topo map. It will enhance your trip.

Unglue your gaze from the nearby peaks on the Great Divide, and you'll overlook Spray Lakes Reservoir, you'll survey most of the Spray and Bryant Creek valleys, you'll peer into the basins harbouring Rummel (Trip 12) and Chester lakes (Trip 13), and you'll see the route up Mt. Chester.

The loop described here follows the entire ridgecrest: south along the east arm, north along the west arm. Though you'll stride effortlessly much of the way, light scrambling is briefly necessary. In particular, surmounting the east arm demands skill and cool. Scrambling up is almost always easier than down, so looping clockwise is preferable.

Tent Ridge basin—a utopian meadow cloistered within the embrace of the ridge—is itself worth visiting should you decline the ridgecrest. You'll likely find solitude at the small ponds beneath the headwall. But the ridge is a vastly more exciting venture. If you're a sure-footed hiker with a little scrambling and routefinding experience, give it a go. If you're daunted by the initial ascent, you can retreat into the basin having wasted little time.

Bear in mind, the beginning of this trip is not clear-cut, because it immediately enters a clearcut. Just follow the detailed *On Foot* description

and know that this less-than-auspicious start belies the wonders awaiting you atop Tent Ridge.

Fact

By Vehicle

In **Canmore**, drive W on Main (8th) Street. Turn left onto 8th Avenue. Follow it over the Bow River bridge. At the T-junction, turn left onto Three Sisters Drive. Ascend, soon forking right onto Smith-Dorrien / Spray Trail (Hwy 742). Pass the Canmore Nordic Centre and reset your trip odometer to 0. Pavement ends at 1.2 km (0.7 mi).

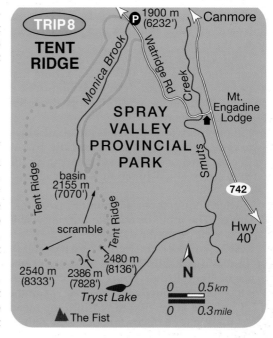

After crossing Whiteman's Gap, proceed generally SE. At 35 km (21.7 mi) turn right (W) at the signs for Mt. Shark and Engadine Lodge.

From the **junction of Hwy 40 and Kananaskis Lakes Trail** (50 km / 31 mi S of Trans-Canada Hwy 1, or 17 km / 10.5 mi N of Highwood Pass), turn SW onto Kananaskis Lakes Trail. Reset your trip odometer to 0. At 2.2 km (1.4 mi) turn right (NW) onto unpaved Smith-Dorrien / Spray Trail (Hwy 742). At 28.6 km (17.7 mi) turn left (W) at the signs for Mt. Shark and Engadine Lodge.

From **either approach**, reset your trip odometer to 0. Pass Mt. Engadine Lodge. Cross the bridge over Smuts Creek. At 0.8 km (0.5 mi) bear right. Reach the trailhead parking area—the grassy clearing on the right—at 1.8 km (1.1 mi), 1900 m (6232 ft).

On Foot

Before departing the trailhead, look NW. Just beyond where you parked, you'll see a grassy, former logging road intersecting the main road. That's the way you'll return upon completing the clockwise loop described here.

To begin, go in the opposite direction. Walk back (SSE) on the main road 200 m (220 yd) to the steep, grassy, former **logging road** on the right (W). It's initially a broad, sloping swath. Ascend right (NW) on the path

photos: *1 Ascending the west arm of Tent Ridge, from the saddle linking the two arms* *2 Gaining the east arm of Tent Ridge* *3 West arm of Tent Ridge. Mount Nestor and Old Goat Mountain are beyond Spray Lakes Reservoir*

bootbeaten through the grass. In a few minutes, the road curves left (S). Enter a re-growing **cutblock** and proceed S. Tent Ridge is visible W and SW above the forest.

Quickly reach a **fork** on level ground. Straight proceeds S along the forest edge. Turn right (SW) onto a route marked by a cairn and a crude teepee of logs. Ascend through young trees and slash. The route remains obvious, climbing the left (E) side of a draw. Spray Lakes Reservoir is visible N. Mt. Sparrowhawk is NE.

Soon enter forest. Where deadfall blocks your progress, the route swerves around it. Ascend generally SW. About 30 minutes from the trailhead, reach a small, level **clearing** at 2076 m (6800 ft). Five minutes farther, arrive at a **T-junction** with a well-trod trail running SE / NW. Go left (SE).

After hiking about 45 minutes, overlook the forested **Monica Brook drainage**. The brook is audible but not visible. You're now among alpine larch. Go left (S) up the draw.

At 2.7 km (1.7 mi), 2155 m (7070 ft), enter the spacious, inviting meadow of **Tent Ridge basin**. Hiking time: about one hour. The two N-trending arms of Tent Ridge wrap around the basin, forming a horseshoe. Wildflowers are abundant here in early summer.

Continue about 100 m/yd into the meadow. Look left (E) along the forest margin for a distinct, bootbeaten path. Follow it left, ascending NNE among trees. About 10 minutes farther, at 2205 m (7234 ft), it curves right (S). The **east arm of Tent Ridge** is now immediately ahead. The ridgecrest route is apparent. Proceed upward. Spray Lakes Reservoir dominates the view behind you (north).

The grade steepens and, for the next 30 minutes or so, the hike becomes a scramble. Exposure is mild. Hand- and foot-holds are prevalent and "juggy"—big and sturdy. Crest the 2480-m (8136-ft) **east-arm summit** about two hours from the trailhead. It's crowned with weather-recording equipment housed in an orange, fiberglass shell. Visible across the Spray Valley are Mt. Chester ESE, and Rummel Pass (Trip 12) ENE.

Resume right (W), descending on scree into the 2386-m (7828-ft) **saddle** linking the two arms of Tent Ridge. Total distance: 4.7 km (2.9 mi). Right (N) is Tent Ridge basin. Left (S) is Tryst Lake basin. On the far side of Tryst Lake basin is The Fist. Nearby, SSW, is 2939-m (9640-ft) Mt. Smuts.

From the saddle, ascend W. About 2½ hours from the trailhead, top-out at 2540 m (8333 ft). This is the **west-arm summit**, the Tent Ridge climax, and the supreme hiker-accessible vantage of Mt. Smuts. A topo map is invaluable for interpreting the mountain vastness extending in all directions. A few of the highlights include heavily forested Bryant Creek Valley (NW), glacier-laden, 3407-m (11,175-ft) Mt. Sir Douglas (S) and, just beyond it, 3097-m (10,158-ft) Mt. Birdwood.

Light scrambling briefly ensues as you continue N atop the **west arm of Tent Ridge**. About 8 minutes farther, at 2480 m (8136 ft), easily skirt a short cliff by dropping left, SW of the crest. The ridge broadens beyond and carefree hiking resumes. A gentle ascent leads to a 2520-m (8268-ft) **bump**, about 3½ hours from the trailhead.

Near the **west arm's north end**, at 7.1 km (4.4 mi), the route angles right and begins descending NNE. About five minutes down, at 2380 m (7808 ft), it veers right (SE), back toward the east arm. About ten minutes farther, at 2318 m (7605 ft), just before the route ascends slightly, abandon it.

Go left (NE), dropping through **stunted, open forest**. In a couple minutes, bear left (N) across a **bare slop**e. Two minutes farther, turn right (NNE) and descend a **larch-filled gully**. Smith-Dorrien / Spray Trail (Hwy 742) is visible far below.

Two minutes farther, intersect a bootbeaten **trail** at 2238 m (7343 ft). Follow it right (E). One minute farther, the trail turns sharply left (N), continuing the steep descent. Stay on it.

Intersect a grassy, former **logging road** at 1930 m (6332 ft). You've now hiked about 4½ hours from the trailhead. Turn right (SE) and walk the old road. A few minutes farther you'll see the main road ahead (SE) and the trailhead parking area just beyond. Swift striders complete the 10.6-km (6.6-mi) loop in about 4¾ hours.

Heading south on west arm of Tent Ridge

TRIP 9
Birdwood Traverse

LOCATION	Spray Valley Provincial Park
	Hwy 742, S of Spray Lakes Reservoir
SHUTTLE TRIP	17.5 km (10.9 mi)
ELEVATION GAIN	710 m (2330 ft)
KEY ELEVATIONS	trailhead 1900 m (6232 ft)
	Smuts Pass 2331 m (7646 ft)
	Birdwood Pass 2445 m (8020 ft)
	Burstall Pass 2380 m (7806 ft)
HIKING TIME	8 to 9 hours
DIFFICULTY	moderate
MAP	Gem Trek *Kananaskis Country*

Opinion

Look for smudges. That's where the earth gets interesting.

On a topo map, smudges are where the contour lines are so near one another there's no visible distance between them. Since the closer the lines the more vertical the land, smudges are your assurance of sheer canyon walls or steep mountainsides, i.e. spectacular scenery.

Glance at any southwest Alberta topo map. You'll see hundreds of thick, dark smudges radiating outward like shock waves. The epicenter of this topographical eruption is, of course, the Rocky Mountains. And one of those smudges represents 3097-m (10,161-ft) Mt. Birdwood, whose distinctively long, northwest ridge is a K-Country landmark and whose west face is the trail-less crux of this enthralling hike.

You'll follow trails up one luxuriant valley and down another. Between, you'll cross four, closely-linked passes, dip into an alpine lake basin, and tip your hat to Mt. Smuts and Snow Peak. And, despite the size and intensity of the surrounding smudges, you'll gain surprisingly little elevation. But you must be a strong hiker and competent navigator. Though the *On Foot* directions are detailed, and the routefinding is across open terrain, bring a topo map. If you must be reminded to bring a compass, sit in the corner with your back to the class.

To spare you a long, boring tramp, the *By Vehicle* directions disregard the official trailhead, suggesting instead that you park on the road and take a shortcut. You'll start cross-country, then follow bits of old logging road. Soon tag onto the trail ascending Commonwealth Creek valley to Smuts Pass. From there, it's a two-hour, off-trail ramble to Burstall Pass (Trip 10). Trail then resumes, allowing a straightforward descent of Burstall Creek valley.

You've rarely ventured off trail? Attaining the col beyond Smuts Pass, above Birdwood Lakes, is a rational but fruitful goal. Birdwood Pass is then in view, as are the alplands you must traverse to reach it. If you hesitate to

Nearing Birdwood Pass, after traversing from the col (left) above Birdwood Lake

proceed, trust your instinct; turn around. If you continue despite qualms, look back every few minutes. You'll feel more secure knowing retreat is always viable.

It's safest to wait until the high-country snow has melted before attempting this trip. Early August is a good bet. The east side of Snow Peak's south ridge (just north of Burstall Pass) will retain snow longest, and it's not visible until you're there. You can get a sense for it, however, by looking southwest, toward the Great Divide, from the Chester Lake trailhead (Trip 13). It's opposite the Burstall Pass trailhead (Trip 10), where this hike ends.

Finally, while most hikes are simply less genial during cloudy, rainy weather, a few—like this one—are a mistake. Save the Birdwood Traverse for a blue-sky day when a high-pressure zone has applied for permanent residence in southern Alberta.

Fact

Before your trip

Be prepared to ford Smuts Creek almost immediately. Though neither deep nor broad, it's frigid, and the bottom is rocky. River sandals or neoprene socks will spare you a few minutes of pain—if you don't mind hauling them the rest of the day. Definitely bring a bandana to dry your feet before rebooting.

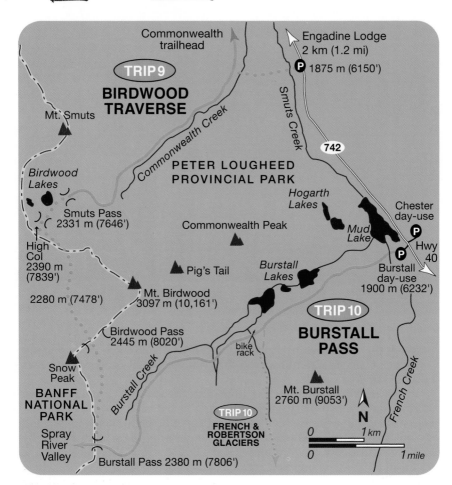

TRIP 9

BIRDWOOD TRAVERSE

Commonwealth trailhead

Engadine Lodge
2 km (1.2 mi)
Ⓟ 1875 m (6150')

Mt. Smuts

Smuts Creek

Commonwealth Creek

PETER LOUGHEED
PROVINCIAL PARK

742

Birdwood Lakes

Hogarth Lakes

Chester day-use
Ⓟ

Smuts Pass
2331 m (7646')

Commonwealth Peak

Mud Lake
Ⓟ

Hwy 40

High Col
2390 m (7839')

Pig's Tail

Burstall Lakes

Burstall day-use
1900 m (6232')

2280 m (7478')

Mt. Birdwood
3097 m (10,161')

TRIP 10

BURSTALL PASS

Birdwood Pass
2445 m (8020')

bike rack

Snow Peak

Burstall Creek

French Creek

BANFF NATIONAL PARK

Mt. Burstall
2760 m (9053')

N

Spray River Valley

TRIP 10

FRENCH & ROBERTSON GLACIERS

0   1 km

0   1 mile

Burstall Pass 2380 m (7806')

By Vehicle

From Calgary, this trip's starting point is nearly the same distance via Hwy 40 or Canmore. But the Hwy 40 approach is quicker and easier. It avoids Canmore congestion and is paved farther.

From the **junction of Hwy 40 and Kananaskis Lakes Trail** (50 km / 31 mi S of Trans-Canada Hwy 1, or 17 km / 10.5 mi N of Highwood Pass), turn SW onto Kananaskis Lakes Trail. Reset your trip odometer to 0. At 2.2 km (1.4 mi) turn right (NW) onto unpaved Smith-Dorrien / Spray Trail (Hwy 742). At 22.2 km (13.8 mi) pass Burstall day-use area, on the left (W). Leave one vehicle here to arrange a shuttle. At 26.4 km (16.4 mi)—near a yellow sign, 70 m (77 yd) after the metal guardrail starts—pull off the road and park.

In **Canmore**, drive W on Main (8th) Street. Turn left onto 8th Avenue. Follow it over the Bow River bridge. At the T-junction, turn left onto Three Sisters Drive. Ascend, soon forking right onto Smith-Dorrien / Spray Trail (Hwy 742). Pass the Canmore Nordic Centre and reset your trip odometer to 0. Pavement ends at 1.2 km (0.7 mi). After crossing Whiteman's Gap, proceed generally SE. At 35 km (21.7 mi) pass the turnoff for Mt. Shark and Engadine lodge. At 37 km (23 mi)—near a yellow sign, 70 m (77 yd) before the metal guardrail ends—pull off the road and park. To arrange a shuttle, leave one vehicle 4.2 km (2.6 mi) farther S, at Burstall day-use area, on the right (W).

From **either approach**, you're now at 1875 m (6150 ft), across the main valley from the tributary valley of Commonwealth Creek. You'll start hiking cross-country, but the route is visible below. Take time to survey it before setting out.

On Foot

From the guardrail at the parking spot, you have an unobstructed view southwest up Commonwealth Creek valley to Smuts Pass. The mountain swooping down to the pass from the left (S) is Mt. Birdwood. Grassy-sloped Tent Ridge (Trip 8) is visible directly W. In the valley below is Smuts Creek. See the short section of creek with gravel on both banks? That's your initial goal. Also fix in your mind the indented clearing in the forest just beyond the creek's gravelly W bank.

Descend W from the road. At the bottom of the slope, the valley floor is soggy but hikeable. Ford **Smuts Creek** where both banks are gravel. Elevation: 1840 m (6035 ft). From the W bank, proceed through the indented clearing in the forest. It's still boggy here. Curve right (NW). Pass a faded metal blaze high on a tree. A bootbeaten route follows the path of least resistance through the brush and trees. Curve W and ascend slightly into a regrowing **cutblock**. Go left (S), gradually curving SW along the edge of the cutblock. Ascend to a clearing and intersect an old **logging road**.

Turn right (N), following the road as it winds SW down to a **creeklet**. Cross the creeklet on a footlog and continue following the road. It curves W and ascends to intersect another old **logging road** at 1 km (0.6 mi), about 12 minutes from Smuts Creek. This road runs N/S. Right (N) leads to Commonwealth trailhead. Turn left (S). The old road gradually dwindles to defined **trail**. Follow it into Commonwealth Creek drainage, where it turns right (SW).

Hike the trail upstream, along the right (NW) bank of moss-lined **Commonwealth Creek**, through beautiful forest. Soon pass a small cascade. The trail is narrow, rooty, and probably muddy. It's on a steep slope with rock outcrops. About 20 minutes upstream, the creek narrows and is lined by willows. The trail levels and improves upon entering a willowy meadow at the mouth of **Commonwealth Creek valley**. Having ascended little, you're now at 1900 m (6232 ft). Ahead (SW) is the headwall below Smuts Pass. Rising above it is 3097-m (10,161-ft) Mt. Birdwood. Left of it is Pig's Tail. Left of that is Commonwealth Peak.

Proceed through luxuriant meadow. Cow parsnip (tall, with white flowers) flourishes here. Re-enter forest. Ascend NW over a rockslide. Return to forest. At 2020 m (6626 ft), about 45 minutes up-valley, reach the base of the **headwall**. The trail to Smuts Pass ascends generally the middle of the headwall—on heather and grass, and through patchy krummholz

Birdwood Lake

(stunted trees). In season, flowers colour the slope. Visible to either side are paths in talus.

At 5.3 km (3.3 mi), about an hour from the base of the headwall, reach 2331-m (7646-ft) **Smuts Pass**. Right (N) is the Mt. Smuts summit ridge. Left (SE) is the Mt. Birdwood summit ridge. Visible SW is a smooth break in the ridge. That's the col you'll cross to traverse Mt. Birdwood's W face. Ahead (W), in the basin 30 m (100 ft) below, is the first and biggest of the two Birdwood Lakes. The second lake is on a terrace just beyond.

Descend to the S shore of **Birdwood Lake**. An easy, ten-minute ascent SW leads to the 2390-m (7839-ft) **col**. Visible SE is Birdwood Pass, with its rock slabs and grass. Survey the terrain between the col and Birdwood Pass, to plan your route and look for bears. Make noise to warn grizzlies of your presence. Bear diggings are common here.

From the col, drop left (E). Contour near treeline on a game trail. In a few minutes reach rock outcroppings. Descend SW, on the right side of a chute. About 12 minutes beyond the col, pick up another game trail. Where the route is obscure, in thick vegetation and profuse flowers, briefly contour at about 2280 m (7478 ft). An obvious trail will resume. Then head SSE toward the pass. Forested Spray River valley is visible west below this upper basin.

About 20 minutes from the col, reach a rocky gully. Descend it to grass and krummholz. Continue to the head of **Birdwood Creek basin**. Mount a low, slabby rib. Hike among larches toward Birdwood Pass. Cross a creeklet in a small defile. Heading SSE, traverse meadows. Soon hop over another creek in a defile. Ascend a grassy depression.

Assault either side of the pass—left or right. We were pulled right, toward the black wall, rather than the gray one. If you are too, climb the scree gully right of the mound in the middle of the pass. About an hour from the col, arrive atop the mound in **Birdwood Pass**, at 8 km (5 mi), 2445 m (8020 ft). Visible NNW, more than 20 km (12.4 mi) distant, is Mt. Assiniboine. ENE, below you, is Burstall Creek valley, which you'll exit from Burstall Pass.

The terrain between Birdwood and Burstall passes is the trip's most precipitous. If all the snow has melted, however, surefooted hikers will encounter no danger. From the SW edge of Birdwood Pass, traverse the grassy, gravelly slope S beneath the east face of **Snow Peak**. Contour at about 2430 m (7970 ft). Visible NE, beyond Hwy 742, is Mt. Chester (Trip 13).

About 15 minutes south of Birdwood Pass, abandon the plunging slope. Angle SW on narrow, rocky, grassy ledges. Ascend about 15 m (49 ft) to surmount the shoulder of Snow Peak. It descends S, in steps. Reach **Burstall Pass** at 10 km (6.2 mi), 2380 m (7806 ft).

A sign here states trail distances to destinations in Banff National Park. Right descends generally W, intersecting the Spray River Valley trail in 4.7 km (2.9 mi). From there, right (NNW) leads to Bryant Creek; left (SE) crosses Palliser Pass. Another trail leads 1 km (0.6 mi) W to Leman Lake. If you started this trip early, and at least four hours of daylight remain, you have time to proceed 1.6 km (1 mi) generally S along the inviting, alpine ridge to South Burstall Pass.

Chipmunk

As for the Burstall Pass view, SSE is glacier-laden, 3407-m (11,175-ft) Mt. Sir Douglas. W, beyond and above Leman Lake, is Mt. Leval. N is Birdwood Pass. NNE is Mt. Birdwood, and just right of it is Commonwealth Peak. NE, beyond Hwy 742, is Mt. Galatea.

From Burstall Pass, a trail leads 7.5 km (4.7 mi) generally NE through Burstall Creek valley. After descending 465 m (1525 ft), it ends at Burstall day-use area, on Hwy 742, where your shuttle vehicle awaits. The following directions are minimal. Read Burstall Pass (Trip 10) for details.

Descend the trail ESE from Burstall Pass. It gradually curves N into **Burstall Creek valley**. Within 15 minutes it levels, heading E through a subalpine meadow at 2131 m (6990 ft). About 30 minutes from the pass, enter forest. A ten-minute descent ends at 2000 m (6560 ft), on the braided stream-channels of Willow Flats. They often flood, but not so deeply as to prevent you from crossing. Robertson Glacier is visible SSE. Signs with red blazes lead E, across the flat. The trail re-enters forest and heads generally NE. It soon widens into an old **logging road**. Follow it out to Hwy 742.

TRIP 10

Burstall Pass

LOCATION	N end Peter Lougheed Provincial Park, Hwy 742
ROUND TRIP	15 km (9.3 mi)
ELEVATION GAIN	480 m (1574 ft)
KEY ELEVATIONS	trailhead 1900 m (6232 ft), pass 2380 m (7806 ft)
HIKING TIME	5 to 7 hours
DIFFICULTY	easy
MAPS	page 60; Gem Trek *Kananaskis Lakes*

Opinion

We once overheard a conversation at the Burstall Pass trailhead. A man who was about to begin hiking approached another who'd just completed the hike.

"How was it?" he asked.

"Eet wazz…"

Clearly he was European, a non-native English speaker, and he hesitated, struggling to respond.

"Eet wazz… very strong," he finally answered, tapping his heart with his fist for emphasis.

What a beautiful answer. With just two words and a simple gesture, this foreigner eloquently described the emotional impact of witnessing the Canadian Rockies from atop Burstall Pass.

The trip begins on an old road where you'll stride easily, probing a forested valley beneath pewter peaks. After hopping across (or de-booting and sloshing through) shallow stream channels, you'll ascend to a hanging, subalpine valley. Then you'll proceed up the headwall to Burstall Pass, where exhilarating mountain scenery extends in all directions.

You'll see saber-sharp peaks slicing the sky. You'll peer over the pass into the southern reaches of Banff Park. You'll have enough visual stimuli to expand your emotions like a spinnaker in a gale.

The grassy alpine environs of the pass will prod you to explore, or induce you to lie down and let your mind walk the lush, lonesome bear haven of the Spray River Valley below. Try to keep moving. The ridge southwest of the pass is an easy, exciting, off-trail ramble where the panorama continues to unfold. In particular, glacier-chested Mt. Sir Douglas is more impressive the farther you go.

Fact

By Vehicle

In **Canmore**, drive W on Main (8th) Street. Turn left onto 8th Avenue. Follow it over the Bow River bridge. At the T-junction, turn left onto Three

photos: **1** *Wandering daisy* **2** *Monkshood* **3** *Burstall Pass alplands* **4** *Bluebell* **5** *Arnica*

1

2

3

4   5

Sisters Drive. Ascend, soon forking right onto Smith-Dorrien / Spray Trail (Hwy 742). Pass the Canmore Nordic Centre and reset your trip odometer to 0. Pavement ends at 1.2 km (0.7 mi). After crossing Whiteman's Gap, proceed generally SE. At 41.5 km (25.7 mi), immediately past Mud Lake, turn right (W) into the Burstall day-use area, at 1900 m (6232 ft). This is across from the Chester Lake day-use area.

From the **junction of Hwy 40 and Kananaskis Lakes Trail** (50 km / 31 mi S of Trans-Canada Hwy 1, or 17 km / 10.5 mi N of Highwood Pass), turn SW onto Kananaskis Lakes Trail. Reset your trip odometer to 0. At 2.2 km (1.4 mi) turn right (NW) onto unpaved Smith-Dorrien / Spray Trail (Hwy 742). At 22.2 km (13.8 mi), turn left (W) into the Burstall day-use area, at 1900 m (6232 ft).

On Foot

The trail departs the N end of the parking lot, where there are no trees. Go left (W), past the gated road, up onto the berm. Follow the berm SW, passing Mud Lake (right). Proceed onto a gravel road curving left (S). Within 70 m (77 ft), where the gravel road continues straight (SSE), fork right (SSW) onto a narrower, dirt road. Cross another berm, this one channeling French Creek (left) into a culvert. Ignore a faint right (SW) fork. Ascend left (S), following hiker signs. Just above, where a trail forks left (SE), stay on the road curving right (SW). You've hiked just five minutes from the trailhead. From here on, the navigating is more straightforward.

Follow the road SW along the N skirt of Mt. Burstall. Commonwealth Peak is right (N) across Burstall Creek valley. At 2.5 km (1.6 mi) pass Burstall Lakes (right / N). At 3.1 km (2 mi) cycling is prohibited beyond the cement bike stands. The road soon tapers to trail. At 3.6 km (2.2 mi) cross braided, shifting, sometimes flooded **stream channels of Willow Flats**. It's wettest in early summer. Expect to wade. The water is shallow, the current gentle, so it's not dangerous.

At 4 km (2.5 mi) begin climbing. Ascend W through dense forest about 30 minutes to emerge in **subalpine meadows**. The trail bends SW here. After a brief, level respite, the ascent resumes: S, curving NW. Reach 2380-m (7806-ft) **Burstall Pass** at 7.5 km (4.7 mi).

N of the pass is Snow Peak. NNE are, from left to right, Birdwood Pass (Trip 9), 3097-m 10,158-ft Mt. Birdwood, Pig's Tail, and Commonwealth Peak. Distant NE, beyond the trailhead, is the 3000-m (9840-ft) Fortress. SSW is 3406-m (11,172-ft) Mt. Sir Douglas.

Continue through the pass, around a sinkhole, to overlook upper Spray Valley. Leman Lake is W across the valley. Distant NW is 3611-m (11,845-ft) Mt. Assiniboine.

For the optimal view, proceed cross-country, ascending about 235 m (720 ft) to the **ridgecrest** SW of the pass. You'll see a huge expanse of Spray Valley, from Bryant Creek in the N to Palliser Pass in the S. Belgium Lake is just N of Palliser Pass. Mts. King Albert and Queen Elizabeth are immediately W of Belgium Lake. Roam the crest S, where Mt. Sir Douglas appears much closer.

TRIP 11
French & Robertson Glaciers

LOCATION	N end Peter Lougheed Provincial Park, Hwy 742
ROUND TRIP	14 km (8.7 mi)
ELEVATION GAIN	740 m (2427 ft)
KEY ELEVATIONS	trailhead 1900 m (6232 ft), col 2510 m (8233 ft)
	knoll 2330 m (7642 ft)
HIKING TIME	5 to 6 hours
DIFFICULTY	moderate due to basic routefinding
MAP	Gem Trek *Kananaskis Lakes*

Opinion

You will not find *Climate Change Col* or *Global Warming Knoll* on any map. The names are unofficial—bestowed by us.

Call them other names of your own choosing, if you prefer. You too are free to play cartographer until enough people have visited these places that a consensus builds regarding how they should forever be known.

That day is unlikely to arrive. Few have hiked here because very few are aware these places exist. And the lack of a formal trail beyond 3 km (1.9 mi) will continue to deter most hikers.

What they'll miss is a beautiful enclave, aerial views of two glaciers, the titillation that comes from exploring terra incognita, and the promise of solitude.

Yet there's nothing here that should deter most hikers. There's only one, minor obstacle: 30 minutes on a bootbeaten route until you surmount treeline and enter the subalpine zone where the way forward is again obvious. You can manage that with sufficient awareness to return the same way? You'll find this hike moderately easy yet hugely rewarding.

You'll ascend into a stark, alpine basin. You'll overlook French Glacier from Climate Change Col—an airy vantage surrounded by massive peaks. You'll hike through alplands studded with karst outcrops and sprinkled with larches. And you'll survey Robertson Glacier from Global Warming Knoll, which also commands a view of the peaks flanking Burstall Pass.

But why the names *Climate Change Col* and *Global Warming Knoll*?

First, because the French and Robertson glaciers are mere remnants— the final vestiges of what were once prodigious rivers of ice. Their recent, rapid demise is the result of forces humanity has contributed to and could, if it mustered the collective will, begin reversing.

Second, because all of us should and can reduce our footprint on Earth, starting right here. Please be vigilant about leaving no trace of your passage in this virginal, fragile setting. Rule number one: walk on rock wherever possible.

French Glacier, from Climate Change Col

Fact

By Vehicle

In **Canmore**, drive W on Main (8th) Street. Turn left onto 8th Avenue. Follow it over the Bow River bridge. At the T-junction, turn left onto Three Sisters Drive. Ascend, soon forking right onto Smith-Dorrien / Spray Trail (Hwy 742). Pass the Canmore Nordic Centre and reset your trip odometer to 0. Pavement ends at 1.2 km (0.7 mi). After crossing Whiteman's Gap, proceed generally SE. At 41.5 km (25.7 mi)—just past Mud Lake, and opposite the Chester Lake day-use area—turn right (W) into the Burstall day-use area at 1900 m (6232 ft).

From the **junction of Hwy 40 and Kananaskis Lakes Trail** (50 km / 31 mi S of Trans-Canada Hwy 1, or 17 km / 10.5 mi N of Highwood Pass), turn SW onto Kananaskis Lakes Trail. Reset your trip odometer to 0. At 2.2 km (1.4 mi) turn right (NW) onto unpaved Smith-Dorrien / Spray Trail (Hwy 742). At 22.2 km (13.8 mi)—opposite the Chester Lake day-use area—turn left (W) into the Burstall day-use area, at 1900 m (6232 ft).

On Foot

The trail departs the N end of the parking lot, where there are no trees. Go left (W), past the gated road, up onto the berm.

Follow the berm SW, passing Mud Lake (right). Proceed onto a gravel road curving left (S). Within 70 m (77 ft), where the gravel road continues straight (SSE), fork right (SSW) onto a narrower, dirt road.

Cross another berm, this one channeling French Creek (left) into a culvert. Ignore a faint right (SW) fork. Ascend left (S), following hiker signs.

Just above, where a trail forks left (SE), stay on the road curving right (SW). You've hiked just five minutes from the trailhead.

Follow the road SW along the N skirt of Mt. Burstall. Commonwealth Peak is right (N) across Burstall Creek valley. At 2.5 km (1.6 mi) pass Burstall Lakes (right /N).

At 3 km (1.9 mi), 2010 m (6593 ft), after rising out of a dip, be alert for an **overgrown, former road** (left / S). If you miss it and proceed SW, you'll immediately pass a large boulder (right), drop into and rise out of a gully, and within two minutes arrive at the cement bike stands (right) beyond which cycling is prohibited. The bike stands are about a 45-minute hike from the trailhead.

Depart the main road by ascending left (SSW) on the overgrown, former road. One minute up, reach a fork. Right is crudely blocked by logs. Ascend steeply left (SE), still on former road.

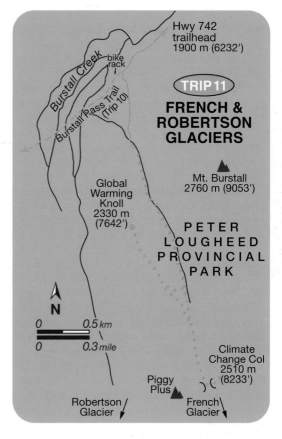

About ten minutes up, the grade eases. Reach another fork. Proceed straight (just left of S) on a bootbeaten route entering a narrow, tree-lined corridor. Ignore the obscure, right fork.

Two minutes farther, a tree-topped rock bluff is visible right. Continue SSW. One minute farther, you're paralleling the rock wall. The stream you'll soon follow is now audible. Enter mature forest.

In another two minutes, having hiked slightly more than one hour from the trailhead, arrive at the **stream** draining the basin ahead. Hop to the far (W) bank, and ascend left (S) on bootbeaten route. Note the small bedrock cascade and tiny pool, so you'll recognize this juncture when you return down-canyon.

The route rises into the trees but soon fades. Abandon it. Drop to the streambed where the hiking is easy. The water is now your guide. Keep following it upstream (generally S), crossing and recrossing as necessary.

Enter the **subalpine zone** where 2760-m (9053-ft) Mt. Burstall is visible above (left / E). It creates the prominent wall of the canyon you've entered.

Expect to encounter icy snow where avalanches careen down Mt. Burstall's scree slopes and slam into vertical bedrock along the right (W) streambank. Hiking atop the snow can speed your progress—if it's thick enough that it won't collapse. Keep to the edges, where it's safest, or skirt left of the snow.

In midsummer, the streamside greenery is lush and wildflowers are prolific. You might see yellow aster, paintbrush, alpine forget-me-not, Lyall's saxifrage, alpine buttercup, grass-of-Parnassus, and valerian.

Continuing up-canyon, the col you're aiming for is visible just left of S. Pass where the stream issues from beneath the talus. The ascent steepens in the **upper basin**. Favour the right (W) side of the draw for the final approach to the col.

Attain **Climate Change Col** at 6 km (3.7 mi), 2510 m (8233 ft), about 2 ¼ hours from the trailhead. The S edge of the col falls away sharply. The peaklet rising abruptly right (W) of the col is 2730-m (8954-ft) Piggy Plus, an outlier on Mt. Robertson's long, N ridge.

French Glacier is visible S, in the upper reaches of French Creek Canyon, between 3194-m (10,476-ft) Mt. Robertson (right / W) and 3234-m (10,608-ft) Mt. French (left / E). To glimpse Roberston Glacier (right / W of Mt. Robertson) ascend a couple minutes up the left (E) side of the col.

Ready for more? Turn N and observe the shelf left (W) of the stream. You'll see an undulating, subalpine meadow broken by karst outcrops and liberally adorned with larches. At the far N end, where the shelf narrows, a bald knoll is visible. That's your next goal.

Descend N from the col. When the grade eases, angle left (NNW) across the **shelf**. Drop into a **sink**, then ascend. Top out on **Global Warming Knoll** at 2330 m (7642 ft), about 2 km (1.2 mi) or 20 minutes from the col. Visible left (S) is Robertson Glacier. Below (E) is the 3-km (1.8-mi) long, rubble-strewn valley that the glacier created and occupied long ago.

The knoll view also comprises Snow Peak (just right of W) rising from Burstall Pass (Trip 10). NW is Birdwood Pass (Trip 9), and beyond it is Mt. Assiniboine. Mt. Birdwood is NNW. Pig's Tail is just left of N. Commonwealth Peak is N.

Robertson Glacier from Global Warming Knoll

Ready to leave? Retrace your steps SSE—descending then ascending—across the **shelf**. In about ten minutes (1 km / 0.6 mi from the knoll, or halfway to the col) curve left and find an easy slope dropping to the **streambed**.

You're now on familiar ground; return the way you came. While hiking down-canyon, remember to watch for where the route crosses then departs the stream (below the small bedrock cascade and tiny pool).

TRIP 12
Rummel Lake

LOCATION	Peter Lougheed Provincial Park, Hwy 742
ROUND TRIP	8.6 km (5.3 mi) to Rummel Lake
	plus 5 km (3 mi) to Rummel Pass
ELEVATION GAIN	355 m (1164 ft) to the lake
	plus 185 m (607 ft) to the pass
KEY ELEVATIONS	trailhead 1865 m (6117 ft)
	Rummel Lake 2220 m (7281 ft)
	Rummel Pass 2405 m (7888 ft)
HIKING TIME	3 to 4 hours for the lake
	plus 1 to 1½ hours for the pass
DIFFICULTY	easy
MAPS	Gem Trek *Kananaskis Lakes*
	Gem Trek *Canmore and Kananaskis Village*

Opinion

Ask Calgarians what they like best about their city, and not one in ten will say "the Rockies." It's like asking Parisians the same question and never hearing "the food."

It's not that Calgarians simply forget what's really important to them. It's that most are only dimly aware they live beside one of the world's great ranges, many rarely visit the mountains, and a substantial number have never (!) set foot on a trail.

That's okay. It's their choice. But it's shocking. And we'd all be better off if it were otherwise. Because hiking makes people healthier, happier, saner, calmer, more aware and appreciative of nature, and better able to deal with the stress and complexity of city life.

Hiking makes people better people.

And in Calgary, of all places, hiking should be celebrated by the masses. Here, you can drive to a Canadian Rockies trailhead in less time than most of us spend checking our email each day.

One of those trails leads to Rummel Lake, a little-known, easy-to-reach, scenic destination that's rarely crowded, usually tranquil, and likely to afford solitude.

Nearby Chester Lake (Trip 13), which is no more impressive than Rummel and arguably less so, has a palatial trailhead parking lot to accommodate a year-round parade of admirers.

Rummel has no parking lot. There's just a small, unsigned pullout across the road. So the trail inauspiciously departs the dusty shoulder of Hwy 742. Then it rises unceremoniously through a cutblock.

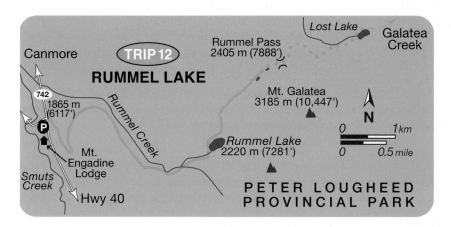

But the cutblock is regrowing vigourously. The view it grants of Spray Lakes Reservoir and the Sundance Range is stirring. And the trail soon enters forest, then delivers you to the grass-fringed lake at the base of soaring Mt. Galatea. The setting epitomizes the golden mean: exciting yet calming.

Plus, if you can resist the park-like lakeshore's curiously strong gravitational pull, or muster the will to resume hiking after you've succumbed, you can proceed to Rummel Pass. A few minutes above the lake, the trail transcends treeline and rolls through an alpine expanse worthy of Jasper National Park. After passing several lakelets, you'll crest the pass and find Lost Lake below the far side.

Fact

By Vehicle

In **Canmore**, drive W on Main (8th) Street. Turn left onto 8th Avenue. Follow it over the Bow River bridge. At the T-junction, turn left onto Three Sisters Drive. Ascend, soon forking right onto Smith-Dorrien / Spray Trail (Hwy 742). Pass the Canmore Nordic Centre and reset your trip odometer to 0. Pavement ends at 1.2 km (0.7 mi). After crossing Whiteman's Gap, proceed generally SE to 34 km (21.1 mi).

From the **junction of Hwy 40 and Kananaskis Lakes Trail** (50 km / 31 mi S of Trans-Canada Hwy 1, or 17 km / 10.5 mi N of Highwood Pass), turn SW onto Kananaskis Lakes Trail. Reset your trip odometer to 0. At 2.2 km (1.4 mi) turn right (NW) onto unpaved Smith-Dorrien / Spray Trail (Hwy 742). Proceed generally NW to 30.2 km (18.7 mi).

From **either approach**, just S of Rummel Creek, turn W onto Mt. Shark Road, signed for Engadine Lodge. Park in the first pullout (left / S). The unsigned trail starts across the highway, ENE from Mt. Shark Road, at 1865 m (6117 ft).

photos: *1 Rummel Lake* *2 Subalpine zone between Rummel Lake and Rummel Pass* *3 Ascending through the cutblock to Rummel Creek*

On Foot

The trail initially leads SE. Pass a sign reminding dog owners to leash their pets. Heading SSE, parallel the highway through a bushy **cutblock** for ten minutes. The young, robust trees are 20 to 25 ft (6 to 7.6 m) high. Still in the cutblock, curve left and ascend NE.

At 20 minutes, Spray Lakes Reservoir is visible left (NW). Mt. Birdwood is the prominent peak right (SSW). At nearly 30 minutes, 2065 m (6773 ft), the trail leads ESE into a **mature forest** of spruce and fir.

About 40 minutes along, the forest is more open and bearberry is profuse. At one hour, the trail grazes Rummel Creek at 2150 m (7052 ft). Follow the trail upstream (E). Ignore the bridge to the left (NE) bank. Stay on the right (S) bank for the more interesting approach.

Where the bank briefly steepens and crowds the creek, the trail traverses it, deteriorating to a rough, narrow route. Comfortable trail resumes just beyond. Pass above the right (S) side of a **cascade**. The trail continues NE along the base of a small rockslide, toward Mt. Galatea. Soon push through brush and rockhop to the creek's left (NNW) bank.

Reach the SW shore of **Rummel Lake**, beside the outlet, at 4.3 km (2.7 mi), 2220 m (7281 ft), about 1½ hours from the trailhead. Rising abruptly from the SE shore is 3185-m (10,447-ft) Mt. Galatea. Grass and alpine larch ring the lake.

For Rummel Pass, follow the main trail left (NNE), away from the lake. After a five-minute ascent left (N), break into the **alpine zone**. The trail curves right (NE). The ground cover includes tiny, white, mountain avens. Mounts Birdwood and Smuts are visible behind you (SW).

Cross an expanse of rocks and ascend a dryfall to arrive at a shallow **lakelet** (possibly dry) at 2350 m (7708 ft). Continue NE, passing another **lakelet** five minutes farther. On its left (N) side is a cairned route leading ENE toward the pass.

Ascend across chunky talus. Follow cairns through a depression. After hiking 2.5 km (1.6 mi) from the SW end of Rummel Lake, crest 2405-m (7888-ft) **Rummel Pass**. Total distance from the trailhead: 13.6 km (8.4 mi).

Hawkweed

Lost Lake is visible down-valley (ENE). From the pass, the route descends left (NE) across scree. It passes Lost Lake in 2.2 km (1.4 mi), then continues NE through forest another 3.2 km (2 mi) to intersect Galatea Creek trail (Trip 18) 2 mi (3.2 km) E of Lillian Lake.

TRIP 13

Chester Lake / Three Lakes Valley

LOCATION	Peter Lougheed Provincial Park, Hwy 742
ROUND TRIP	9 km (5.6 mi) to Chester
	13.5 km (7.4 mi) to third lake
ELEVATION GAIN	315 m (1030 ft) to Chester
	555 m (1820 ft) to third lake
KEY ELEVATIONS	trailhead 1910 m (6265 ft)
	Chester Lake 2220 m (7282 ft)
	third lake 2460 m (8070 ft)
HIKING TIME	3 to 4 hours for Chester
	4 to 5 hours for third lake
DIFFICULTY	easy
MAP	Gem Trek *Kananaskis Lakes*

Opinion

Countless Calgarians have hiked to Chester Lake. Many have done it repeatedly. It's the most popular trail in K-Country. For good reason: the difficulty / reward ratio is out of whack. A child can do it. Yet even mountaineers are moved by the splendour of the lake setting. Be thankful camping is prohibited. Otherwise a tribe of devoted Chesterites would establish a tent city here every summer.

Upon arrival at Chester Lake, most hikers stop and plop. It *is* a premier destination, particularly if you lack time or energy for a more vigourous, solitudinous outing, or if you're a parent toting infants or herding young-sters. But adventures beckon beyond. After admiring Chester Lake, persist to Three Lakes Valley, The Fortress, or Mt. Chester.

The initial 2 km (1.2 mi) to Chester Lake is on a former logging road reincarnated as a hiking and ski trail. It's broad, smooth, not too steep, quickly and easily dispatched while enjoying occasional mountain views. Above the regenerated clearcut, enter mature forest. The way finally levels out in meadows known for their dazzling, late-June display of glacier lilies and alpine buttercups. Autumn oranges and mauves are also delightful here. Approaching Chester Lake, the alps forming the cirque are visible ahead. Visual tension—stark, imposing cliffs, contrasting with lush, welcoming meadows—creates a scene of compelling drama.

Venturing north to Three Lakes Valley should be compulsory. A mere two-hour round trip from Chester Lake, it doubles the day's scenic reward. This intimate-but-awesome enclave is guarded by soaring Mt. Galatea and patrolled by stolid mountain goats. The lakes are small, just tarns really, and the third is often dry. But the first two are lovely. And the second offers a

Chester Lake, from Mt. Chester summit

superb view of grand, glacier-laden peaks on the Great Divide. En route, you'll pass a heap of colossal boulders. Scurry onto a flat one to lounge in the sun, relish your red-pepper hummus, or evade marmots jostling for attention. Bring your rock shoes for a little bouldering.

The canyon NE above Chester Lake leads to The Fortress—a distinctive, lofty bastille that, from Hwy 40, appears unassailable. But from this side, it's simply a moderate scramble to the big-grin view on top. Allow a full day. From the summit-ridge col, keen explorers loop back to the trailhead via Headwall Lakes (Trip 14). Even if your goal isn't The Fortress, nipping into the canyon is worthwhile. A 1½-hour round-trip from Chester Lake allows you to appreciate the fetching, grassy environs of upper Chester Creek.

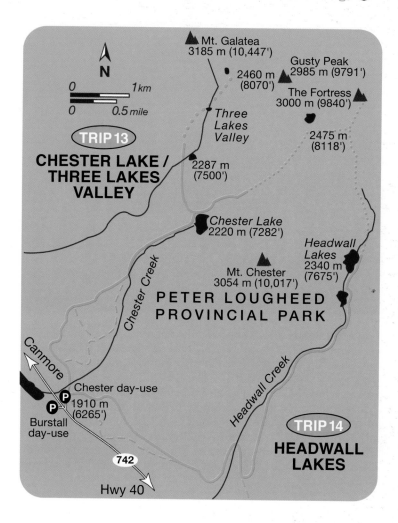

Swooping above Chester Lake's SE shore is Mt. Chester. Where the trail to the lake crosses the last meadow, look right (SE). The Mt. Chester scramble begins up that draw. It's a rugged ascent, gaining 834 m (2736 ft) from the meadow. If you're capable, however, you'll need no directional advice; it's straightforward. The summit panorama includes an arresting view of the Great Divide.

Fact

By Vehicle

In Canmore, drive W on Main (8th) Street. Turn left onto 8th Avenue. Follow it over the Bow River bridge. At the T-junction, turn left onto Three Sisters Drive. Ascend, soon forking right onto Smith-Dorrien / Spray Trail (Hwy 742). Pass the Canmore Nordic Centre and reset your trip odometer

Glacier lilies

to 0. Pavement ends at 1.2 km (0.7 mi). After crossing Whiteman's Gap, proceed generally SE. At 41.5 km (25.7 mi)—just past Mud Lake, and across from Burstall day-use area—turn left (E) into the enormous Chester Lake day-use area at 1910 m (6265 ft).

From the **junction of Hwy 40 and Kananaskis Lakes Trail** (50 km / 31 mi S of Trans-Canada Hwy 1, or 17 km / 10.5 mi N of Highwood Pass), turn SW onto Kananaskis Lakes Trail. Reset your trip odometer to 0. At 2.2 km (1.4 mi) turn right (NW) onto unpaved Smith-Dorrien / Spray Trail (Hwy 742). At 22.2 km (13.8 mi)—just before Mud Lake, and across from Burstall day-use area—turn right (E) into the enormous Chester Lake day-use area at 1910 m (6265 ft).

On Foot

From the NE corner of the parking lot (above the toilets and info kiosk), follow the unpaved road NE. Pass a gate in 40 m/yd. Quickly reach a fork. The narrow, overgrown road (right / E) leads to Headwall Lakes. For Chester Lake, bear left (N) on the broad, gravel road and immediately cross a bridge over **Chester Creek**. Likewise, go left at all subsequent junctions. The road climbs at a moderate grade through forest of primarily Engelmann spruce and alpine fir.

At 1942 m (6370 ft), about ten minutes up, reach a signed junction. Turn left (NW), as the hiker sign directs. At 2073 m (6800 ft), about 30 minutes up, French Creek is visible south. Burstall Pass (Trip 10) is southwest. Just north of it is Smuts Pass (Trip 9).

A few minutes farther, bear left (NE) at the next junction where right leads S. Your general direction of travel is NE. At 2.2 km (1.4 mi) the **road narrows to a wide trail**. It soon levels at 2140 m (7020 ft) in a small meadow.

You've now hiked about 45 minutes. Ups and downs are few and gentle the rest of the way. Meadows and trees alternate.

Descend into a large, tussocky meadow at 2.7 km (1.7 mi). Looking NNE you can see 3185-m (10,447-ft) Mt. Galatea at the head of Three Lakes Valley. From the next meadow, Mt. Chester is visible E. The trail then slips back into forest for 10 minutes before emerging in another meadow. Lavender fleabane (daisy shaped) thrive here.

At 4 km (2.5 mi) enter a sweeping, willowy **meadow below Mt. Chester**. The alps forming Chester Lake cirque are in view. Left (NNE, between Chester Lake and Three Lakes Valley) is 2985-m (9791-ft) Gusty Peak. Ahead (NE) is the 3000-m (9840-ft) Fortress. Right (E) is 3054-m (10,017-ft) Mt. Chester. The scramble route up Chester begins in the conspicuous draw SE. Behind you (SSW) is French Glacier, between Mt. Robertson and Mt. French.

An elevated pit toilet on the left heralds your arrival at **Chester Lake**. Reach the SW shore, near a footlog over the outlet stream, at 4.5 km (2.8 mi), 2220 m (7282 ft). Fleet-footed hikers eager to explore farther will be here about 1¼ hours after leaving the trailhead.

Three Lakes Valley

From Chester Lake to the third and highest lake in Three Lakes Valley is a 4.5 km (2.8 mi) round trip gaining 240 m (787 ft). Start at the footlog over the outlet stream on Chester Lake's SW shore. Follow the trail left, around the W shore. In 60 m (66 yd) turn left (NW) and ascend the first of two forks. The shoreline trail leads to upper Chester Creek. The two ascending forks soon merge. Proceed uphill among larches. At 2238 m (7340 ft), about five minutes above the lake, emerge from forest and encounter an array of **giant boulders**. It's reminiscent of southern California's Joshua Tree National Park. The trail passes left of the boulders.

In another five minutes, at 2256 m (7400 ft), enter a meadowy basin harbouring a stream-fed pond. The trail curves right (NNE) into Three **Lakes Valley**. Zigzag up rocky steps. Attain a view SW to Burstall Pass (Trip 10) and, just N of it, the distinctively long, NW ridge of Mt. Birdwood (Trip 9). The slopes here are lush green, adorned with wildflowers including yellow columbine and white Sitka valerian.

Though called *lakes*, the pools in this valley are actually small tarns. Reach the **first tarn** at 2287 m (7500 ft). Round its left side to ascend a narrow trail N through a grassy depression between trees on the left and rock slabs on the right. Where the trail fades above, pick your way over the slabby hump.

About 10 minutes above the first, reach the **second tarn** at 2410 m (7900). Gusty Peak forms the valley's right (E) wall. SSW is an excellent view of the Great Divide. The highest peak in that direction is 3407-m (11,175-ft) Mt. Sir Douglas.

Grass and moss campion (tight, green cushions, studded with tiny pink flowers) enliven the slabby terrain en route to the **third tarn**. Though shallower than the others and often dry, this last tarn, at 2460 m (8070 ft), is a worthy goal. It's deeper in the valley, where you can fully appreciate the intricacies and magnitude of 3185-m (10,447-ft) Mt. Galatea, directly N. The head of the valley, above the third tarn, is an austere, gray, talus bowl.

Upper Chester Creek

Follow the trail left, around the NW shore. Bear right (E), passing two left forks that ascend to Three Lakes Valley. Climb into the forest on a rough, twisting path. From here on, your general direction of travel is NE. At 2223 m (7290 ft), drop to and cross a meadow. Ascend the grassy slope beneath the scree on the left (N). At 2271 m (7450 ft), about ten minutes up, you're among larches, near **treeline**. Chester Lake is visible below. Among many notable landmarks on the Great Divide, Burstall Pass is SW. Just N of it, is the distinctively long, NW ridge of Mt. Birdwood (Trip 9). At 2363 m (7750 ft), about 20 minutes up, The Fortress is visible NE. Over the next rocky rib, you can see deeper into the canyon. The meadows here are small, delicate, exquisitely picturesque. Hints of bootbeaten path continue. **Upper Chester Creek** is above ground for only about 50 m/yd, at 2400 m (7872 ft). Strong hikers will be here within 30 minutes of departing Chester Lake. Negotiating the bouldery expanse beyond is no fun, but it's necessary if proceeding to The Fortress or Headwall Lakes (Trip 14).

The Fortress

About 2 km (1.2 mi) up the canyon NE above Chester Lake, turn right (E) and scramble up steep scree to the 2710-m (8889-ft) **col**. You're now 490 m (1607 ft) above Chester Lake; 290 m (951 ft) below The Fortress. Turn left (NNE) and ascend the **ridgecrest**. Loose scree atop rock slabs demands attention. The ridge then widens and the angle of ascent eases. Toil onward. The angle further relaxes, but the crest narrows. Bear left below the summit crags, then angle right over blocks and scree to the 3000-m (9840-ft) **summit**. Total elevation gain: 780 m (2558 ft) from Chester Lake, 1090 m (3575 ft) from the trailhead. Total distance: 8.2 km (5.1 mi) from the trailhead. A few of the panorama highlights are Mt. Assiniboine (W), Mt. Joffre (S), the Opal Range (SE), Mt. Kidd (NNE), and Mt. Galatea (nearby NW).

Headwall Lakes

From the 2710-m (8889-ft) col on the ridgecrest leading to The Fortress, it's possible to drop E, then S down-canyon, looping back to the Chester Lake trailhead via Headwall Lakes. The day's total mileage—15 km (9.3 mi)— makes the journey sound easier than it is. The col is extremely steep; both the ascent and descent are demanding. Most of the 4 km (2.5 mi) from Chester Lake to upper Headwall Lake is on untracked, rocky terrain. Navigation, however, should pose no problem if you have a topo map in hand, or you're an experienced cross-country rambler.

TRIP 14
Headwall Lakes

LOCATION	Peter Lougheed Provincial Park, Hwy 742
ROUND TRIP	14 km (8.7 mi) to upper lake
ELEVATION GAIN	430 m (1410 ft)
KEY ELEVATIONS	trailhead 1910 m (6265 ft)
	upper lake 2340 m (7675 ft)
HIKING TIME	5 to 6 hours
DIFFICULTY	moderate
MAPS	page 77; Gem Trek *Kananaskis Lakes*

Opinion

Hiking whittles away at people, chipping them down to their essence. That's why true hikers, those for whom hiking is a bright, strong thread in the fabric of their lives, are authentic, without pretense or facade. Almost never will you meet a hiker who's a monster of self-regard. Maybe that's why Canmorites are so amiable. Many can start hiking at their doorsteps. And some of the Rockies' most rewarding trails are nearby. Like this one, to Headwall Lakes.

It begins at the same trailhead that serves Chester Lake. The trip to Chester, just one canyon north, is easier, shorter, more popular, and therefore siphons off most of the crowd. Headwall Lakes canyon, however, is equally beautiful. It's just a little longer, a bit more challenging, and feels wilder. But the Three Lakes Valley extension of the Chester hike also fits that description. So, you've a decision to make. Go to Chester if you're feeling social, in the mood for meadows. Go to Headwall if you're drawn to austerity and want to see waterfalls.

Your first 45 minutes hiking to Headwall Lakes will be on former logging roads reincarnated as hiking and ski trails. Though less than lovely, they allow brisk striding and an occasional mountain view. Then you'll follow an undeveloped trail along a creek to a cascade crashing down the first headwall. An abrupt ascent then vaults you into alplands. The view explodes all the way to the Great Divide. After a rest at lower Headwall Lake, climb past the cascade adorning the next headwall to arrive at the upper lake.

Before booting it home, consider your options. The head of the canyon above upper Headwall Lake is not a dead end. It's possible to scramble to a col and, from there, either assault The Fortress or loop back to the trailhead via Chester Lake.

Looping over the col, without detouring to The Fortress, your total day's mileage will be 15 km (9.3 mi). It makes the journey sound easier than it is. The col is extremely steep; both the ascent and descent are demanding. Most of the 4 km (2.5 mi) from upper Headwall Lake to Chester Lake is on untracked, rocky terrain. Navigation, however, should pose no problem if you have a topo map in hand, or you're an experienced cross-country rambler. Reading Chester Lake (Trip 13) will help you fully appreciate what the loop entails.

Fact

By Vehicle

Follow the directions for Chester Lake (Trip 13). Chester and Headwall lakes share the same trailhead, at 1910 m (6265 ft).

On Foot

From the NE corner of the parking lot (above the toilets and info kiosk), follow the unpaved road NE. Pass a gate in 40 m/yd. Quickly reach a fork. The broad, gravel road (left / N) crosses bridged Chester Creek and leads to Chester Lake. For Headwall Lakes, turn right (E) onto the narrower, overgrown road marked with a blue cross-country ski-trail sign. It snakes through forest before heading generally SSE. Peaks across the valley are occasionally visible.

In about 15 minutes, at 1.4 km (0.9 mi), 1966 m (6450 ft), cross a regrowing clearcut and reach a fork. There's a map-sign here. Left (NE) ascends sharply and is marked with an orange ski-trail sign. Go right (E), following the blue ski-trail sign.

At 1.9 km (1.1 mi) intersect the road marked with a yellow ski-trail sign. Right descends W. Go left (SE). The gentle ascent continues.

A tight curve left (NE) rises to a junction at 2.6 km (1.6 mi), 2021 m (6630 ft), in another regrowing clearcut. Your destination, Headwall Creek canyon, is visible ahead (NE). Mt Chester is NNE. The road marked with an orange ski-trail sign ascends left (N). Descend right (NE) on the road marked with a yellow ski-trail sign.

After a short, easy ascent, drop to a **bridge over Headwall Creek**, at 3.2 km (2 mi), 2037 m (6680 ft), about 45 minutes from the trailhead.

Cross the bridge and bear left. Shortly upstream, above the SE bank, the road curves right (S) and ascends steeply. In a couple minutes, the road levels at 3.7 km (2.3 mi). Look left for a **cairn** indicating where to abandon the road and turn E onto a trail.

Ascend through rooty, disenchanted forest. Your general direction of travel is soon NNE. At 2073 m (6800 ft), about an hour from the trailhead, enter the subalpine zone near boisterous Headwall Creek. The peak-lined valley is visible ahead. Left (N) is 3054-m (10,017-ft) Mt. Chester. Right (NE) is 3035-m (9958-ft) Mt. James Walker.

In another 15 minutes, the trail goes left, along the creek, at the base of a **rockslide**. It heads toward the cascade on the first headwall, then climbs very steeply right (E). Zigzag up steps and ledges. Curve N.

Crest the **first headwall** at 6.8 km (4.2 mi), 2296 m (7530 ft), about two hours from the trailhead. The first of the two Headwall Lakes is just ahead. Sharp limestone karst is underfoot. Visible behind you (SW) are glacier-laden, 3050-m (10,000-ft) peaks on the Great Divide.

At 2260 m (7413 ft) round the W shore of **lower Headwall Lake**. A rough, steep path climbs right of the cascade on the second headwall. Though there's no exposure, the ascent demands sure footing and might require you to grapple with roots and rocks. Crest the second headwall and arrive at **upper Headwall Lake** about 15 minutes after leaving the lower lake. Elevation: 2340 m (7675 ft). Total distance: 7 km (4.3 mi).

To scramble up The Fortress, or to loop back to the trailhead via Chester Lake (Trip 13), proceed up-canyon. Start by rounding the E shore of upper Headwall Lake. Ascend steadily. The terrain gradually tilts skyward. Scramble up the scree. Aim for the left gap in the low point NW. Keep toiling until you reach the 2710-m (8889-ft) col on the ridgecrest leading to The Fortress. You've gained 370 m (1214 ft) in 1.9 km (1.2 mi) since leaving upper Headwall Lake.

From the col, **The Fortress** is right (NNE), 290 m (951 ft) higher and 1.6 km (1 mi) farther. If that's your goal, follow the directions in Trip 13.

Your other option is **Chester Lake**, 490 m (1607 ft) below you and 2.1 km (1.3 mi) distant. To loop back to the trailhead that way, begin the sharp descent W. Upon reaching the jumbled canyon floor, bear left (SW). Pass upper Chester Creek at 2400 m (7872 ft). It's above ground for only 50 m/yd. Then pick up the path dropping to Chester Lake (visible below). The rest of the way to the trailhead is well defined and popular. If you need directions, follow those for Trip 13 in reverse.

Ascending from lower to upper Headwall Lake. Great Divide in background.

TRIP 15
James Walker Creek Basins

LOCATION	Peter Lougheed Provincial Park, Hwy 742
CIRCUIT	15.8 km (9.8 mi)
ELEVATION GAIN	600 m (1968 ft)
KEY ELEVATIONS	trailhead 1875 m (6150 ft)
	confluence of upper basins 2300 m (7544 ft)
	basin highpoints 2450 m (8036 ft)
HIKING TIME	5 to 6 hours
DIFFICULTY	moderate
MAP	Gem Trek *Kananaskis Lakes*

Opinion

This isn't a trail. It's a psycho path. Oh, the trailhead looks normal enough. It even affords views as impressive as those you typically must hike to attain. But a few minutes into the journey you'll discover the psychotic nature of the path itself.

It begins as an old, abandoned logging road, one in a network of industrial scars snaking all over this slope. The roads were eventually reclaimed by the provincial park for cross-country skiing and signed with colour-coded trail symbols. But that use was abandoned too. It remains an overgrown, seemingly aimless road accessing not a constructed trail but a bootbeaten route: narrow, rough, briefly steep, possibly muddy, but always distinct, easy to follow.

So the path's psychosis is due to the same cruelties—abuse and neglect— that induce psychopathic behaviour in humans. And, just as psychologically aberrant people sometimes exhibit startling brilliance, so does this psycho path: it leads to a pair of scenically splendid, tarn splashed, alpine basins, both of which you can savour on a dayhike.

These are the headwater basins of James Walker Creek. A mere 90 minutes from the trailhead, you'll spurt out of the forest into the rolling, park-like expanse beneath the basins' confluence. From there on, you can romp the alplands.

You'll enjoy constant views. The 3000-m (9840-ft) peaks walling-in the basins are impressive glimpsed from Hwy 742 but spectacular up close. And you might roam in delicious solitude, because the deranged approach deters crowds.

Though similar, the basins are unique, so probe them both. The basin mouths are wet, green, welcoming havens, while the upper reaches are dry, barren, forbidding lunarscapes. If you have time for only one, go left (NNW) into the basin beneath Mt. James Walker's long, south ridge.

Be keenly aware of bears. Though an encounter here is no more likely than elsewhere in the Canadian Rockies, it could have more serious

Great Divide, from James Walker Creek basins

consequences. That's because the confluence of the James Walker basins is prime grizzly habitat, as evidenced by profuse "bear tear" (ground cover disturbed by feeding bears). And the area is small, with only one narrow point at which people or bruins can easily enter or exit.

So be vigilant upon entering the alpine zone. If you spot a bear, leave immediately: quickly but quietly. Otherwise the bear might feel cornered, perceive you as a threat, and respond aggressively.

Fact

By Vehicle

In **Canmore**, drive W on Main (8th) Street. Turn left onto 8th Avenue. Follow it over the Bow River bridge. At the T-junction, turn left onto Three Sisters Drive. Ascend, soon forking right onto Smith-Dorrien / Spray Trail (Hwy 742). Pass the Canmore Nordic Centre and reset your trip odometer to 0. Pavement ends at 1.2 km (0.7 mi). After crossing Whiteman's Gap, proceed generally SE to 47.6 km (29.5 mi).

From the **junction of Hwy 40 and Kananaskis Lakes Trail** (50 km / 31 mi S of Trans-Canada Hwy 1, or 17 km / 10.5 mi N of Highwood Pass), turn SW onto Kananaskis Lakes Trail. Reset your trip odometer to 0. At 2.2 km (1.4 mi) turn right (NW) onto unpaved Smith-Dorrien / Spray Trail (Hwy 742) and drive to 16.6 km (10.3 mi).

From **either approach**, turn NE into the Sawmill day-use-area parking lot. Elevation: 1875 m (6150 ft).

On Foot

Begin on the abandoned road departing the NNE corner of the parking lot, behind the toilets. Follow it uphill to a nearby gate. Fifteen paces beyond the **gate**, fork left (NE). The ascent is gentle but steady. Ignore the cross-country skiing / snowshoeing signs.

About 20 minutes from the trailhead, reach a **junction**. Right leads SE. Go left (N). Five minutes farther, at 2 km (1.3 mi), reach a **fork**. Left (NNW) descends to **James Walker Creek** (audible, not yet visible) in the canyon below. Go right (N) and ascend.

About ten minutes farther, the former road curves right (NE), enters James Walker Creek canyon, and dwindles to a bootbeaten trail. Expect to encounter deadfall.

At 4.2 km (2.5 mi), 2128 m (6980 ft), arrive at what can be—depending on the previous winter's snowfall—either a large, beautiful **tarn, or mud flat** cleaved by a creek.

Round the tarn's right (E) shore. Proceed to the NE corner of the clearing, where the tarn's **inlet creek** emerges from forest. The trail re-enters the trees here. Follow it upstream, generally NE.

The ascent steepens. Plunge pools are visible in the gorge below. Follow cairns along the base of a **rockslide**. Hop a **spring** cascading from a **limestone cliff**. Enter the **alpine zone** at 5.5 km (3.4 mi), 2300 m (7544 ft), about 90 minutes from the trailhead.

Cross-country travel ensues above treeline. So stop, turn around, and fix in your mind where you exited the trees. After exploring the **upper basins**, you must return here and find the trail.

Ahead (NNE) is 3035-m (9958-ft) Mt. James Walker (JW). Right (W) is 3000-m (9843-ft) Mt. Inflexible. Those two giants define your options. A gradual ascent left (NNW) leads to the basin beneath JW's long, S ridge. A steeper ascent right (E, then NE) leads to the basin beneath Inflexible's N ridge.

Confluence of James Walker Creek basins

In either direction, you'll hike over rock and heather, pass tarns, and find countless inviting places to stop, rest and gaze. If time allows, probe both basins. Start by going left (N).

Ideally, complete a 4.8-km (3-mi) circuit. From the first basin, contour SE, then ascend NE into the second basin. Your highpoint in either basin likely won't exceed 2450 m (8036 ft).

When leaving the second basin, descend left (SW), aiming for where the trail initially deposited you in the alpine zone. You're then on familiar ground. Retrace your steps to the trailhead.

TRIP 16
Mt. Allan

LOCATION	Bow Valley Wildland Provincial Park
	Hwy 40 near Kananaskis Village
ROUND TRIP	14.6 km (9 mi)
ELEVATION GAIN	1313 m (4307 ft)
KEY ELEVATIONS	trailhead 1506 m (4940 ft)
	Olympic Summit 2457 m (8059 ft)
	Mt. Allan 2819 m (9246 ft)
HIKING TIME	7 to 8 hours
DIFFICULTY	challenging due only to elevation gain
MAPS	page 94; Gem Trek *Canmore & Kananaskis Village*

Opinion

Methylsulfonylmethane is a sulphur compound known by the abbreviation MSM. It's easy to remember. Think of it as *Mountain Suffering Minimized*.

MSM helps prevent joint inflammation while enhancing the efficacy of another dietary supplement, glucosamine, which rebuilds damaged joint cartilage.

Just thought you'd want to know that before you go charging up the south ridge of Mt. Allan on the highest trail in the Canadian Rockies.

Few ridges in this or any other mountain range loft hikers above treeline for so long. But this one's rarely level. Summitting 2819-m (9246-ft) Mt. Allan requires a sustained, uphill assault.

This is the Centennial Trail, built by Calgary's Rocky Mountain Ramblers to commemorate Canada's 1967 Centennial. It's efficient, leading you so quickly to a grand, alpine panorama high above Nakiska Ski Area that you might wonder, "Why go higher?"

True, some hikers turn around at Olympic Summit, about two kilometres shy of Mt. Allan, feeling proud and satisfied. At this point, however, most of the ascent is behind you yet most of the reward is ahead.

You'll soon stride past huge, moonscape pinnacles. The big-mountain scenery continues expanding. And a new view awaits you on top: north, up the Bow Valley, beyond Canmore, into Banff National Park.

Except at a couple momentarily craggy passages, the trail poses no obstacle but ballistic steepness. So enlist your arms and shoulders in this campaign, not just your legs. Bring a pair of poles.

Old ski poles will suffice, but positive-angle, adjustable-length trekking poles are better. Poles not only help you climb faster with less effort, they absorb much of the impact that such a sustained, sharp descent will otherwise inflict on your body.

On our last Mt. Allan hike, most people we saw atop the peak arrived there with trekking poles. Everyone who turned back early did so empty handed.

Mt. Lougheed, from the ridgecrest leading to Mt. Allan summit

Below Olympic Summit

Ideally, hike Mt. Allan before mid-August, while the grassy, summit ridge remains an emerald carpet woven with colourful wildflowers.

Want to traverse the entire peak? A trail continues off the summit, down the north ridge. It leads to a trailhead near Deadman's Flats and Trans-Canada Hwy 1. But it soon plunges into forest. Better to relish the hard-won vistas longer by returning the way you came.

Fact

Before your trip

Be aware that hiking Mt. Allan is prohibited April 1 through June 21, when bighorn sheep are lambing on the summit ridge.

By Vehicle

From Trans-Canada Hwy 1, drive 23 km (14.3 mi) S on Hwy 40. Or, from the junction of Hwy 40 and Kananaskis Lakes Trail, drive 27 km (16.7 mi) N on Hwy 40. From either approach, turn W at the sign for Kananaskis Village. Reset your trip odometer to 0. Cross a bridge over the Kananaskis River. At 0.8 km (0.5 mi) turn left. At 1 km (0.6 mi) turn right. Pass the hostel and a picnic shelter, both on the right. At 1.6 km (1 mi) enter the Ribbon Creek day-use area. Park at the near (E) end, close to the toilets (left) and trailhead kiosk (right). The elevation here is 1506 m (4940 ft).

On Foot

From the kiosk at the NE corner of the parking lot (near the toilets), hike NNW on a former road entering forest.

Ahead is a network of former roads where junctions are frequent. This is a popular hike, however, so it's signed, and the way forward is evident due to the passage of many boots.

Until you're on a straightforward trail, about 30 minutes up, here's what to do if uncertain at those junctions: (1) Turn left (W). (2) Bear left (NW). (3) Cross a former road and proceed straight (WNW). (4) Intersect a former road, jog right, then ascend left on trail. (5) Cross a former road and continue ascending. (6) Contour left (SW) on a former road.

At 2.1 km (1.3 mi) 1735 m (5691 ft), reach a **viewpoint on a meadowy slope** (left). Resume right (SW) and switchback upward.

You're now following an actual trail (not a former road) and will encounter no junctions. The trail surges abruptly above treeline, keeps to the alpine ridgecrest, and heads generally NW all the way to the summit of Mt. Allan.

Significant sights en route include 2958-m (9702-ft) Mt. Kidd (S), Ribbon Creek valley (SSW), 3144-m (10,312-ft) Mt. Bogart (SW, above and just beyond 2880-m / 9446-ft Ribbon Peak), 3121-m (10,237-ft) Mt. Sparrowhawk (W), 3107-m (10,191-ft) Mt. Lougheed (NW), 2450-m (8036-ft) Mt. McGillivray (NNE), and 2487-m (8157-ft) Mt. Lorette (NE).

After negotiating a short cliffband, the trail crests **Olympic Summit** at 4.3 km (2.7 mi), 2457 m (8059 ft). Pass weather-data gizmos. Enjoy easy striding W over gentle slopes. SW, across North Ribbon Creek valley, upper Memorial Lake is visible on the chest of Mt. Bogart.

From the W edge of Olympic Summit, turn right (NW), descend, then begin climbing again. At 5.4 km (3.3 mi) pierce a corridor created by the ridgecrest (right) and a fin comprising **rock pinnacles** (left).

The trail briefly requires easy scrambling off a rock shelf, then traverses scree, regains the ridgecrest, and ascends talus. Crest the 2819-m (9246-ft) summit of **Mt. Allan** at 7.3 km (4.5 mi). The four peaks of Mt. Lougheed loom nearby (W and NW).

Mt. Allan

TRIP 17
Memorial Lakes

LOCATION	Bow Valley Wildland Provincial Park
	Hwy 40, near Kananaskis Village
ROUND TRIP	14.8 km (9.2 mi) to middle lake
	16 km (10 mi) to upper lake
ELEVATION GAIN	599 m (1965 ft) to middle lake
	759 m (2490 ft) to upper lake
KEY ELEVATIONS	trailhead 1506 m (4940 ft), middle lake 2105 m
	(6904 ft), upper lake 2265 m (7429 ft)
HIKING TIME	5 to 6 hours for middle lake, 6 to 7 for upper
DIFFICULTY	moderate to middle lake, challenging to upper
MAP	Gem Trek *Canmore & Kananaskis Village*

Opinion

Hiking evolves beyond recreation. Fostering calm and clarity, it becomes meditation. Revealing how nature manifests the divine, it becomes reverent, a form of worship. It can even usher us into mystical terrain—our feet taking us as far as it's possible to go.

In pursuit of that loftier goal, aim for upper Memorial Lake. You'll find the tranquility that allows for a deeper experience, because the trail is too obscure and challenging to attract a crowd. And the climax is beautiful. The upper lake adorns an austere, alpine cirque—headwaters of Ribbon Creek's north fork—beneath massive peaks.

The trip begins at Ribbon Creek day-use area, beside the boisterous creek. From here, a broad, former road ascends mercifully. It shadows the creek for about 8 km (5 mi) to Ribbon Falls. Early on, it twice crosses the creek on sturdy bridges and passes a creekside picnic table. This initial stretch—walkable May through November—is a soothing, 45-minute, out-and-back amble, ideal for anyone soft as meringue.

You're tough as beef jerky? Veer off the road onto an unsigned, primitive trail: brushy, rocky, rooty, narrow. At times, it's just a scratch in the earth. And it tilts increasingly skyward, following Ribbon Creek's rowdy north fork. The first Memorial Lake is a bush-bound puddle—a disappointment, though it does afford a tantalizing view of the high country. Only a scurfy route continues. Expect a steep, moderately-difficult rock romp to the turquoise middle lake in a classically beautiful, subalpine bowl. But even there, you might feel overworked and under compensated. Push on. Just above is the upper lake, guarded by a short, precipitous scramble on gritty, unstable terrain.

If you're fit and capable, you'll enjoy grappling with this final obstacle and surmount it quickly. You can then celebrate your accomplishment with a lakeshore victory lap. Admire the surrounding alplands. Gaze up at the lake's guardian peaks. Perhaps savour a few precious moments of calm and clarity.

Scrambling above middle Memorial Lake

Fact

By Vehicle

From the Trans-Canada (Hwy 1), drive 23 km (14.3 mi) S on Hwy 40. Or, from the junction of Hwy 40 and Kananaskis Lakes Trail, drive 27 km (16.7 mi) N on Hwy 40. From either approach, turn W following signs for Kananaskis Village. Reset your trip odometer to 0. Immediately cross a bridge over the Kananaskis River. At 0.8 km (0.5 mi) turn left. At 1 km (0.6 mi) turn right. Pass the hostel, then a covered picnic shelter, both on the right. At 1.6 km (1 mi) reach the Ribbon Creek day-use area and trailhead parking lot. Continue to the far (W) end, at 1506 m (4940 ft).

On Foot

The Ribbon Creek trail, a former road, departs the far (W) end of the parking lot. After two bridged creek crossings, pass a picnic table and begin a gradual ascent. Reach a signed junction at 2.5 km (1.6 mi), 1595 m (5230 ft). The Kovach ski trail drops left to a bridge. Continue straight.

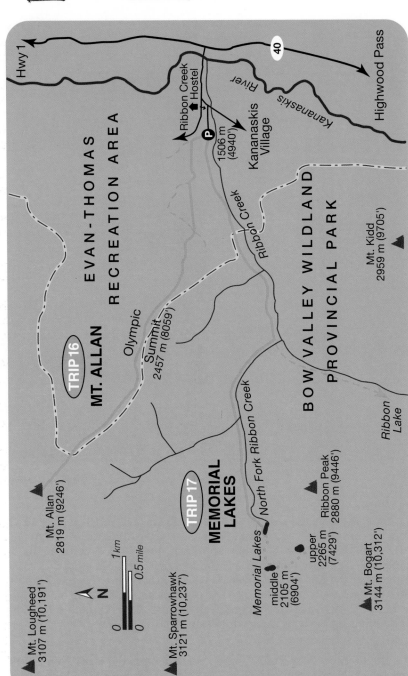

Where the road levels again and the forest opens, look for a **cairned trail** (right / NW). It's at 3.7 km (2.3 mi), about 40 minutes along. The road parallels Ribbon Creek SW to Ribbon Falls. For Memorial Lakes, follow the trail into Ribbon Creek's **north-fork drainage**.

The trail plows through small trees, climbs above the N fork's NE bank, and soon forks. Left is easier. A few minutes farther, stay high, on the better trail. Ahead, cross a steep, eroded slope.

At 1726 m (5660 ft), about 1¼ hours along, the trail levels briefly along the creek bank, then ascends right. Cross a footlog spanning a **tributary**. Proceed W.

At 1890 m (6200 ft), about 1¾ hours along, the trail is comfortably broad and level, heading W. A left spur detours to a showy **cascade** where the N fork plummets through a rocky gorge.

Resume on the trail, ascending steeply, skirting the right (N) edge of the gorge. Above the cascade, enjoy a level respite along the creek bank. Turn left, hop a **tributary**, and hike SSW.

The **first Memorial Lake** is at 6.8 km (4.2 mi), 1955 m (6412 ft). Strong hikers arrive here in about two hours. It's just a pond in a willow-choked bowl with muddy banks, but formidable mountains surround it.

Left (SE) is 2880-m (9446-ft) Ribbon Peak. On the horizon (SSW) is 3144-m (10,312-ft) Mt. Bogart. Nearby (WSW) is Bogart Tower. Far right (NW) is 3121-m (10,237-ft) Mt. Sparrowhawk. A multi-stage cascade drops beneath Bogart Tower to the far (S) side of the first lake.

Begin an athletic 30-minute clamber to the middle lake. The trail, diminishing to route, rounds the first lake's W end. Rough but discernible, it leads through willows. Hop the inlet stream.

Above the stream's S bank, turn right (W). Ascend along the base of Bogart Tower. Cairns guide you up a rockslide. Reach a cairned boulder at the edge of a small, treed bench, beneath another rockslide.

Ascend steeply left (generally SW). Follow a bootbeaten path above the rockslide, angling left beneath an overhanging rock shelf then curving right above it. At 7.4 km (4.6 mi), 2105 m (6904 ft), overlook **middle Memorial Lake** (right / N) from its S shore.

Only strong, experienced scramblers should continue. If you're capable, the way forward is obvious. From the middle lake, ascend S. The route steepens and narrows dramatically. Soon bear left and scramble (yes, hands-on) through a vertical gully. A few minutes above, the grade eases but remains steep.

A path leads SW through a meadowy draw. It levels, then ascends the right side of a tiny basin. At 8 km (5 mi), 2265 m (7429 ft), overlook **upper Memorial Lake** (E).

The lake occupies an alpine cirque beneath Ribbon Peak (ESE) and Mt. Bogart (SSW). The namesake memorial—a heart-rending **cenotaph** honouring the 13 victims of a tragic, 1986 aviation disaster—is atop a knoll above the NE shore.

1

2

3

4

TRIP 18
Galatea Lakes / Guinn's Pass

LOCATION	Spray Valley Provincial Park, Hwy 40
ROUND TRIP	17 km (10.5 mi) to upper Galatea Lake
	16 km (10 mi) to Guinn's Pass
ELEVATION GAIN	670 m (2198 ft) to upper Galatea Lake
	870 m (2854 ft) to Guinn's Pass
KEY ELEVATIONS	trailhead 1550 m (5084 ft)
	lower Galatea Lake 2180 m (7150 ft)
	Guinn's Pass 2420 m (7940 ft)
HIKING TIME	5½ hours for Galatea Lakes
	7 hours for Guinn's Pass
DIFFICULTY	moderate to Galatea Lakes
	challenging to Guinn's Pass
MAP	Gem Trek *Canmore and Kananaskis Village*

Opinion

Hiking is more than what you see, who you're with, or what you accomplish. It's what you bring back, mentally, emotionally, spiritually. Returning from Guinn's Pass—despite that it's actually not far from civilization—we've felt that alchemic blend of exhilaration and serenity that the big wild, at its purest and sharpest, always stirs in us.

The final ascent from Galatea Creek to Guinn's Pass is demanding enough to feel purifying. The new view from the pass is into consummate Canadian Rockies high country: the basin harbouring Ribbon Lake. The peaks visible from the pass are as rousing as any that K-Country has tossed at the sky. And the pass itself is an unusually freeing one, allowing you to easily wander ever higher up a gentle, alpine slope toward Mt. Kidd until you find a place to marinate in the powerful yet ineffable influences here.

Yet Guinn's is often ignored because of the steep climb, and because people fixate on the Galatea Lakes, which are better known and easier to reach. Most hikers blow by the turnoff to Guinn's with only a sideways glance. Sure, the Galateas are beautiful. But to reach Guinn's Pass is to touch the distinguishing essence of the range. It's not just that there's more to see from the pass. There's more to feel, thus more to bring home within you.

The trail to Galatea and Guinn's starts by crossing a bridge over the Kananaskis River. It then romps up Galatea Creek canyon, where you'll partake of K-Country's most cheerful creekside hiking. The signed Guinn's Pass fork peels off just before Lillian Lake.

Lillian, thickly girdled by trees, is unattractive. It doesn't compare to the Galatea Lakes, ringed by immense peaks in the alpine basin above. But when weighing the comparative merits of the Galatea Lakes and Guinn's

photos: *1 Memorial above upper lake's northeast shore 2 Middle Memorial Lake
3 Wild blue flax 4 Cascade en route to Memorial Lakes*

Pass, consider that the shoulder of Mt. Kidd—a short, easy walk-up from Guinn's—grants a view of the Galatea Lakes, plus a lot more.

The Guinn's Pass trail will work you. That's apparent when you gaze up at its skyward trajectory. Switchbacks are minimal. The lower reaches are bouldery. It's thirsty work on a hot day, and you'll find no water at the pass. There might be a trailside trickle, but don't rely on it. Bring all the water you'll need.

Though steep, the ascent itself offers rewards. Wildflowers sprout with surprising alacrity in the rocky terrain. And the anticipation aroused on such an intense climb can be as delicious as the climax. Savour it. The traverse of green, alpine slopes, just before the trail tops out, is exhilarating.

Highlights of the stupendous Guinn's Pass view include Mt. Galatea, The Fortress, Mt. Bogart (Trip 17), the inviting alplands beneath Buller and North Buller passes (Trip 7), and the nearby, towering, sheer wall of an unnamed peak. A few minutes higher and farther, at the upper edge of the pass, you can survey the Ribbon Lake basin and appreciate more of Mt. Kidd.

Okay, options. If you cross Guinn's Pass, you can make this a loop or a one-way through trip. You can backpack or dayhike the loop. You can backpack or dayhike the one-way trip. We advise against all of the above, for these reasons:

• There's no point in hauling a full pack over Guinn's to see what's well within dayhiking range if you're strong and start early. Yet even if dayhiking fast and light, the loop and one-way trips are less appealing than the round trip.

• Looping past Ribbon Lake, down Ribbon Creek, back to Hwy 40, requires only a short, easy shuttle. And Ribbon Lake is wonderful. But standing on the shore is less impressive than peering down at it from Guinn's Pass. (See photo on page 17.) And from Ribbon Falls out (nearly half the loop), you'll plod an old road through forest. We didn't include that section as a dayhike in this book, because it's not premier.

• Hiking one-way to Hwy 742, via either of the Buller Passes, would be excellent if it didn't necessitate a tediously long shuttle. Enjoying the Bullers on a dayhike circuit, as described in Trip 7, is easier and therefore increases the likelihood you'll complete the exciting, scenic detour above North Buller Pass.

• The loop and one-way trips discourage you from tagging both Guinn's Pass and Galatea Lakes in a single day, which we recommend if you're physically capable.

So instead of proceeding over Guinn's Pass, continue up the ridgecrest about 20 minutes or so toward Mt. Kidd, until your aerial survey is complete. After descending back to the Galatea Creek trail, if you still have time and energy, spurt up to Galatea Lakes. By then it should be late afternoon and the crowd will have dispersed. Hiking to Guinn's Pass *and* Galatea Lakes entails a 22-km (13.6-mi) round trip gaining 1127 m (3697 ft). It's a feel-it-the-next-day outing but feasible for athletic hikers.

photos: **1** *Ascending from Lower Galatea Lake to upper lake* **2** *Upper Galatea Lake* **3** *700-m wall of unnamed peak above Guinn's Pass* **4** *Spotting bighorn sheep* **5** *Bighorn sheep above Guinn's Pass*

Fact

By Vehicle

From Trans-Canada Hwy 1, drive S 32.7 km (20.3 mi) on Hwy 40. Or, from the junction of Hwy 40 and Kananaskis Lakes Trail, drive N 17.2 km (10.7 mi) on Hwy 40. From either approach, turn SW into the Galatea trailhead parking lot, at 1550 m (5084 ft).

On Foot

Descend the wide path departing the NW corner of the parking lot, near the info kiosk. In two minutes, cross a suspension bridge over the Kananaskis River. Mt. Kidd's stark, swirling cliffs are visible NNW. The trail briefly heads SW, then crosses a **bridge over Galatea Creek** at 0.5 km (0.3 mi), 1524 m (5000 ft).

On the creek's N bank is a **T-junction**. Turn left (SW) on the Galatea Creek trail. From here, all the way to lower Galatea Lake, it ascends generally W. It closely follows the rambunctious creek as far as Lillian Lake. Turning right at the T-junction would put you on the Terrace trail. It goes generally NNE through forest, beneath the E slope of Mt. Kidd, reaching Kananaskis Village in 7 km (4.3 mi).

While gently undulating through forest, the Galatea Creek trail crosses the creek seven times on sturdy bridges within the next 2.6 km (1.6 mi). About 30 minutes from the trailhead, ascend a **rockslide** at 1680 m (5510 ft) on the canyon's N wall and attain views. The S-facing cliffs of Mt. Kidd are above you. The Wedge is visible ESE, across Hwy 40. Slightly farther, overlook the deep inner gorge and a short waterfall.

At the sixth bridge since the T-junction, **log benches** on the N bank offer comfort to the weary. Elevation: 1769 m (5800 ft). You're now about an hour from the trailhead, entering Galatea Creek's NW-fork drainage. In a few minutes, traverse a lush avalanche path, then a grassy, flowery slope. Soon, at 1860 m (6100 ft), a more earnest ascent begins. You can look forward to a few level respites about ten minutes after the trail steepens.

At 5.5 km (3.4 mi), 1960 m (6430 ft), reach a **signed junction**. Moderately fast hikers will be here 1½ hours after leaving the trailhead. Straight (W) leads to Lillian and Galatea lakes. Right (N) leads to Guinn's Pass.

Galatea Lakes

In 0.6 km (0.4 mi) reach the E end of **Lillian Lake**, at 2030 m (6658 ft). The trail rounds the N shore, then forks at the lake's NW corner. Left (SW) enters the **campground**. For Galatea Lakes bear right (NW) and resume ascending through forest.

Attain a view of Lillian Lake below and Galatea Creek canyon beyond in about 15 minutes. Steep scree ensues. Within another 15 minutes, overlook **Lower Galatea Lake** from 2180 m (7150 ft), just above its NE shore. The trail continues around the N shore, descending gradually across talus. After curving S around the W shore at the water's edge, the trail ascends to the low ridge—2220 m (7282 ft)—overlooking **Upper Galatea Lake** (W). Total distance from the trailhead: 8.5 km (5.3 mi).

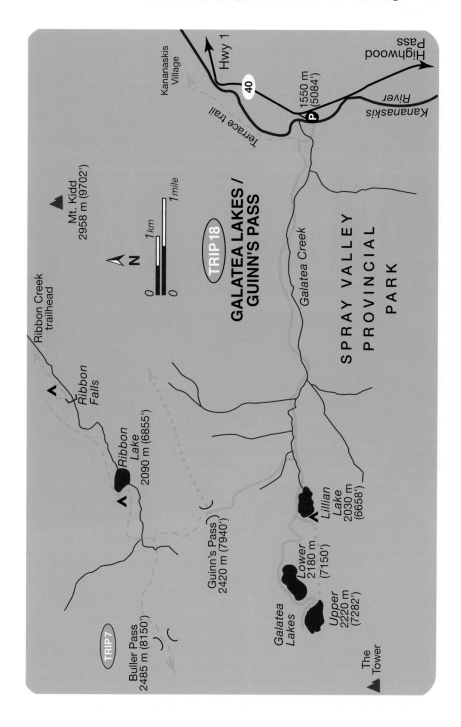

TRIP 18

GALATEA LAKES / GUINN'S PASS

SPRAY VALLEY PROVINCIAL PARK

Highwood Pass

Hwy 1

Kananaskis River

Kananaskis Village

40

P 1550 m (5084')

Terrace trail

Galatea Creek

Mt. Kidd 2958 m (9702')

Ribbon Creek trailhead

Ribbon Falls

Ribbon Lake 2090 m (6855')

Guinn's Pass 2420 m (7940')

Lillian Lake 2030 m (6658')

Lower 2180 m (7150')

Upper 2220 m (7282')

Galatea Lakes

The Tower

Buller Pass 2485 m (8150')

TRIP 7

N

0   1 km

0   1 mile

Departing Upper Galatea Lake, you can of course retrace your steps all the way to the trailhead. But if you prefer to vary the return to Lillian Lake, you can do so on a rough, sketchy, ultimately very steep route. From the low ridge above Upper Galatea, the route contours E across the talus slope high above Lower Galatea's S shore. It then plunges along the forest margin, continues generally E, and ends near the outhouse at Lillian Lake campground. It's possible to descend from Upper Galatea to Lillian in about 30 minutes this way. Most hikers, however, should follow the route only onto the talus slope above Lower Galatea's S shore, appreciate this perspective of the basin, then return the way they came.

Guinn's Pass

From the signed junction on the Galatea Creek trail, Guinn's Pass is 2.5 km (1.6 mi) farther and 457 m (1500 ft) higher. Turn right (N). Briefly descend to cross bridged Galatea Creek. Fill water bottles here. Just five minutes farther, Guinn's Pass is visible ahead (NNW).

The narrow trail ascends moderately above a grassy slope burgeoning with flowers mid-July to early August. You might see white spirea, lavender harebells, nodding onion (light pink bells), orange false dandelions, purple scorpionweed, cobalt monkshood, lavender fleabane, willow-herb, plus red, orange and fuchsia versions of the seemingly omnipresent Indian paintbrush.

Continue upward through a steepening dirt-and-talus gully. Pockets of flowers brighten the stark rock. Two-thirds of the way to the pass, where water dribbles through the talus, look for another display of purple flowers: fleabane, willow-herb, and penstemon. Watch for yellow columbine and baby-blue alpine-forget-me-not sheltered beneath small, trailside boulders.

Nearing the pass, hop to the W side of a creeklet. The trail is now dirt. It sweeps across flower-dense slopes of heather and grass. Mt. Kidd's long, smooth scree slopes are ENE, across the draw. Strong hikers will arrive at 2420-m (7940-ft) **Guinn's Pass** one hour after turning off the Galatea Creek trail. Total distance from the trailhead: 8 km (5 mi). Immediately WSW of the pass is a stupefying presence: the towering, sheer, 700-m (2296-ft) wall of a massive, unnamed, 3052-m (10,015-ft) peak. Right (NE) of the pass, grassy slopes give way to scree cascading from Mt. Kidd's SW outlier. Peaks visible behind you while ascending are now in better view: 3185-m (10,447-ft) Mt. Galatea is SSW, the 3000-m (9840-ft) Fortress is SE, and the serrated Opal Range is SE across Hwy 40. (Explore the Opals by hiking to King Creek Ridge, Piper Pass, or Paradise Pass: Trips 19, 27, and 38.) The N side of Guinn's Pass overlooks the upper basin of Ribbon Lake. NNW is 3144-m (10,315-ft) Mt. Bogart.

Before dropping your pack and collapsing, proceed a few minutes farther NE. Ascend toward the **ridgecrest**. Then go left (WNW) descending slightly to the edge of the crest. Here, Ribbon Lake is entirely within view, far below. Mt. Bogart looms beyond the lake. Forested Ribbon Creek valley

photos: *1 Galatea Creek 2 Mt. Galatea, from Guinn's Pass 3 Bighorn sheep at Guinn's Pass*

descends NE. Mt. Kidd forms the valley's S wall. Mt. Allan (Trip 16) is in the distance, NNE. Looking NW, into the grassy, upper basin above Ribbon Lake, you can see Buller Pass. Just N of it, between two knobs, is North Buller Pass. Trip 7 describes both passes and the traverse linking them. Underfoot, look for pink moss campion, mountain buttercup (taut, bright-yellow bunches), and white asters.

Above Guinn's Pass

For a superior prospect, ascend the ridgecrest E about 20 minutes. Follow scraps of bootbeaten path. After gaining 160 m (545 ft) in 0.8 km (0.5 mi), top out on the 2585-m (8480-ft) **SW outlier of Mt. Kidd**. Lillian Lake is visible SW, beneath an outlier of The Tower. In the basin above and W of Lillian, you can see both Galatea lakes, closer to the 3117-m (10,224-ft) Tower. Distant SW, you can identify the distinctively long, NW ridge of Mt. Birdwood (Trip 9). From Mt. Kidd's SW outlier, brave, adept scramblers proceed along the crest—NE, W, then NE again—to summit 2959-m (9705-ft) Mt. Kidd. But the outlier will be the day's crowning achievement for most hikers.

Beyond Guinn's Pass

If pursuing the one-way or loop extensions described but not recommended in the *Opinion* section, the following directions will be helpful.

From Guinn's Pass, the trail descends steep talus NNW. It skirts the flank of Mt. Kidd, then drops through subalpine forest and meadow to a junction in **Ribbon Lake's upper basin**. At this point, you're 0.7 km (0.4 mi) beyond the pass.

A right turn at the junction leads to **Ribbon Lake** and, a bit farther, **Ribbon Falls**. The trail then descends NE through Ribbon Creek valley, reaching Ribbon Creek trailhead in 11.2 km (6.9 mi). Total loop distance (up Galatea Creek, over Guinn's Pass, out Ribbon Creek) is 20.6 km (12.8 mi), not counting a one-hour round-trip detour to the outlier above the pass.

Left at the junction in Ribbon Lake's upper basin ascends open slopes generally W, cresting **Buller Pass** in 2 km (1.2 mi). The trail then follows Buller Creek downstream to Buller Mtn trailhead, on Hwy 742. The trailhead is 8 km (5 mi) from the junction. Total one-way distance (up Galatea Creek, over Guinn's Pass, out Buller Pass) is 16.7 km (10.4 mi).

Here's further detail on the Ribbon option. From the junction in Ribbon Lake's upper basin, right goes N. Soon cross to the N side of Ribbon Creek. Descend through forest. The trail bends right (E), traversing willowy meadow to reach **Ribbon Lake campground** in 1.2 km (0.75 mi), on the lake's NW shore. You'll find 20 tent pads, a cooking shelter, metal fire pits, metal food-cache, food-hanging cable, and an outhouse here. After rounding Ribbon Lake's N shore, the trail heads NE beneath Mt. Bogart. Reach Ribbon Falls headwall 1.8 km (1.1 mi) from the lake. Downclimb with the aid of a handrail and fixed chain. From the falls, it's 8.2 km (5.1 mi) NE to the trailhead at Ribbon Creek day-use area, just W of Hwy 40. This stretch is easy but uneventful—a broad track through forest, following Ribbon Creek downstream. For *By Vehicle* directions to Ribbon Creek trailhead, read Mt. Allan (Trip 16).

TRIP 19
King Creek Ridge

LOCATION	Peter Lougheed Provincial Park, Hwy 40
LOOP	7 km (4.3 mi)
ELEVATION GAIN	729 m (2390 ft)
KEY ELEVATIONS	trailhead 1692 m (5550 ft)
	second summit 2421 m (7940 ft)
HIKING TIME	4 to 5 hours
DIFFICULTY	challenging
MAP	Gem Trek *Kananaskis Lakes*

Opinion

Zen Buddhists refer to our incessant, mental chatter as "monkey mind." It's pointless distraction and futile worrying. It keeps us anxiously fixated on the past or future, preventing us from living fully in the present moment. They quell monkey mind by meditating. You can also do it by hiking. When your body takes your brain for a ride, it just stares calmly out the window. Steep, rough terrain is best. King Creek Ridge is ideal.

Though the distance here is short, the ridge is a slender, precipitous fin: excruciating to mount and dismount. The ascent demands maximal effort. The descent requires intense concentration. Only if you're experienced at scrambling and routefinding will you be confident on this awkward terrain.

In short, you'll grind up to the ridgecrest, stride along the spine, ease down the other side, work through a canyon, then complete the loop by piercing a deep gorge cut by King Creek. Fit, experienced, sure-footed hikers love it. If that's not how friends would describe you, you'll struggle to appreciate this hike. You might not even complete it.

You can, of course, make this a simple, round trip by hiking up and down the front (west) face of the ridge. But that would just be a masochistic workout. The loop feels like a genuine journey. It avails you of much more scenery and earns you a strong sense of accomplishment.

Either way—round trip or loop—your chief reward will be a nonpareil view of the unique Opal Range. Imagine a mountain wall created by layer upon layer of gigantic, skyward-pointing arrowheads. That's the Opals. They're an arresting sight from Hwy 40. But once you crest the ridge, they'll vacuum every speck of your attention. Your travail below will suddenly seem worthwhile.

After following the crest, enjoying frequent, panoramic views despite the trees, you'll plummet off the back (east) side of the ridge, into the canyon beneath the Opals. This slope, too, feels nearly vertical but is different from the front (west) side. On the front, you'll follow a trail—boot-beaten, gravity-swept, but distinct. On the back, you'll follow a route that's initially obvious but drops onto a vegetated slope where the tread is obscure.

Once you tag onto the path descending the canyon between King Creek Ridge and the Opal Range, you can relax physically but must remain alert. The angle of descent is gentle. The hiking is easy. The path, however, is not constant. It occasionally dwindles, requiring you to cast about to see where it resumes. Meanwhile you'll enjoy a deliciously remote atmosphere that belies your proximity to the highway.

Upon reaching King Creek, you'll exit via a sheer-walled slot resembling those in southern Utah. The trail repeatedly crosses the creek. At low flow, rockhopping is easy. At high flow, you'll have to keep your balance on the numerous foot-logs improvised by previous hikers. The other high-flow option is to ford. The cold-but-narrow creek probably won't be more than knee deep, and wet boots aren't a concern because you'll soon reach your vehicle. Better to ford than to slip, fall, and injure yourself.

However you negotiate the creek, you'll be more fully engaged with the lively water than you would on a taciturn trail that stayed above one bank. It's a fun, celebratory finale to an otherwise exacting hike.

Wildlife Alert: Before departing the trailhead, scan the crags across the creek for mountain goats or bighorn sheep. They're a common sight here. Later, when exiting through the gorge, watch for dippers. They're tiny birds that do a knee-bending dance before plunging into running water to snatch food.

Fact

By Vehicle

From Trans-Canada Hwy 1, drive 50 km (31 mi) S on Hwy 40. Or, from Highwood Pass, drive 17 km (10.5 mi) N on Hwy 40. From either approach, turn E into the signed, paved, King Creek day-use area trailhead parking lot, at 1692 m (5550 ft). It's 100 m (110 yd) N of where Kananaskis Lakes Trail intersects Hwy 40.

On Foot

Ignore the signed trail departing the E end of the parking lot. It probes the gorge cut by King Creek. You'll loop back that way. Your initial goal is to begin ascending the slope N of the parking lot, on the far side of the creek.

If the creek's shallow, rockhop it. Otherwise, walk out to the highway. Immediately before the stop sign, leave the pavement by turning right (N) onto the bootbeaten path crossing the grassy slope below the guardrail.

The path drops then rises, curving upstream (away from the highway) onto a level bench well above the creek's N bank. Ahead you'll see two diverging paths. Go right (E) and descend toward the creek. Just before the final drop to the bank, look left (E). Follow the defined trail rocketing up the treed slope.

About two minutes up, the path traverses N and the grade briefly eases. From here on, precise directions for the ascent are difficult to provide and would be tedious to decipher. In short, stay on this trail. It leads to the ridgecrest.

photos: **1** *The Opals, from King Creek Ridge* **2** *King Creek gorge* **3** *King Creek Ridge*

1

2

3

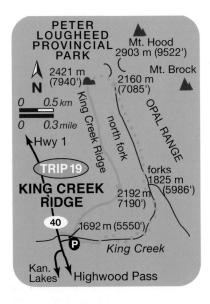

You might feel the trail drifts farther N than is necessary, but in doing so it skirts small rock bands, avoids most of the forest, and grants an ever-improving view of Lower Kananaskis Lake. Also, the trail lands you on the crest where it's level, which is nearly a kilometer N of the creek gorge.

After ascending northward, the trail turns right and climbs generally ENE. It zigs and zags but never relaxes into comfortable switchbacks. Because it was boot-built rather than properly constructed, it keeps aiming up-slope like a rambunctious child.

You'll see diverging paths, but the main trail is evident because it's wider, more frequently trod. Keep to the main trail. Sporadic but substantial cairns offer assurance you're on course.

Crest **King Creek Ridge** at 2192 m (7190 ft) about one hour after departing the trailhead. Take note of this juncture if you intend to return the way you came.

The Opal Range is E, across the canyon. It comprises several peaks. The one directly opposite you and immediately above King Creek gorge is 2993-m (9820-ft) Mt. Blane. The others, continuing left (N) along the range, are 2902-m (9521-ft) Mt. Brock, 2903-m (9525-ft) Mt. Hood, and 3000-m (9843-ft) Mt. Packenham.

Right (S) is 2700-m (8859-ft) Mt. Wintour. It rises out of King Creek gorge and towers above the trailhead parking lot. Farther right (SW), beyond Upper Kananaskis Lake, is the Mangin Glacier on Mt. Joffre.

Resume hiking left (N). The trail atop the crest is prominent, easy to follow. Reach the **first summit** at 2332 m (7650 ft). Reach the **second summit** at 3 km (1.9 mi), 2421 m (7940 ft). Immediately ahead (N) is the **third summit**—only a couple boulders higher than the second summit.

The **descent route** into the canyon is the gully right (E) between the second and third summits. Immediately below the crest, the route is a scar: pounded by the passage of many boots into a swath of bare dirt. It funnels you between outcroppings.

Near the outcroppings, traction improves on rock. Below that, follow the route boot-beaten into the grass. Where it appears you have a choice— left or right?—angle left. The grade remains very steep. The final descent is on a broad, vegetated slope bordered on the left by a wall of trees.

After bailing off the ridgecrest, it takes about 30 minutes to bottom-out at 2160 m (7085 ft) in the **N fork of King Creek canyon**. The saddle linking the ridge with the Opals is left (N) just above you.

Look right (S). You can see where the canyon's N and S forks split from the E-W gorge cut by King Creek. That's your next goal. At a moderate pace, you'll be there in about an hour. There's a discernible path most of the way.

The path initially stays right (W) of the N fork of King Creek, descending through grass. In a few minutes, it crosses the rocky creekbed and resumes descending above the left (E) bank. It crosses and re-crosses the creek a couple more times. If you're uncertain where the path continues, stop. Scout ahead, and on the opposite bank, until you find it.

The final stretch is in mature spruce forest above the left (E) bank. The path then appears to end in a chaotic, rocky ravine immediately above King Creek gorge. Rockhop to the right (W) bank of the N fork (the creek you've been following down-canyon). From there, the path quickly drops to the **mouth of King Creek gorge** and the confluence of the creek's N and S forks, at 6 km (3.7 mi), 1825 m (5986 ft).

Rockhop to the far (S) bank of King Creek. The trail leads downstream, curving right (W) between the sheer, soaring walls of the narrow gorge. You'll arrive at the trailhead—1 km (0.6 mi) distant—in about 40 minutes.

Your hiking time in the gorge will depend on the water level, the number of times you must cross the creek, and the presence or lack of exposed, stepping-stone boulders or improvised, log bridges. Just before exiting the gorge and reaching the trailhead parking lot, the trail is on the left (S) bank.

King Creek Ridge, Opal Range beyond, from Hwy 40

TRIP 20
Mt. Indefatigable

LOCATION	Peter Lougheed Provincial Park
	between Upper and Lower Kananaskis lakes
ROUND TRIP	7.6 km (4.7 mi) to summit ridge
ELEVATION GAIN	920 m (3018 ft)
KEY ELEVATIONS	trailhead 1725 m (5658 ft), NE outlier 2485 m (8150 ft)
	summit ridge 2645 m (8676 ft)
HIKING TIME	3½ to 4½ hours
DIFFICULTY	moderate
MAP	Gem Trek *Kananaskis Lakes*

Opinion

Mt. In-duh-FAT-igabull. Mt. In-duh-fuh-TEEG-a-bull. Mt. Unpronounceable. Or simply *Mt. Fatty.* Call it what you will, the summit ridge affords a majestic vantage of Upper and Lower Kanananskis lakes and countless surrounding alps. To reach it, however, you must endure an unmaintained, labouriously vertical trail and abide a higher-than-usual possibility of a bear encounter.

If you're unable to surmount treeline on Fatty's east face, there are consolation viewpoints: (1) about a third of the way up, and (2) two-thirds of the way up, at trail's end. But try to keep motoring west, to the premier panorama above. The final, steep, rocky ascent to the ridgecrest is not quite a scramble and can be dispatched in 30 to 45 minutes.

Another option beyond trail's end is the generally northwest ascent through a meadowy basin to Fatty's northeast outlier. Though slightly farther than Fatty's summit ridge, the outlier is a less strenuous goal. It's also less scenic. The basin's wildflower display, however, can be kaleidoscopic. Purple fleabane, red paintbrush, white Sitka valerian, yellow glacier lilies, and white mountain avens abound in early summer.

Before fixing Fatty as your destination, be aware that the trail is gradually deteriorating to a mere route because the provincial park discourages its use. Their concern is legitimate: This is critical, grizzly-bear habitat, where sows with cubs typically linger for weeks. If you go, carry pepper spray. Remain vigilantly alert. Make noise frequently. If you see a bear, or fresh scat indicating a bear is present, abort your trip. Hike elsewhere. Visit Fatty another time.

Alpine sorrel

Fact

By Vehicle

From Trans-Canada Hwy 1, drive 50 km (31 mi) S on Hwy 40. Or, from Highwood Pass, drive 17 km (10.5 mi) N on Hwy 40. From either approach, turn SW onto Kananaskis Lakes Trail. Reset your trip odometer to 0.

0 km (0 mi)

Starting SW on Kananaskis Lakes Trail.

2.2 km (1.4 mi)

Proceed straight where Smith-Dorrien / Spray Trail (Hwy 742) forks right.

9.8 km (6.1 mi)

Proceed straight where right leads to Lower Kananaskis Lake and Boulton Creek campground.

12.6 km (7.8 mi)

Proceed straight where left leads to the trailhead parking lot on the SE shore of Upper Kananaskis Lake.

14.8 km (9.2 mi)

Bear left, uphill. Straight leads to Panorama. Right leads to Interlakes campground.

15.2 km (9.4 mi)

Reach the trailhead parking lot at North Interlakes day-use area. It's on the NE shore of Upper Kananaskis Lake. Elevation: 1725 m (5658 ft).

On Foot

From the trailhead kiosk at the N end of the parking lot, walk NW atop the dam. Soon cross the **spillway bridge**. Turn left (W) onto an old road. Reach an **unsigned junction** just beyond, at 0.3 km (0.2 mi). The old road continues W, above the lake's N shore. It leads to Trips 21, 22, 23 and 24. Turn right here onto the Mt. Indefatigable trail, initially blocked by boulders.

The trail undulates generally NW in subalpine forest. Climbing through rock bands, several paths diverge but rejoin above. A severe ascent N (dirt and scree) leads to a rocky **promontory** at 1.3 km (0.8 mi), 1980 m (6495 ft). It overlooks Upper and Lower Kananaskis lakes. Also visible are Mt. Sarrail (SSW) and Mt. Lyautey (SW).

The rocky route continues ascending steeply N, above the E-facing limestone escarpment that rises from Lower Kananaskis Lake.

The view is panoramic. The Opal Range is NE, the Elk Range SE. Larch trees begin to appear.

Nearly an hour up, at 2207 m (7240 ft), pass a minor, left (W) spur. Proceed straight (N). One minute farther, the narrow, rooty path forking left (W) leads to Fatty's summit ridge. But before going that way, continue a few minutes farther N to the **trail's end viewpoint** at 2.5 km (1.6 mi), 2210 m (7250 ft). The serrated Opal Range dominates the NE horizon. For directions to Fatty's NE outlier, skip below.

Now back at the fork: Fatty's summit ridge is W, 1.3 km (0.8 mi) farther and 415 m (1362 ft) higher. Follow the narrow route uphill through spruce, larch and heather. Where it levels, bear left on a narrower route. Proceed through a glade, then up a broad, grassy slope. The route veers right, granting a view of Fatty's NE outlier, then left across grass and patches of shale. Where the ridge becomes steeper and rockier, the route splits in a shallow depression. An angling ascent, right to left, leads to a cairn on the **ridgecrest** at 2645 m (8676 ft). Total distance from the trailhead: 3.8 km (2.4 mi).

You can continue right (NNW) from the cairn, but the view does not improve significantly. Beyond the communications gizmo, you must negotiate a couple hundred meters of knife-edge if you're intent on reaching Fatty's 2670-m (8760-ft) summit.

Ah, the view. Upper Kananaskis Lake is S, far below. SW of it is smaller Hidden Lake. Beyond that is Mt. Sarrail (left) and Aster Lake basin—the descent route from Northover Ridge (Trip 24). Reigning over the peaks, glaciers and snowfields in that direction is Mt. Joffre. W is the valley leading to Three Isle Lake. NW, below you, is Invincible Creek canyon, which drains Invincible Lake (Trip 21). NE, beyond Lower Kananaskis Lake and Hwy 40, is the Opal Range. WSW is Pocaterra Ridge (Trip 30) in the Elk Range. SW are the Elk passes (Trip 26).

Northeast Outlier

From the trail's end viewpoint, at 2.5 km (1.6 mi), 2210 m (7250 ft), you'll ascend 280 m (918 ft) in 1.5 km (0.9 mi) to reach Fatty's NE outlier in about 45 minutes.

Proceed N. Four strides ahead, ignore a minor path. During the next eight minutes, bear right at two forks. Your general direction of travel is NW. (On the way back, go left on the path with orange flagging.)

Ten minutes beyond trail's end, enter a wet, verdant basin. Right (W) is a drainage plummeting to Lower Kananaskis Lake. Round the right (NE) side of a seasonal **pond** and hop across its narrow outlet stream. Ascend NW on grassy, flowery slopes beside stands of larch.

Curve N for the final approach. Soon top out at 2485 m (8150 ft) on the **NE outlier**. Total distance from the trailhead: 4 km (2.5 mi). Total elevation gain: 760 m (2493 ft).

King Creek Ridge (Trip 19) is NNE, beneath the Opals. The Smith-Dorrien road is NNW. Mt. Indefatigable's true summit is SW. Separating you from the true summit is a col. Vary your return by descending that way.

photos: *1 Ascending Fatty's NE outlier, Upper Kananaskis Lake in background 2 Basin beneath Fatty's NE outlier 3 Starting the ascent from Upper Kananaskis Lake to Mt. Fatty*

1

2 3

TRIP 21
Invincible Lake

LOCATION	Peter Lougheed Provincial Park
	NW of Upper Kananaskis Lake
ROUND TRIP	14 km (8.7 mi)
ELEVATION GAIN	635 m (2082 ft)
KEY ELEVATIONS	trailhead 1725 m (5658 ft)
	highpoint 2375 m (7790 ft), lake 2255 m (7396 ft)
HIKING TIME	7 to 8 hours
DIFFICULTY	challenging
MAP	Gem Trek *Kananaskis Lakes*

Opinion

On a rough road in Bhutan, a sign warns of worse conditions ahead and suggests what to do. "Treacherous road," it says. "Bash on regardless."

That's the human condition, isn't it? Bash on regardless. Which is why an off-trail hike, such as this one to Invincible Lake, is an apt metaphor for life. It's a physical reminder that faith and determination are necessary to overcome the inevitable difficulties.

En route to Invincible Lake, the difficulties are not treacherous. And, given the assurances of a guidebook, faith comes easily. But you'll still feel you're bashing on regardless.

You'll start by hiking the old road maintained as trail around the north shore of Upper Kananaskis Lake, just as you would for Three Isle Lake (Trip 23). Then you'll veer onto the road's rougher, unmaintained, upper reaches. Soon you'll abandon the road and commit to a steep, arduous, cross-country ascent on an eerily beautiful slope swept by fire long ago. The terrain is bristling with silver snags. The grass is lush. Fuschia fireweed is profuse. Deadfall is a frequent obstacle. The views are inspiring. Your goal is skyward: a ridgecrest that looks discouragingly distant.

Though the navigation is not puzzling, to enjoy this trip you'll need either off-trail experience or a keen desire to begin extending your hiking range. The ascent ends on a ridgecrest overlooking Invincible Lake sequestered in a lonely basin and guarded by titans: Mounts Indefatigable, Invincible, and Warspite. Decision time: call it a day, or proceed to the lake?

You can turn back at the ridge pleased with your reward: a rousing panorama that includes Upper Kananaskis Lake, the Great Divide, and the mountains extending into Elk Lakes Provincial Park. Or you can continue the exploration all the way to Invincible Lake. That necessitates descending via game trail, then briefly ascending cross-country yet again. A lakeside lunch is a reasonable goal for a full dayhike. Probing farther, into Invincible Creek's meadowy, north-fork basin, however, is a no-dinner-plans-in-the-city dayhike requiring an early start and a constant, determined pace.

Invincible Lake and Spray Mountains

Fact

By Vehicle

Follow directions for Mt. Indefatigable (Trip 20) to the trailhead parking lot at North Interlakes day-use area. It's on the NE shore of Upper Kananaskis Lake. Elevation: 1725 m (5658 ft).

On Foot

From the trailhead kiosk at the N end of the parking lot, walk NW atop the dam. Soon cross the bridge over the spillway. Turn left (W) onto an old road. Reach a **signed junction** just beyond, at 0.3 km (0.2 mi). The trail forking right ascends Mt. Indefatigable (Trip 20). Continue W on the old road above Kananaskis Lake's N shore. Soon bear right at the map-sign.

At 0.8 km (0.5 mi) and 2.2 km (1.4 mi), where left forks drop to the lakeshore trail, bear right and stay high on the rocky, old road. The lake is visible below. Also attain a view left (SSW), beyond the lake, up Aster Creek canyon (Trip 24), formed by 3174-m (10,414-ft) Mt. Sarrail on its E side and 3082-m (10,112-ft) Mt. Lyautey on its W.

Cross the Palliser rockslide. After curving NW, the road descends. About an hour from the trailhead, reach a bridge over **Invincible Creek** at 3.8 km (2.3 mi), 1750 m (5740 ft). Mountainbikers must stop here. The trail to Three Isle Lake (Trip 23), Northover Ridge (Trip 24) and North Kananaskis Pass (Trip 22) continues across the bridge. Turn right for Invincible Lake.

About 25 m/yd upstream from the bridge, the old road continues on the far (W) bank. Rockhop across and proceed NW on the gently ascending road. If the creek is too deep, cross the bridge, go right (upstream), regain the road and follow it left (NW). The forest is slowly reclaiming the road.

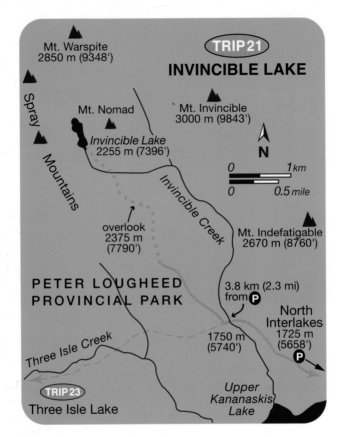

It's choked with young trees and cluttered with deadfall. Note the following landmarks so you know precisely where to begin the cross-country ascent.

The road bends left (W). About 15 minutes beyond Invincible Creek, an enormous **log jam** on the right testifies to nature's might. Two minutes farther, at a small **clearing**, Mt. Lyautey is visible again SW. Mt. Putnik is WSW. One minute past the clearing, at 1857 m (6090 ft), reach a **cairn**. Depart the road here by turning right. Ascend the steep sand-and-dirt bank into open forest. This departure point is immediately before the road curves right and dips.

You're now hiking trail-less terrain. Ascend N on the steep, snag-strewn slope. Follow the crest of the **rib** running all the way to the ridgecrest. The view WSW is up Three Isle Creek valley. At 2240 m (7347 ft), continue upward beside small rock outcrops and a ribbon of trees. Fireweed and asters festoon the grass. Keep heading N.

Top out on the **ridgecrest** at about 2375 m (7790 ft), slightly right (E) of and just above a treed gap. Turn left, pass a cairn, drop into the gap, and ascend the crest WNW to attain a better **vantage point**. Within five minutes, overlook Invincible Lake NW. The great cliffs of an unnamed ridge rise above scree left (W) of the lake. Mt. Nomad, the small, conical peak right (E)

Upper Kananaskis Lake, from ascent to Invincible Lake

of the lake, is N. Sculpted Mt. Invincible is NE. Mt. Indefatigable is E. Upper Kananaskis Lake is SE. Hidden Lake is SSE. The farther you ascend the crest, the better the view.

To reach Invincible Lake, follow the elk trail starting on the NE side of the gap. It rounds a knob and descends into larch forest on the N side of the ridge. After crossing shale and scree, the path fades in grass near the bottom of the draw. Rockhop to the N bank of Invincible Creek (the lake's outlet stream), then begin a gentle ascent WNW on grassy slopes. Curve NW across a rockslide. The terrain steepens on the final approach. Reach **Invincible Lake** at 7 km (4.3 mi), 2255 m (7396 ft). Cross the low ridge N of the lake to explore Invincible Creek's meadowy N-fork basin below 2850-m (9348-ft) Mt. Warspite.

Willow-herb

TRIP 22

North Kananaskis Pass Haig Glacier

LOCATION	Peter Lougheed Provincial Park
	NW of Upper Kananaskis Lake
ROUND TRIP	34.4 km (21.3 mi) to North K Pass
	plus 5.6 km (3.5 mi) to Haig Glacier
ELEVATION GAIN	660 m (2165 ft) to pass, plus 390 m (1280 ft) to glacier
KEY ELEVATIONS	trailhead 1725 m (5658 ft), Forks campground 1785 m (5855 ft), Turbine Canyon 2210 m (7250 ft), pass 2368 m (7767 ft), glacier trail's end 2600 m (8528 ft)
HIKING TIME	10-hour dayhike to pass or glacier
	2- to 3-day backpack for both
DIFFICULTY	challenging dayhike, moderate backpack
MAP	Gem Trek *Kananaskis Lakes*

Opinion

Trendy restaurants, blaring concerts, terrifying movies, and recreational drugs are inadequate substitutes for the adventure missing from modern life. You'll find authentic adventure when you begin stripping *modern* from *life*. And here's a beautiful hike where you can easily do that for a couple days.

North Kananaskis Pass and Haig Glacier are among a handful of premier K-Country destinations sharing the same trailhead and initial approach. Before planning a journey here, broaden your understanding of the backpacking options in the area by reading about South Kananaskis Pass (Trip 23), and Northover Ridge (Trip 24).

If you're fit, fleet and focused, North K Pass or Haig Glacier is hikeable in a day. But even the swiftest dayhikers must choose to see only one, and both are rewarding. So it's best to wag a full pack and camp at Turbine Canyon. The Turbine Canyon campground is equally close to North K Pass and the basin beneath Haig Glacier. Pitching your tent for a single night at Turbine allows you to see the pass on the afternoon you arrive, the glacier basin on the morning you leave. If a weekend-package-tour pace isn't necessary, throttle back. Camp two nights at Turbine.

Bound for North K Pass and Haig Glacier, you'll begin on a former road, now a broad, rocky trail. A few striking vistas are motivation to keep chugging around the north shore of Upper K Lake. At Invincible Creek, continue on a soft path winding through lovely forest. After Forks campground, follow the Upper K River, then gear down for a long ascent.

Views expand while you assail an avalanche slope. Escape the trees and enjoy a long, nearly level traverse through rock gardens, subalpine

photos: **1** *Maude Lake in North Kananaskis Pass* **2** *Just above Turbine Canyon* **3** *En route to Haig Glacier, beneath Mt. Jellicoe* **4** *Porcupine* **5** *Haig Glacier, from near route's end*

meadows, and a princely stand of larches. Peaks roar to life around you. Pass a tarn, then Lawson Lake, before reaching Maude Brook. Turbine Canyon campground is immediately beyond. The canyon, a couple minutes downstream, is not a destination-status sight. It's a small chasm through which Maude Brook briefly squeezes and roars. But do peer into it sometime during your stay at the campground.

Venturing onward, Maude Lake is essentially *in* North K Pass. Rounding it's shore, the trail climaxes just above, on an alpine ridge, high on the Great Divide, where Alberta gives way to British Columbia. It's a grand and lonely vantage from which to see our sacred star waft toward the horizon as day gives way to evening.

The far (west) slope of the pass falls sharply into a lonely, lush, B.C. valley. And you'll see a trail plunging down that slope. Yes, the trail (dwindling to a route) proceeds to South K Pass (Trip 23) via LeRoy Creek and Beatty Lake. Yes, a dual-pass circuit is possible. But it entails an elevation loss of 620 m (2034 ft), and a gain of 555 m (1820 ft), so accepting the invitation to plunge is a commitment.

The foray toward Haig Glacier is best undertaken on the morning you depart for home or on day two of a three-day trip, so if you want to explore deeper and higher into the glacial basin, you might have time and will certainly have daylight.

The ice is visible from atop a former terminal moraine, about 30 minutes from the campground. Attain a better view by crossing the bridge spanning the stream below and ascending to the helipad just beyond. To approach the ice and see much more of it, ascend the cairned trail starting behind the ski-camp huts.

Fact

Before your trip

If you're staying overnight, bring a stove. Open fires are prohibited at Turbine Canyon.

By Vehicle

Follow directions for Mt. Indefatigable (Trip 20) to the trailhead parking lot at North Interlakes day-use area. It's on the NE shore of Upper K Lake. Elevation: 1725 m (5658 ft).

On Foot

Follow directions for Three Isle Lake (Trip 23) to **Forks junction and campground** at 7.2 km (4.5 mi), 1785 m (5855 ft). Left (W) leads to Three Isle Lake, South K Pass (Trip 23), and Northover Ridge (Trip 24). Bear right and proceed NNW for North K Pass and Haig Glacier.

Forks campground is in forest, beside the Upper K River. It has 15 tent pads, four tables, outhouses, benches around a fire pit, and bear-proof food storage. The optimal site is #15, at the NW end of the campground, between the creek and the trail.

The trail parallels the **Upper K River** gorge for about the next 20 minutes, heading upstream above the W bank. Your general direction of

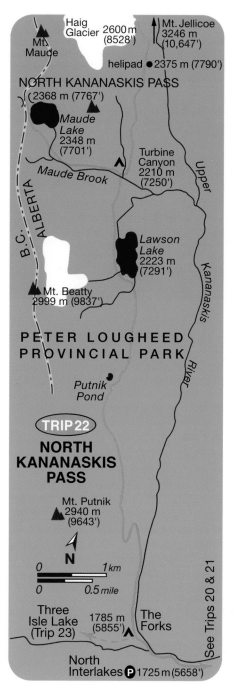

Haig Glacier 2600 m (8528')
Mt. Maude
Mt. Jellicoe 3246 m (10,647')
helipad ● 2375 m (7790')

NORTH KANANASKIS PASS
(2368 m (7767')

Maude Lake 2348 m (7701')

Maude Brook

Turbine Canyon 2210 m (7250')

Upper

Lawson Lake 2223 m (7291')

Mt. Beatty 2999 m (9837')

B.C.
ALBERTA

Kananaskis River

PETER LOUGHEED PROVINCIAL PARK

Putnik Pond

TRIP 22
NORTH KANANASKIS PASS

Mt. Putnik 2940 m (9643')

N

0   1 km
0   0.5 mile

See Trips 20 & 21

Three Isle Lake (Trip 23)
1785 m (5855')
The Forks

North Interlakes ℗ 1725 m (5658')

travel will remain NNW all the way to Turbine Canyon campground.

At 8.5 km (5.3 mi), just after a cascade flowing off Mt. Putnik (left), begin ascending steeply. The trail soon switchbacks up an **avalanche slope**, through head-high willows and alders. Attain views S to 3081-m (10,112-ft) Mt. Lyautey. Nearly an hour from the Forks, re-enter forest near 2150 m (7050 ft), where larches signal treeline is near. Cross a bridged stream beneath the massive walls of a cirque on your left (W), between Mounts Putnik (S) and Beatty (NW). Continue switchbacking.

At 11.5 km (7.1 mi) the trail emerges from forest onto a small saddle on a larch-covered ridge overlooking **Putnik Pond**. The Spray Mtns, including Mt. Black Prince, are NE. Descend into the valley to begin a long, nearly level traverse—through rock gardens, subalpine meadows, and an impressive larch forest—on a 2240-m (7347-ft) bench beneath Mt. Beatty's E slope. Visible ahead (just left of N) is 3246-m (10,647-ft) Mt. Jellicoe. NNW are 3042-m (9978-ft) Mt. Maude and Haig Glacier.

Reach **Lawson Lake** at 13.2 km (8.2 mi), 2223 m (7291 ft). Part of Beatty Glacier is visible W. The twin summits of Mt. Maude are a spectacular sight NW beyond the lake. The trail curves left, then continues NNW, up the lake's W shore. Near the N end of the lake, at 14.7 km (9.1 mi), pass a ranger cabin (left).

Lawson Lake below Mounts Sarrail and Lyautey, from trail to Haig Glacier

At 15 km (9.3 mi), cross a bridge over Maude Brook and reach **Turbine Canyon campground** at 2210 m (7250 ft). Fast hikers will arrive here 3½ hours after departing the trailhead. It has 12 tent pads, two tables, outhouses, bear-proof food storage, and a view of Beatty Glacier (SW). Just downstream is Turbine Canyon—the slender, snaking chasm through which Maude Brook plummets 330 m (1082 ft) E into Upper K River canyon.

North K Pass

The trail to North K Pass leads left (W) from Turbine Canyon campground. Staying above the N bank of Maude Brook, it climbs gradually through meadows and stunted trees. Crest a rocky, alpine **ridge** at 16.5 km (10.2 mi), 2370 m (7774 ft)—the trip's highpoint. Then drop NW to **Maude Lake** (2348 m / 7701 ft) beneath the steep, desolate, S slope of 3042-m (9978-ft) Mt. Maude. Round the W shore to arrive at 2368-m (7767-ft) **North K Pass**, 17.2 km (10.7 mi) from the trailhead.

The pass straddles the boundary distinguishing Alberta's Peter Lougheed Provincial Park from B.C.'s Height of the Rockies Provincial Park. The N arm of Mt. Beatty drops to the S edge of the pass. Visible NW, across Leroy Creek valley, are Mounts LeRoy (left) and Monro (right). SW, across the Palliser River valley, are Mounts Prince Henry (right), Prince Edward (middle), and Prince Albert (left) in the Royal Group. A severely steep, rough trail dives off the W side of the pass and curves SW, following LeRoy Creek downstream to the Palliser River.

Haig Glacier

From the Turbine Canyon campground tables, follow the trail dropping past the lower tentsites. In a couple minutes, reach the confluence of an unnamed, shallow, tributary stream and Maude Brook, near where the brook cascades into **Turbine Canyon**. Hop the tributary stream and—immediately left (N) of the canyon—ascend the narrow trail NE. Climbing through forest, the trail leads generally N, emerging onto **glacial rubble**.

In about 20 minutes, pass a cairn in the alpine zone at 2354 m (7720 ft). Proceed N a few more minutes to the 2385-m (7823-ft) crest of what, long ago, was a **terminal moraine**. Visible ahead is Haig Glacier (NW) and summer ski-camp huts (N). Visible behind are Beatty Glacier (right / SSW) and Lawson Lake (left / SSE).

Continuing toward the ski-camp huts, descend to the roaring, **glacial-meltwater stream**. Cross it on a metal bridge at 2357 m (7731). On the far bank, ascend N to a **helipad** at 2375 m (7790 ft), about 45 minutes from Turbine Canyon campground.

The **ski-camp huts** are a couple minutes N of the helipad. Behind the huts, a **cairned trail** boot-beaten into scree ascends N. Skiers use it to access the glacier. Follow it.

Near 2500 m (8200 ft) the trail bends left (NW). After pushing through a final, steep section of loose rock, attain a commanding view from **trail's end** at 2600 m (8528 ft), 2.8 km (1.7 mi) from the campground, or about 40 minutes from the helipad. **Haig Glacier**, now directly below you, is visible nearly to its apex. Above you (N) is 3246-m (10,647-ft) Mt. Jellicoe.

Lawson Lake, en route to Turbine Canyon

TRIP 23

Three Isle Lake
South Kananaskis Pass

LOCATION	Peter Lougheed Provincial Park
	W of Upper Kananaskis Lake
ROUND TRIP	20.8 km (12.9 mi) to lake, 24.8 km (15.4 mi) to pass
ELEVATION GAIN	475 m (1558 ft) to lake, 610 m (2000 ft) to pass
KEY ELEVATIONS	trailhead 1725 m (5658 ft), lake 2160 m (7085 ft)
	pass 2305 m (7560 ft)
HIKING TIME	8 hours to 2 days
DIFFICULTY	moderate
MAP	Gem Trek *Kananaskis Lakes*

Opinion

Drive a paved road, shamble a few steps from your car, and magnificence greets you: vast Upper Kananaskis Lake haloed by lofty mountains. So why leave it and plod into the wilderness beyond? For the same reason you don't just gaze at your lover. You make love, meld, become one.

Hiking propels you from sightseeing to experience; from spectator to participant; from taking a snapshot with your eyes, to putting yourself in the picture. Here, the picture is multi-faceted. Like a painting by Hieronymus Bosch, it contains worlds within worlds. You must choose among them.

Shortly beyond Upper Kananaskis Lake, you have the choice of detouring to Invincible Lake (Trip 21). At Upper Kananaskis River, the choice is North Kananaskis Pass (Trip 22), or Three Isle Lake? At the lake, the choice is Northover Ridge (Trip 24), or South Kananaskis Pass? At South Kananaskis Pass, you have the choice of continuing to Beatty Lake. On Northover Ridge, you have the choice of proceeding to Aster Lake and looping back to Upper Kananaskis Lake. The following synopses will help you decide.

Think of the Invincible Lake hike as distinctly separate, though it shares the same initial approach as the other options. It merits a start-early, go-far, finish-late daytrip. The rugged route requires navigational skill, so it promises solitude.

The trip to North K Pass is beautiful and lenient. It's hikeable in a day from the trailhead, if you're strong and determined, but your reward for lugging a full pack and spending a night out is the opportunity to also see Haig Glacier.

photos: *1 Looking NNW to South Kananaskis Pass, from Northover Ridge ascent*
2 Final ascent to Three Isle Lake 3 Three Isle Lake

Three Isle Lake is simply a landmark en route to superior scenery and greater adventure. The lake is pretty when full-pool, but expect to see a broad, muddy shoreline lending a ring-around-the-tub appearance. If you go, keep going at least into the gorgeous, South K Pass meadows. Time permitting, heed the meadowy invitation, press onward to Beatty Lake, where your foray in that direction will feel complete. Dayhiking to Beatty demands vigour and resolve. Burdened with a backpack, however, surmounting the headwall that guards Three Isle Lake is a chore.

To visit both North and South K passes, shoulder your backpack 7.2 km (4.5 mi) to Forks campground. Start early. After pitching your tent, dayhike to South K Pass and possibly Beatty Lake. On day two, light out for North K Pass and Haig Glacier. It's possible for zealots to compress this trip into a weekend by exiting on evening two. If you decline to hike at race pace, hike only as far as the campground on day one. Three days makes this a much less demanding trip. The leisurely ideal is to spread it out over four, allowing yourself to sleep in late on the final morning before heading home.

Now hear this. The real reason to hike to Three Isle Lake is because it's on the way to Northover Ridge. Nowhere in K-Country, perhaps nowhere in the entire Canadian Rockies, is there a more sensational hike than the Northover loop. If you're a gladiator capable of marching with Caesar, you can pull it off in a single, ambitiously long, arduously challenging, gloriously fulfilling day. Backpacking Northover in two or three days is equally splendid, though less of a crowning achievement. But Northover is strictly for confident scramblers and proficient cross-country navigators.

If the Northover loop exceeds your ability or desire, try a one-way trip: attain the supremely scenic ridge, then turn back before descending to Aster Lake. It's possible to do this as a long dayhike from Upper Kananaskis Lake trailhead, but much easier if you start at Three Isle Lake campground. Camping at Three Isle also gives you the option of dayhiking to Northover one day, and South K Pass on your day out.

Finally, here's a brief summary of the hike to Three Isle Lake. It follows a rocky road littered with stones that jackhammer your joints. Occasional impressive vistas help keep you motivated. A soft path then winds through lovely, mature forest. After Forks campground, views of surrounding mountains expand while you ascend out of the trees. Assault an avalanche slope. Toil over a very steep headwall. Then catch your breath during a short, gentle descent to the lake.

Fact

Before your trip

If you're staying overnight at Three Isle Lake, bring a stove. Open fires are prohibited.

By Vehicle

Follow directions for Mt. Indefatigable (Trip 20) to the trailhead parking lot at North Interlakes day-use area. It's on the NE shore of Upper Kananaskis Lake. Elevation: 1725 m (5658 ft).

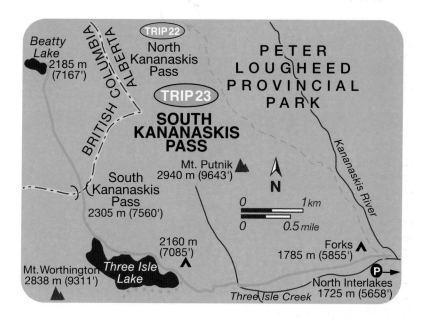

On Foot

From the trailhead kiosk at the N end of the parking lot, walk NW atop the dam. Soon cross the bridge over the spillway. Turn left (W) onto an old road. Reach a **signed junction** just beyond, at 0.3 km (0.2 mi). The trail forking right ascends Mt. Indefatigable. Continue W on the old road above Upper Kananaskis Lake's N shore. Soon bear right at the map-sign.

At 0.8 km (0.5 mi) and 2.2 km (1.4 mi), where left forks drop to the lakeshore trail, bear right and stay high on the rocky, old road. The lake is visible below. Also attain a view left (SSW), beyond the lake, up Aster Creek canyon. Scrutinize it if you intend to complete the entire Northover Ridge loop (Trip 24), because the route descends the left (SE) wall of that canyon, from high above the falls. This is your only chance to assess the route conditions. If the left wall of the canyon is snow covered, descending could be treacherous. You want to know that now—not near the end of the loop, when turning back would require you to spend the night out and repeat the entire arduous hike in reverse.

Resuming your trip to Three Isle Lake, cross the Palliser rockslide. After curving NW, the road descends, reaching a bridge over **Invincible Creek** at 3.8 km (2.3 mi). Mountainbikers must stop here. Right leads to Invincible Lake (Trip 21). For Three Isle Lake, cross the bridge and follow the dirt trail generally W through ancient forest. Among the spruce is a stand of 400-year-old lodgepole pine.

At 5.8 km (3.6 mi), 1780 m (5838 ft), cross a bridge over the cascading **Kananaskis River**. Proceed generally W. The headwall you'll ascend to reach the lake is soon visible ahead. In quick succession, cross several bridged streams, all flowing into the river. The trail skirts a rockslide at the base of Mt. Lyautey (left / S).

Beatty Lake

Shortly after crossing the bridged river again, enter **Forks campgrown** at 7.2 km (4.5 mi), 1785 m (5855 ft). It's in forest, just above Kananaskis River. You'll find 15 tent pads, outhouses, tables, benches around two communal fire pits, and bear-proof food storage. There's a junction here. Right leads NNW to Lawson Lake, Turbine Canyon campground, North Kananaskis Pass, and Haig Glacier (Trip 22). Go left (W) for Three Isle Lake and South Kananaskis Pass. The lake is 3.2 km (2 mi) farther. Right (NW) is Mt. Putnik.

About ten minutes past Forks campground, the trail begins climbing. The grade is increasingly steep. Soon cross an avalanche slope overgrown with willow and alder. Attain views down-valley to Mt. Indefatigable (ENE). At 1980 m (6495 ft), about an hour from Forks campground, begin a skyward ascent of the headwall—a strenuous 15-minute task for strong dayhikers. Stairs assist you over awkward rock bands. Arrive **atop the headwall** at 10 km (6.2 mi), 2200 m (7216 ft).

Proceeding WNW, descend 30 m (100 ft) in the next 200 m (220 yd) to a signed junction. Left keeps descending to reach the E shore of **Three Isle Lake** at 10.4 km (6.4 mi), 2160 m (7085 ft). Right enters Three Isle Lake campground (16 tent pads well above the lake, bear-proof food storage) and continues to South Kananaskis Pass.

After delivering you to the lake, the trail leads W, around the S shore. South Kananaskis Pass is visible NW, beyond the lake. A left spur climbs to a ranger cabin above the S shore. At the lake's SW corner, shortly past the spur, the route to **Northover Ridge** (Trip 24) curves left (S) up-valley. The ridge is then visible ahead on the skyline.

For South Kananaskis Pass, follow the trail generally NW from Three Isle Lake campground. It rounds the lake's N shore. Mt. Putnik is right (NE) above you. Mt. Worthington is left (SW) beyond the lake. Near the lake's NW corner, Northover Ridge is visible S. The trail then turns right, heading generally N, ascending moderately through subalpine forest. Surpass treeline and reach **South Kananaskis Pass** at 12.4 km (7.7 mi), 2305 m (7560 ft), on the Great Divide. There's a large cairn here and a sign HEIGHT OF THE ROCKIES WILDERNESS AREA. WELCOME TO B.C. Meadows extend N toward pyramidal, 3000-m (9840-ft) Mt. Beatty.

The trail continues NNW from the pass. It descends 120 m (394 ft) in 2 km (1.2 mi) to **Beatty Lake** at 2185 m (7167 ft). Total distance: 14.4 km (8.9 mi). The lake is enclosed by forest and a cliff.

Trail to Beatty Lake

TRIP 24

Northover Ridge / Aster Lake

LOCATION	Peter Lougheed Provincial Park
	W of Upper Kananaskis Lake
LOOP	33.7 km (20.9 mi)
ELEVATION GAIN	1180 m (3870 ft)
KEY ELEVATIONS	trailhead 1725 m (5658 ft)
	Three Isle Lake 2160 m (7085 ft)
	highpoint 2830 m (9282 ft)
	Aster Lake 2305 m (7560 ft)
HIKING TIME	11-hour dayhike, or 2-3 day backpack
DIFFICULTY	challenging
MAP	Gem Trek *Kananaskis Lakes*

Opinion

Earth is speeding through space at 107,320 kph (66,700 mph). Good thing this galactic vehicle of ours has spoilers. The Himalayas. The Andes. The Alps. The Sierra Nevada. The Rockies. Surely these skyscraping protuberances slow the planet and keep it from spinning out of control. No? Well, maybe not. But on this adventure, into the heart of one of the world's great mountain ranges, it's easy to imagine.

The approach to Northover is via Three Isle Lake (Trip 23). The description of that hike is a helpful preface to this one. Read the *Opinion* section, particularly the last three paragraphs. Go ahead. Do it now. We'll wait here for you.

You're back? Okay. As we were saying, the Northover loop affords an ecstatic sense of exploration. Between Three Isle and Aster lakes, you'll be deep in the wilderness. On trail-less terrain. Labouring up steep scree. Following a sustained high-elevation route. Surrounded by peaks grinding their teeth on passing clouds. Peering into deep, remote, bear-haven valleys. Below Aster Lake, you'll descend an alarmingly steep route into an exciting, severe canyon. Then, if Hidden Lake is full-pool, you might have to thwack 'n thrash around its forested shore to reach Upper Kananaskis Lake and the groomed path that leads back to the trailhead.

So, this thrill ride's price of admission is competence born of backcountry experience. To safely attempt the Northover loop, you must be a strong hiker, able to navigate cross-country. No matter how confident you are, bring a topo map and compass—for enjoyment as well as insurance. If you intend to flash the entire loop in a single day, be prepared to bivouac. Essentials include surplus food, extra layers of warm clothing, and a headlamp.

You're acrophobic? Whoa. For you, Northover would be a mistake. The ridge itself is 2.7 km (1.7 mi) long. A significant stretch is shoulder width and outer-space airy. This amplifies the thrill if you're sure-footed and unafraid of heights. Otherwise it will reduce you to quivering Jello. The Aster Creek

Ascending Northover Ridge. Three Isle Lake below.

Northover Ridge. Royal Group beyond.

canyon descent route is equally exposed, but unstable, even narrower, and therefore more perilous. If you're rattled by the ridge, you'll be petrified at the prospect of edging along the canyon's heart-stopping cliffs.

Truly hardy hikers: fear not. For you, the challenges described above are reasonable and make the journey more rewarding. And some of the way is as easy as it is sublime. Once the ridge broadens, and foot placement is no longer your focus, you'll simply be walking in the sky, enjoying operatic vistas. You'll see why the Royal Group deserves its august name. You'll see 3450-m (11,319-ft) Mt. Joffre shouldering the Mangin Glacier. You'll see a lonely, lovely, tarn-dappled sanctuary beneath Warrior Mtn. After dismounting the ridge, you'll drop into the sprawling basin harbouring Aster Lake. You'll stride through meadows while skirting the lake's shore. It was here that a well-traveled American friend of ours summed up the Northover experience in just three words: "Who needs Alaska?"

Delay your Northover assault until August. By then, the snow should have melted off most of the route, making it safer. It's critical that Aster Creek canyon be free of snow, or the risk of slipping off that precarious descent route will be deadly serious. The second paragraph under *On Foot* in Trip 23 describes where you can view the descent route and assess conditions. If it looks snow-covered, don't go. Also call the park office (403-591-6322) and ask to speak to a ranger who has current information about the route.

If you backpack, it's logical to camp at Three Isle Lake your first night out. You can then be atop Northover Ridge before noon on day two, in time for optimal photographs of the Royal Group. If you make this a three-day trip, camp at Aster Lake the second night. Approaching the lake basin in the afternoon is best for photography, because you'll have an aerial view, plus the lake and Mt. Sarrail will be bathed in low-angle light.

Fact

Before your trip

If you're staying overnight, bring a stove. Open fires are prohibited. Also be aware that you must ford Aster Creek. Though shallow, it's broad, frigid and rocky. River sandals or neoprene socks will spare you a few minutes of pain, if you don't mind hauling them the whole way. Bring an extra bandana to dry your feet before rebooting.

By Vehicle

Follow directions for Mt. Indefatigable (Trip 20) to the trailhead parking lot at North Interlakes day-use area. It's on the NE shore of Upper Kananaskis Lake. Elevation: 1725 m (5658 ft).

Although not strictly necessary, you should arrange a shuttle. You'll be glad you did at the end of this trip. Follow directions for Rawson Lake (Trip 25) to leave a vehicle in the trailhead parking lot at Upper Kananaskis Lake day-use area, on the SE shore. This will spare you a 3.2-km (2-mi) hitchhike or road-walk to link the trailheads and complete the loop.

On Foot

Follow directions for Three Isle Lake (Trip 23). Above the headwall, at the signed junction where right enters Three Isle Lake campground, bear left. Descend to reach the E shore of **Three Isle Lake** at 10.4 km (6.4 mi), 2160 m (7085 ft). Your total elevation gain so far is 475 m (1558 ft).

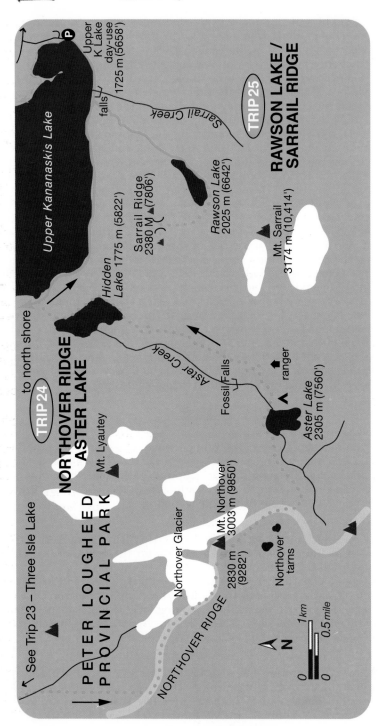

Follow the trail W, around the S shore. Pass a left spur that climbs to a ranger cabin above the S shore. At the lake's SW corner, curve left (S) into a **valley.** Northover Ridge is now visible ahead (S) on the skyline. Right (W) is 2838-m (9311-ft) Mt. Worthington.

The valley floor is level and treeless. Your general direction of travel will remain S to the ridgecrest. Visible on the valley's right, rear wall is the steep, scree slope you must surmount to reach the obvious pass on the crest.

Initially follow a path along the left (E) side of the valley. It soon disappears in the rocky, bushy, muddy **flats**. Where comfortable, work your way to the right (W) side of the valley, still continuing S.

If clear water is coursing through the flats, top-up your water bottles. Though you might find a snowmelt pool on the ridge, don't count on it. The next reliable water source is the Northover tarns, below the far end of the ridge, a couple hours distant.

Note where a mudslide ripped through a tributary drainage on the valley's right (W) slope. Just beyond (S), in the next **tributary drainage**, a bootbeaten path ascends right (SW). Follow it into the alpine zone.

Reach a **tussocky bench** at 2410 m (7905 ft). The view N is dramatic: over Three Isle Lake basin to South Kananaskis Pass and beyond to Mt. Beatty and neighbouring peaks. From the bench, proceed S—over talus and possibly snow—toward the steep, **scree slope**. Tag onto the distinct path bootbeaten into the scree and toil upward.

Atop the 2630-m (8626-ft) **pass**, drop your pack, relax, and congratulate yourself for attaining the **crest of Northover Ridge**. Defender Mtn is on the W side of the pass. Here at the NW end of the ridge, however, you're still well below the highpoint. You've hiked 3.8 km (2.4 mi), or about 1½ hours, from Three Isle Lake's E shore. Your total distance is 14.2 km (8.8 mi).

Turn left at the pass and trudge up the talusy ridgecrest SE. Though it looks dauntingly steep, it's easier than the slope you vanquished below the pass. The ascent route, bootbeaten into loose rock, favours the right (SW) side. At 2760 m (9053 ft) regain the crest for good. Ups and downs are now minimal. But the crest briefly narrows to a slender **arete**. At one point, you must step from one dinner-plate-size stone to the next, with the earth falling away dramatically on either side. Acrophobes might come unglued here. Surefooted hikers cruise on unconcerned. The crest then broadens, affording easy, carefree, spectacularly scenic hiking. Proceed ESE. Keep following the crest.

Dominating the mountainous panorama is the Royal Group (WNW) across the deep, forested, Palliser River valley. The massif comprises eight peaks and shoulders a couple glaciers. Visible W, beyond the Rockies, is the Purcell Range in the Kootenays. Mt. Joffre and the Mangin Glacier are SE. Mt Lyautey is E. These are but a few highlights. Your map will reveal all.

The route closely follows the ridgecrest, which divides Alberta from B.C. Allow time to sit and gaze. The scenery ahead is wonderfully vast and wild, but you're now at the scenic climax of the trip. Looking S, Joffre Creek valley is 1150 m (3772 ft) below you. Above it, SSW, is the little-visited Shangri-La of Limestone Lakes basin.

After passing the top edge of Northover Glacier, reach the **North–over Ridge highpoint**: 2830 m (9282 ft). It's just WNW of 3003-m (9850-ft)

Hike south to the ridgecrest lowpoint.

Mt. Northover. Descend talus slopes, then ascend along the SW side of the ridge. Looking NNW, beyond Northover Glacier, you can again see South Kananaskis Pass. Visible N of the pass is Beatty Glacier, on Mt. Beatty's right (E) side.

The route heads E briefly, toward Mt. Northover, then SE, dismounting the ridge, plunging into the small basin harbouring the two **Northover tarns**. It's a long, steep, rocky descent, possibly snow covered. After losing about 160 m (535 ft), pick up a path bootbeaten into the scree. It curves S, traversing just left (E) of the tarns, passing about 50 m (164 ft) above the smaller, higher one. S of the basin is 2973-m (9754-ft) Warrior Mtn.

After passing the tarns, the bootbeaten path ascends S to a prominent, 2585-m (8480-ft) **gap**. There's an Alberta provincial-park boundary sign here, announcing your re-entry into Alberta from B.C. Proceed through the gap. Then descend S, following a faint path on the left (E) wall of the rocky **gorge**. It curves E, dropping toward Aster Lake basin. The lake is visible ahead. Beyond it (E) is 3174-m (10,414-ft) Mt. Sarrail. Pause here to survey the next leg of the journey. Identify the outhouse on the SE bank of Aster Creek—the lake's outlet. That's your immediate goal. Get there by rounding the lake's N shore.

Where scree gives way to dryas, the path disappears. Keep descending the steep, heather-and-dryas slope. Head NE, curving N. Aim for the delta created by the creek flowing from the left (NW) drainage. Push through the brush in the delta. Find a place to rockhop across the stream. Then bear right (E). Your total distance is now 20.6 km (12.8 mi). You've hiked 10.2 km (6.3 mi) from the E end of Three Isle Lake.

Pick up scraps of path along the creek's N bank while you hike generally E to **Aster Lake**. Elevation: 2305 m (7560 ft). A more defined path rounds the N shore. Reach the mouth of the outlet—**Aster Creek**—at 22 km (13.6 mi). Ford to the SE bank. Then go left (NE) to the outhouse. Trail resumes here, above where the creek cascades into a rocky gorge. A few minutes farther, pass **Aster Lake campground** (5 tent pads, bear-proof food storage).

Descend a rocky declivity beside the rampaging falls. The trail zigzags, dropping steeply beside Fossil Falls gorge. Enter trees. Proceed through a grassy gully beneath a water-worn escarpment. Turn right (SE) following the distinct trail. Soon turn left (NE) and hop over a stream. The trail goes up and down beneath a cliff, over and around rock ribs. Stay on the main trail; needless ones have been blocked.

About 25 minutes beyond Aster Lake, pass a right spur leading to a **ranger cabin** tucked into Foch Creek basin. Then pass Foch Pond. Your general direction of travel is now NE and will remain so until Hidden Lake. Soon leave the trees behind and gain an aerial view of Hidden and Upper Kananaskis lakes. Steel yourself for an arduous descent of the formidable **canyon** ahead.

The trail careens down the canyon's E wall—the lower scree slopes of Mt. Sarrail's W face. The terrain is very steep. The trail is obvious, but narrow. Early on, several sections are exposed, meaning the trail is immediately above a vertical drop. A fall could be fatal. Stay alert. Be aware of every step.

At 2076 m (6810 ft) cross a stream in a vertical gully beneath a short cliff. Descend another 122 m (400 ft) and you're on safer ground. There's a lot more talus to negotiate, but the canyon wall is now reclining. At 1900 m (6232 ft), about 1½ hours from Aster Lake, the trail is dirt. Re-enter forest for the final 15-minutes down to Hidden Lake.

Reach the S shore of **Hidden Lake** at 26.5 km (16.4 mi), 1775 m (5822 ft). Mt. Indefatigable is visible N. Follow the rough trail around the right (E) shore—about a 20-minute task. (If it's been a rainy summer, the water level could be high, forcing you to bash through the trees, slowing your progress.) Just beyond the lake's N end, pick up a trail leading NE into the forest. Within ten minutes, at 28.5 km (17.7 mi), 1718 m (5635 ft), intersect the broad, virtually level trail encircling **Upper Kananaskis Lake**. Turn right (SE), ignoring any sign suggesting otherwise.

The narrowest section of Northover Ridge

Rounding the S shore, the trail curves E. Only during the final 1 km (0.6 mi) is the lake significantly visible. From where you intersected the lake trail, it takes about 1⅓ hours to reach the trailhead parking lot at **Upper Kananaskis Lake day-use area**, on the SE shore. Your total distance is now 33.7 km (20.9 mi). If you arranged a vehicle shuttle, as suggested in the *By Vehicle* section, you'll have wheels waiting for you here. Otherwise you must hitchhike or road-walk about 3 km (1.9 mi) generally NNW to where you began this trip: the trailhead parking lot at **North Interlakes day-use area**.

TRIP 25
Rawson Lake / Sarrail Ridge

LOCATION	Peter Lougheed Provincial Park S of Upper Kananaskis Lake
ROUND TRIP	7.8 km (4.8 mi) to lake, 11.3 km (7 mi) to ridge
ELEVATION GAIN	300 m (984 ft) to lake, plus 355 m (1164 ft) to ridge
KEY ELEVATIONS	trailhead 1725 m (5658 ft), lake 2025 m (6642 ft) ridge 2380 m (7806 ft)
HIKING TIME	2 to 3 hours for lake, 4½ to 5½ hours for ridge
DIFFICULTY	easy to lake, challenging to ridge
MAPS	page 134; Gem Trek *Kananaskis Country*

Opinion

"I'm not in shape for hiking." "I don't have any boots." "I've got out-of-town guests." Rawson Lake trashes these worn-out excuses. You can start getting in shape here, on a measured ascent. Wear your runners; the trail to Rawson is broad and smooth. Bring your guests, let the Canadian Rockies relieve you as host for an afternoon.

Your burden lighter now that you left all that rationalizing behind, you'll stride briskly along a level trail following the shore of mountain-ringed Upper Kananaskis Lake. Then you'll turn into the forest and switch-back upward on a city-park quality path. The elevation gain is significant, but the grade is moderate.

Expect to encounter a steady flow of hikers on summer weekends because this is a short trip starting at a favoured day-use area. Some people don't even intend to hike. They just start walking, see the Rawson Lake sign, and say "Why not?" But despite the lake's popularity, if you proceed along its rocky, southeast shore, you'll likely find a quiet spot where you can meditate on the serene beauty of this cirque clasped in the awesome arms of Mt. Sarrail.

Rawson's too tame to satisfy your appetite for adventure? Keep going. From the southwest shore, storm the steep slope to Sarrail Ridge. It over-looks Upper and Lower Kananaskis lakes, affords an excellent view of Haig Glacier, and boosts you high enough to see over Mt. Sarrail's shoulder to Mt. Foch—an astounding sight. Though you can try the ascent in late June, it might be early July before this southeast-facing slope is hikeable without an ice axe.

It's a hot, summer day? After returning from Rawson Lake, stop just before reaching your vehicle. Drop your pack on the gravel beach below the trailhead. Kick off your footwear, strip to your shorts and halter-top, and plunge into glacier-cold Upper Kananaskis Lake. Your initial gasping shock will soon ease, leaving you relaxed and refreshed. Ahhh.

Looking down the Sarrail Ridge ascent route, above Rawson Lake

Fact

By Vehicle

From Trans-Canada Hwy 1, drive 50 km (31 mi) S on Hwy 40. Or, from Highwood Pass, drive 17 km (10.5 mi) N on Hwy 40. From either approach, turn SW onto Kananaskis Lakes Trail. Reset your trip odometer to 0.

0 km (0 mi)

Starting SW on Kananaskis Lakes Trail.

2.2 km (1.4 mi)

Proceed straight where Smith-Dorrien / Spray Trail (Hwy 742) forks right.

9.8 km (6.1 mi)
Proceed straight where right leads to Lower Kananaskis Lake and Boulton Creek campground.

12.6 km (7.8 mi)
Turn left. Straight leads to the trailhead parking lot on the NE shore of Upper Kananaskis Lake.

12.9 km (8 km)
Bear left. Right is a boat ramp.

13 km (8.1 mi)
Bear right. Left is a parking lot for boat trailers.

13.2 km (8.2 mi)
Arrive at Upper Kananaskis Lake day-use area, on the SE shore. Turn left (S) onto dirt. Right is a paved parking lot and public phone. Both sides have picnic tables above the lake.

13.4 km (8.3 mi)
Park at the far S end of this unpaved lot, near the trailhead sign for Kananaskis and Rawson lakes. Elevation: 1725 m (5658 ft).

On Foot
The wide trail leads SW around the shore of Upper Kananaskis Lake. Breaks in the forest grant views. Curve W. Mt. Indefatigable (Trip 20) is visible NNW, across the lake. At 1.2 km (0.75 mi), just W of the bridge over **Sarrail Creek falls**, fork left at the sign for Rawson Lake.

The trail climbs via moderate switchbacks through a mature forest of Engelmann spruce and subalpine fir. Your general direction of travel will remain SW to the lake. About 20 minutes up, the ascent eases for the final 1 km (0.6 mi). Stretches of boardwalk start 0.5 km (0.3 mi) before the lake. Reach the NE shore of **Rawson Lake**, near the outlet stream, at 3.5 km (2.3 mi), 2025 m (6642 ft). Fast hikers will be here in less than an hour. An outhouse is 100 m (110 yd) farther.

The wall just beyond the far (SW) end of the lake belongs to 3174-m (10,411-ft) Mt. Sarrail. The mountain's flanks clench the lake. Follow the path at least another 300 m (328 yd) SW, along the SE shore. The view improves, and you'll find comfortable places to sit and enjoy it. A sign indicates the **end of official trail** and warns that grizzly-bear sightings are common. There's a rock-slab bench here.

A bootbeaten route continues below cliffs and scree slopes, around the **SW shore**, to an inlet stream created by early-summer snowmelt. Sarrail Ridge looms 355-m (1164-ft) above, NNW. Scan the lush slope for feeding bears. If you see one, turn around. Leave quietly without disturbing it. If you proceed, be observant. Make noise to warn unseen bears of your presence.

Hop the inlet stream. Follow the path through krummholz, over the knoll. Pick your way across a rocky, bushy area. Bootbeaten path resumes between the stream gully (left, possibly snow-filled) and the forest edge (right). Ascend NNW.

The path leads to a rocky pour-off at the head of the **gully**. Veer right. Scramble out of the gully, up the dirt slope. The path resumes in the grass above. Turn left and follow it NNW, up the green **draw** bordered by krummholz. It's very steep, but solid footholds allow you to keep stair-stepping upward to the ridgecrest between Mt. Sarrail's sheer face and a small, rocky tower. Top out on 2380-m (7806-ft) **Sarrail Ridge** about 45 minutes after leaving the lake.

Upper and Lower Kananaskis lakes are visible below (N and NE). Haig Glacier is NW, up the Kananaskis River Valley, between Mounts Maude (left) and Jellicoe (right). SSE, just past dual-peaked Mt. Sarrail, is 3180-m (10,430-ft) Mt. Foch.

Now look right (NE), along Sarrail Ridge. Just beyond and above you is the ridgecrest highpoint. That little outlier offers the supreme vantage. Surmount it by first retracing your steps as if descending to Rawson Lake. Approaching treeline, watch left for a **game trail** traversing left (E). Follow it to a fork just shy of a **rock band**. Go either way to gain the 2465-m (8085-ft) **outlier summit**. Left is a no-exposure, scramble route piercing a cleft. Right skirts the rock band, accessing a steep, grassy, hikeable ramp.

TRIP 26

Elk Lakes / Petain Basin

LOCATION	S end Peter Lougheed Provincial Park
	N end Elk Lakes Provincial Park
ROUND TRIP	16.4 km (10.2 mi) to Upper Elk Lake
	29.4 km (18.2 mi) to Petain Basin
ELEVATION CHANGE	185-m (608-ft) gain / 140-m (460-ft) loss to lake
	plus 521-m (1710-ft) gain to basin
KEY ELEVATIONS	trailhead 1720 m (5642 ft)
	Upper Elk Lake 1765 m (5790 ft)
	basin 2287 m (7500 ft)
HIKING TIME	6 hours for lake, overnight for basin
DIFFICULTY	easy to lake, challenging to basin
MAP	Gem Trek *Kananaskis Lakes*

Opinion

Nature isn't a destination. It's not merely a place you enjoy visiting occasionally. Nature is the energy manifested in all of life, including you. So when you're awed by nature at its most pure and grand, such as when hiking through wildly beautiful Petain Basin, remember: you and it share the same life force. This awareness can help sustain you—long after your trek into B.C.'s Elk Lakes Provincial Park—during those inevitable times when nature is less powerfully evident.

Just don't be discouraged by the journey's inauspicious start: an old road plowing into dense, viewless forest. The hiking is soon surprisingly engaging. And the access described here, from the north, spares you the tedious, southern approach, which entails a 1½-hour drive from Sparwood, mostly on an unpaved backroad. The trail should be sufficiently snow-free from late May through October as far as Upper Elk Lake. Within that comparatively wide window, you have many appealing options for dayhiking or backpacking.

Just 5.2 km (3.2 mi) from the trailhead is a steep, 1.3-km (0.8-mi) spur climbing to Frozen Lake. Gripped in a spectacular cirque on the northeast face of Mount Fox, the lake is shaded from afternoon sun and therefore resembles a daiquiri much of the year. Expect the route to be partly snow-covered but discernible by mid-June, snow-free by mid-July. Whether dayhiking or backpacking, definitely detour to Frozen Lake on your way back from Upper Elk Lake.

If you're dayhiking here in early June, plan to turn around at Upper Elk Lake, where you can eat lunch at the water's edge beneath the sheer south face of Mount Fox. By mid-July, strong dayhikers might go beyond Upper Elk, crossing impetuous Petain Creek and ascending to a flowery meadow beneath impressive Petain Falls. But you're cheating yourself to go that far

Lower Elk Lake

and not make the final vault into Petain Basin. To accomplish that goal and relish it requires a two-night backpack trip: late July through early October.

If you're backpacking, you can choose from three campgrounds: Lower Elk Lake, Petain Creek, or Petain Basin. All are appealing. Lower Elk Lake, however, is a bit out of the way. Petain Creek is the logical choice. Petain Basin is the most scenic. But before deciding where to plunk your temporary home, consider the 410-m (1345-ft) headwall guarding the basin. It's seemingly vertical, exceedingly rough. You don't just hike it; you assault it. Carrying only a daypack, it's a challenge. Bearing the weight of a full backpack, it's a chore. Most hikers will be glad they camped two nights below—either at the lake or beside the creek—and enjoyed a lightly-laden, one-day venture into the basin.

After clambering over the headwall, you'll enter an alpine Eden. Once again you'll be striding freely—over rock slabs, across meadows—but only if you aren't knocked off your feet by the beauty of it all. Petain Glacier is just one of the enthralling sights. The temptation to lounge is the only obstacle between you and the basin's upper reaches, at 2440 m (8000 ft).

Fact

Before your trip

Be aware that camping is prohibited at Frozen Lake. Mountain bikes are allowed only as far as West Elk Pass, at 4.8 km (3 mi), because they're not permitted in Elk Lakes Provincial Park.

By Vehicle

From Trans-Canada Hwy 1, drive 50 km (31 mi) S on Hwy 40. Or, from Highwood Pass, drive 17 km (10.5 mi) N on Hwy 40. From either approach,

Upper Petain Basin

turn SW onto Kananaskis Lakes Trail. Reset your trip odometer to 0 and proceed generally S. At 12 km (7.4 mi) turn left into the signed Elk Pass trailhead parking lot, at 1720 m (5642 ft).

On Foot

Immediately right (S) of the outhouse is a gated gravel road. Follow it ESE. In about seven minutes, near the first rise, ignore the ski trail forking left (N). Proceed straight. In about 15 minutes, the road passes beneath power lines and grants a view NNW over Lower Kananaskis Lake to Mt. Indefatigable (Trip 20). The road then curves right and descends. Several minutes farther, ignore a smaller road veering left.

About 30 minutes from the trailhead, cross a bridge over **Fox Creek** at 2 km (1.2 mi), 1785 m (5855 ft). On the far (E) bank are three options. Left (NNE) ascends to the hydroline. The trail ahead (SE) is blocked by a berm. Go right (S) on the diminishing road marked by a hiker sign. Just 15 minutes farther, cross two more bridges over Fox Creek.

About an hour from the trailhead, reach a three-way junction at 3.8 km (2.4 mi), 1880 m (6166 ft). Mt. Fox is visible SW. Behind it (W) is Mt. Sarrail. Ignore the distinct road ascending left (SE) and what appears to be an overgrown road right (W). Proceed straight (SSW) over a low shoulder, on a trail marked by a hiker sign.

About 50 m/yd farther, the trail merges with an old road. Follow it left and quickly reach a junction at 4.3 km (2.7 mi), near a picnic table, immediately NE of a bridge. Don't cross the bridge; the trail beyond ascends SW, then curves NW to Blueberry Hill. Instead, proceed straight (SSE) on the level, overgrown road, past a brushy clearing (right) with a stream meandering through it.

Within five minutes, reach another junction. The road proceeds straight (E). Turn right (S) onto a trail marked by a hiker sign. Drop in and out of a drainage. A bit farther, at 4.8 km (3 mi), 1905 m (6250 ft), reach a signed junction in **West Elk Pass**, where you'll leave Peter Lougheed Park and enter Elk Lakes Park.

At the pass, left (SE) descends the Elkan Creek drainage 4.2 km (2.6 mi) to the N terminus of Elk River Road, which is 1.6 km (1 mi) E of the backcountry campground on Lower Elk Lake. Don't go that way, even if you intend to camp at Lower Elk. Instead, turn right (SW), following the sign for Upper Elk Lake via Fox Lake.

In a couple minutes, reach a signed fork at 5.2 km (3.2 mi). Right (SW) leads to Frozen Lake. Skip below for details. Go left (S) for Fox and Upper Elk lakes.

Proceeding S toward Upper Elk Lake, soon reach a lengthy boardwalk traversing marshy terrain. Just beyond, at 5.6 km (3.5 mi), a short, right spur leads to **Fox Lake**. From the shore, at 1940 m (6363 ft), you can peer up at where Mount Fox clutches Frozen Lake. Departing Fox Lake, the trail is fairly level for about 15 minutes before starting the long descent to Upper Elk Lake.

About ten minutes into the descent, attain a view of Lower Elk Lake and Mt. Aosta. A bit farther, the trail drops sharply through an avalanche swathe granting a broader view of Upper Elk Valley. After briefly resuming in forest, the trail plunges across a rockslide affording a view SW of Upper Elk Lake and Castelneau Glacier beyond. The Petain Basin route ascends beneath that glacier.

At the bottom of the rockslide, reach the NE end of **Upper Elk Lake**. Cross the bridged outlet stream to reach a T-junction on the S bank. You've hiked 8.2 km (5.1 mi) from the trailhead. The elevation here is 1765 m (5790 ft). Left (ESE) passes Lower Elk Lake campground in 1 km (0.6 mi), at 1740 m (5707 ft). Go right (SW) along the upper lake's SE shore for Petain Basin. The S face of Mount Fox rises abruptly from the N shore.

When the water is high, you'll be stepping across flooded sections of trail. After recent rain, scan the mountain's folded limestone face for spouting cascades. From the lake's S shore, hike about 12 minutes—generally SW, across gravel beds, then back into forest—to a signed fork. Left follows Nivelle Creek upstream (S) 6 km (3.7 mi) to Coral Pass. Go right (SW). Two minutes farther is a bridged crossing of **Petain Creek**. The trail continues upstream (SW), on the W bank. In another eight minutes, reach **Petain Creek campground**. It's between the trail and the creek, at 11 km (6.8 mi).

For Petain Basin, resume SW. At 12.7 km (7.8 mi), 1835 m (6020 ft) arrive at a signed fork. Left (NW) is a spur to the base of **Petain Falls**. Even if you don't want to tag the falls, briefly probe the meadow. Mid-July through early August, it explodes with wildflowers: tall, light-blue alpine forget-me-nots, yellow columbine, graceful lavender clematis on long stalks, yellow hedysarum, and white spirea.

Heading to Petain Basin? At the waterfall fork, bear right (NE) and ascend. Soon cross a rocky gorge and continue up its left (W) side. Heading generally N, the trail rapidly deteriorates to a route and dramatically steepens. Traction is hard won even when the route is dry. If it's wet, good luck.

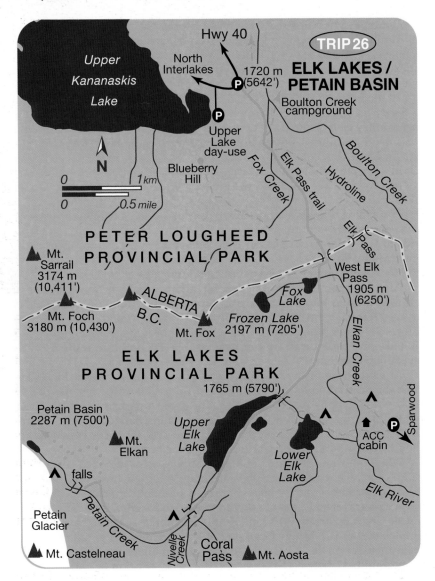

Tunnel through krummholz (stunted trees) for about 15 minutes. Negotiate a short, awkward stretch. Enjoy a short reprieve where the ascent eases among bigger trees. Resume labouring skyward. The route soon exits the trees and enters a rocky chute—the upper reaches of the gorge you crossed below. Keep powering higher, over the loose boulders.

Near 2200 m (7216 ft) a cairn indicates where to turn left, out of the chute, onto a path traversing a steep, grassy slope. Wfffeww! The hard part's behind you. Wildflowers are again profuse: deep purple larkspur, lavender sky pilot, purple penstemon, red paintbrush. The hanging

Petain Basin

Castelneau Glacier is visible S. Mt. McCuaig is on the glacier's SE edge. Keep following the narrow but well-defined path. Crest the lip of **Petain Basin** at 14.7 km (9.1 mi), 2287 m (7500 ft).

Ascend another 61 m (200 ft) over rock slabs and grass for improved glacier-views. Mt. Nivelle is visible SW of Castelneau Glacier. Pointy Mt. Castelneau is NE of it. A bit of Petain Glacier is visible W. Ignore the cairned route descending left (SW) to upper Petain Creek, unless you're spending the night in the treed campground on the far bank (fires prohibited). Instead, go N, cross-country, up gentle, green, slabby ridges, toward the right (E) side of the basin.

The deeper you probe the basin, the more you'll see of broad Petain Glacier. Even 15 minutes makes a big difference. Mt. Petain is W. Keep ascending to see Mount Joffre SW, rising at the upper edge of the ice. Given sufficient daylight, energy and will, it's possible for hikers to summit 3180-m (10,430-ft) Mt. Foch—the basin's northernmost guardian and the ultimate vantage from which to survey Petain Basin.

Frozen Lake

The signed spur to Frozen Lake initially follows the Alberta / British Columbia boundary. It departs the main trail 0.4 km (0.2 mi) N of the spur to Fox Lake, or 0.4 km (0.2 mi) SW of the signed junction in West Elk Pass.

Follow the trail WSW. Within five minutes, cross a broad, marshy clearing. Upon re-entering forest, a steep, rough ascent ensues. After gaining 90 m (296 ft) in about 20 minutes, ignore a minor, overgrown path crossing your ascent route. Eventually your trail angles SW, contouring momentarily then tilting skyward again. In about 45 minutes, reach Frozen Lake at 1.3 km (0.8 mi), 2197 m (7205 ft). It's cupped in a cirque on the NE face of Mount Fox.

TRIP 27
Elbow Lake / Piper Pass

LOCATION	Elbow-Sheep Wildland Provincial Park
	Hwy 40, N of Highwood Pass
ROUND TRIP	19.2 km (11.9 mi) via short approach
ELEVATION GAIN	617 m (2024 ft)
KEY ELEVATIONS	trailhead 1963 m (6440 ft), lake 2105 m (6905 ft)
	pass 2580 m (8462 ft)
HIKING TIME	7 to 8 hours
DIFFICULTY	easy to moderate
MAP	Gem Trek *Kananaskis Lakes*

Opinion

Despite proof that the earth is round, apparently we kept wishing it were flat. Because we've succeeded in pounding much of our world flat again. You now spend your life staring at flat surfaces: computer screens, smartphone screens, tablet screens, TV screens, movie screens, the pages of books, magazines, and newspapers. Even car windshields create the impression of watching a film. And all this one-dimensional imagery, though mentally stimulating, requires you to be motionless, with your eyes focused on a fixed distance. But you're a creature designed to move. So here's a hike as multi-dimensional as they come, leading you through forests and meadows, past a lake, along a river and a creek, down a valley, up a canyon, above a tarn, to a lonely, scenic pass among lofty, jagged peaks.

Most people will arrive at Elbow Lake in about 30 minutes. Like all lakes, it holds a seemingly pheromonal attraction for hikers, campers and anglers. You won't be here alone. If all you're seeking is a short walk in the woods, however, you'll find Elbow Lake a splendid destination. Though the lake is below treeline, the open shore allows you to appreciate the mountainous setting.

Continue at least 1.6 km (1 mi) beyond the lake, into Elbow River valley. The hiking is close-your-eyes easy, on a level road-trail, yet the expansive meadowlands are bug-eyes beautiful. The massive shoulders of Elpoca Mtn and Mt. Rae rise on either side. Solitude is likely here, because the crowd stops at the lake.

The view from the Elbow River meadows extends northwest into Piper Creek canyon, which harbours delights not evident to those prying from a distance. That's why all capable hikers should allow a full day, scurry past Elbow Lake, and scamper into the upper canyon. It's a meadowy, alpine haven, carpeted with grass, heather and wildflowers, at the base of the two Tombstone Mtns. Can you eke out a little more oomph? Dash up to Piper

Pass, gaze at the ragged Opal Range, and peer into the upper reaches of West Fork Little Elbow River valley (Trip 39).

Between Elbow River valley and the mouth of Piper Creek canyon, you have a choice of two routes. We recommend a direct, cross-country shortcut. It entails only a little, light bushwhacking. Elevation gain and loss is minimal. It takes just 35 to 45 minutes. Or you can hike the longer, circuitous, up-and-down route that stays on road and trail. It might take 1½ hours. For the shortcut to be faster, easier and more fun, you must be an experienced pilgrim. You've never navigated by compass? Around you go.

Study the Gem Trek map. You'll see a potential backpack circuit: from Elbow Lake, north into Elbow River valley, northwest through Piper Creek canyon, over Piper Pass, down the West Fork Little Elbow River Valley, northeast to Mt. Romulus campground, up the south fork of Little Elbow River, south over Tombstone Pass, down to Tombstone campground in Elbow River valley, then southwest back to Elbow Lake. It fails to earn premier status because so much of it's on former road, and the 10.4 km (6.4 mi) between Romulus and Tombstone campgrounds is popular with mountainbikers. Nevertheless, if you're keen to stay out a couple nights, and you fancy combining the Elbow Lake / Piper Pass dayhike with its counterpart—West Fork Little Elbow River (Trip 39)—this makes a fine trek. Compared to separately dayhiking Trip 39, the backpacking circuit spares you the 25-km (15.5-mi) round-trip bike ride between the end of Hwy 66 and Romulus campground.

You intend to backpack this circuit? On day one, hike over Piper Pass. Camp in the West Fork Little Elbow River valley, near where the Paradise Pass (Trip 38) trail departs. On day two, enjoy the wonderful dayhike to Paradise Pass before continuing to Romulus campground. On day three (ideally midweek, to avoid bike traffic) hike up the south fork of Little Elbow River,

Elbow River meadows, Piper Creek Canyon beyond

detour to Tombstone Lakes, then proceed to Tombstone campground. Continue hiking out past Elbow Lake to the trailhead, and your day-three mileage will be 17.2 km (10.7 mi). The entire circuit, including the Paradise Pass side trip, totals 37.6 km (23.3 mi).

Fact

Before your trip

Be aware that Hwy 40, from Kananaskis Lakes Trail to Highwood Junction, is closed December 1 through June 15.

By Vehicle

From Trans-Canada Hwy 1, drive 62 km (38.4 mi) S on Hwy 40. (Pass the junction with Kananaskis Lakes Trail at 50 km / 31 mi.) Or, from Highwood Pass, drive 5.1 km (3.2 mi) N on Hwy 40. From either approach, turn E into the trailhead parking lot at Elbow Pass day-use area. Elevation: 1963 m (6440 ft).

On Foot

From the middle of the parking lot's E side, ascend the steep, old road through forest. It leads SE, then curves NE. After climbing to 2090 m (6855 ft), the road dips. Reach **Elbow Lake** at 1.3 km (0.8 mi), 2105 m (6905 ft). Strong hikers, eagerly pushing on to Piper Pass, will arrive at the lake in 20 minutes. Those sauntering no farther than the lake might take 40 minutes. There's a campground with 15 tent pads behind the S shore.

Follow the road-trail along the left (W) shore. At the lake's N end, cross a bridged creeklet, then bear left. Proceed generally N on the level road-trail, into an expansive **meadow** dominated by willow but also sustaining fuschia moss campion, yellow buttercup, magenta willow-herb, and white western anemone. Ignore the trail veering right. It climbs 405 m (1328 ft) in 2.7 km (1.7 mi) to unimpressive Rae Glacier, which is visible from Piper Pass.

After hiking 4.3 km (2.7 km) from the trailhead, you can see left (NW) into Piper Creek canyon. Fast hikers will be here roughly an hour after leaving their vehicle, or 35 minutes after leaving the lake's N end. You now have a choice. The recommended *Short Approach* goes cross-country 1.4 km (0.9 mi), directly to the trail ascending the canyon. If you prefer to reach the canyon trail by hiking a more circuitous, up-and-down 3.6 km (2.2 mi) but staying entirely on road and trail, skip to the *Long Approach* below.

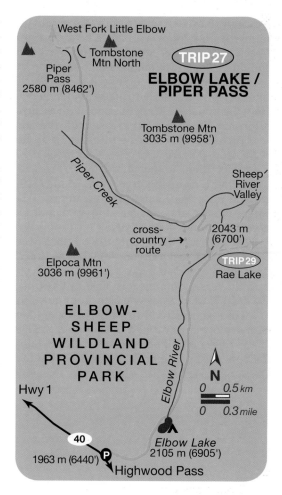

Short Approach

When you're directly opposite the mouth of Piper Creek canyon (looking into it NW), survey the terrain between you and the canyon. Generally, you'll descend, cross the Elbow River, ascend N, descend again, cross Piper Creek, then briefly ascend to pick up the trail at the base of Tombstone Mtn, which forms the canyon's NE wall. It'll take 35 to 45 minutes. Got the overall picture? Okay, let's go. Here's a detailed route description.

Abandon the road-trail by turning left (N). Follow a descending depression. Rockhop across the **Elbow River** where it breaks into multiple, narrower channels. It's more difficult to cross the single channel farther upstream. Elephant heads (see image on page 161) grow in the boggy meadows here; look closely to distinguish the trunks.

From the river's NW bank, hike N. Ascend 21 m (70 ft). Pick your way through rolling, stunted forest. You'll find passages through the tight trees.

Descend 15 m (50 ft) into a gully. You might tag onto a path leading NW, but follow it only 50 m/yd before bearing right and continuing N to **Piper Creek**. At 5 km (3.1 mi), 2060 m (6757 ft), cross Piper Creek. In summer it should be shallow enough here to rockhop over. From the creek's N bank, ascend the hillside through tight alpine fir. Within a few minutes, intersect the **canyon trail**. Athletic hikers will be here about 1 hour and 40 minutes from the trailhead. Mark this spot with a cairn, so you can recognize it when returning. But remember to dismantle the cairn on your way out.

Turn left (WNW). The trail climbs steadily beneath the canyon's NE wall. At 2149 m (7050 ft) cross a dry creek drainage. Ascend NW. Soon cross a creeklet, then another shortly after. Proceed upstream above Piper Creek cascading through a gorge. At 2226 m (7300 ft), about 30 minutes up the canyon trail, enter **subalpine meadows**. Wildflowers here include alpine forget-me-not, shooting star, Indian paintbrush, and yarrow. The moderate ascent continues generally N.

At 2311 m (7580 ft), about 15 minutes from the meadows, crest the lip of **upper Piper Creek canyon**. Total hiking time: 2½ hours at a vigourous pace. The upper canyon is a meadowy, alpine haven, carpeted with grass, heather and flowers. Looming S is 3030-m (9938-ft) Elpoca Mtn. East is 2997-m (9830-ft) North Tombstone Mtn. Your goal, Piper Pass, is visible ahead (N).

Hike generally N toward the lone, giant boulder at the base of the brown slope. Just beyond the boulder, at 2439 m (8000 ft), begin ascending the very steep trail beaten into the loose talus by boots and hooves. Reach 2580-m (8462-ft) **Piper Pass** about 20 minutes from the giant boulder. Total distance: 9.6 km (6 mi), which is hikeable within 3¼ hours.

Elbow Lake

Atop Piper Pass, the new view is NNW, into the upper reaches of West Fork Little Elbow River valley. The ragged Opal Range forms the West Fork valley's left (W) wall. Left (WNW) is 2997-m (9830-ft) Mt. Jerram. Directly below the N side of the pass is a tarn. Visible SSE is 3218-m (10,558-ft) Mt. Rae (Trip 29) and its tiny glacier. Another tarn is below the SE side of the pass.

A faint route veers left (W) from Piper Pass, steeply descending scree and talus on the N slope. For details, read West Fork Little Elbow River (Trip 39), which describes ascending to the pass from N to S.

Returning to the trailhead from Piper Pass, you again have a choice. Either take the cross-country shortcut starting at the cairn you built (remember to dismantle it), or exit the roundabout way staying on trail and road. To go the long way, follow the trail ESE around the S slope of Tombstone Mtn. It leads to Piper Creek, which you must ford. The trail then undulates and needlessly zigzags, heading generally SE. Ford the Elbow River at 2043 m (6700 ft). Continue ascending the trail out of the river gorge to intersect the road-trail you originally hiked from Elbow Lake. Turn right (SW). Elbow Lake is 3.5 km (2.2 mi) distant—about 45 minutes at a brisk pace. You'll soon be on familiar ground.

Long Approach

From where the cross-country shortcut abandoned the road-trail (directly opposite the mouth of Piper Creek canyon), proceed northeast on the road-trail, slightly downhill, 1 km (0.6 mi), or about ten minutes at a good clip. At 5.3 km (3.6 mi), 2000 m (6560 ft), fork left onto a distinct, cairned and flagged **trail**. It's a couple minutes past an obscure, uncairned trail also forking left.

Before following the trail through a wall of trees, look NW across the valley. Identify the trail rising on a grassy slope. That's where you'll soon be hiking, between fords of the Elbow River and Piper Creek.

Descend to the **Elbow River** and ford it. Ascend out of the gorge. The trail undulates and needlessly zigzags. It leads to **Piper Creek**, which you must also ford. It then curves NW beneath Tombstone Mtn and enters the mouth of **Piper Creek canyon**.

—Marmots

After steadily ascending for about ten minutes from the Piper Creek ford, you'll be near where the cross-country shortcut intersects the canyon trail. Continue following the *Short Approach* directions, beginning with the second sentence of the fourth paragraph. Keep in mind that your hiking time will be longer than the stated cumulative estimates. Your total distance to Piper Pass will be 12 km (7.4 mi).

TRIP 28
Tombstone Lakes

LOCATION	Elbow-Sheep Wildland Provincial Park
	Hwy 40, N of Highwood Pass
ROUND TRIP	22.1 km (13.7 mi) including Tombstone Pass
ELEVATION GAIN	545 m (1988 ft)
KEY ELEVATIONS	trailhead 1963 m (6440 ft)
	lower Tombstone Lake 2186 m (7170 ft)
	Tombstone Pass 2238 m (7340 ft)
HIKING TIME	6 to 7½ hours
DIFFICULTY	moderate due only to distance
MAP	Gem Trek *Kananaskis Lakes*

Opinion

Hikers, almost without exception, drive automobiles to trailheads. Yet it's the automobile, and everything pulled along in its wake, that hikers seek to escape by hiking. We're a conflicted bunch, aren't we? So try to suspend your not-always-logical judgment when you learn that fully 90% of the Tombstone Lakes hike is on a road.

"A road!" you say. "A road?" Yup. But it's a road that might make you recant the hikers' dogma that all roads are abhorrent. Because this is an old road, from which motorized vehicles were banned long ago. It's broad, fairly level and mostly smooth, so instead of fixating on what's underfoot, as trails often force you to do, you can lift your eyes and appreciate the scenery while you stride. And the scenery here is grand.

Elbow Lake, a mere half-hour from the trailhead, is an image suitable for framing. Beyond, you'll hike through upper Elbow River Valley, past the mouth of Piper Creek canyon (Trip 27), and across the north end of Sheep River Valley. Even if you've been to Piper Pass, this approach bears repeating. Much of the area is rolling, sparsely-treed meadowland that's not only beautiful itself but allows nearly constant views of the surrounding peaks: Elpoca Mtn, Mt. Rae, Tombstone Mtn, and Cougar Mtn. They're a visual feast. From Tombstone campground, you'll ascend into forest and turn onto an actual trail for the final approach to Tombstone Lakes. The upper lake, tucked into the bosom of full-breasted Tombstone Mtn, is lovely.

From Tombstone Lakes, you should lengthen and vary your return by detouring through Tombstone Pass, and/or to Rae Lake. Both options significantly boost the day's spectacle quotient. The pass, a sprawling heather-and-grass meadow ringed by larches, affords an impressive, elevated perspective of Mt. Rae and Tombstone Mtn. And Rae Lake is gorgeous, surrounded by subalpine meadow, clutched by mighty Mt. Rae. The Rae Lake detour also includes a brief, enjoyable stretch of hiking on a trail and a less-defined route.

photos: **1** *Upper Tombstone Lake* **2** *Columbine* **3** *Sheep River Valley and Mt. Rae*

1

2

3

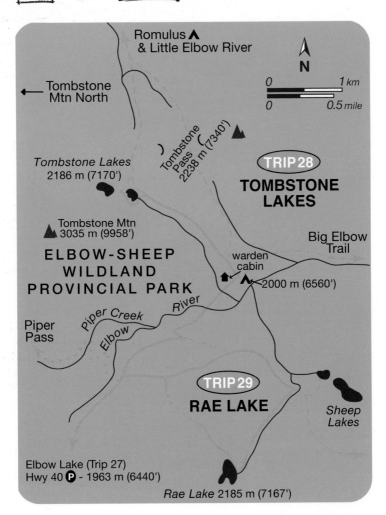

Tagging the Tombstone Lakes, returning via Tombstone Pass, and detouring to Rae Lake is not a Herculean dayhike. The total distance is 25.5 km (15.8 mi). The total elevation gain is 730 m (2395 ft), all of it gradual. Strong hikers who start early will find this a full but not exhausting day. The Rae Lake detour accounts for only 4.4 km (2.7 mi) of the total mileage, so definitely include it. Read Trip 29 for a motivating description. Detour directions are at the bottom of the *On Foot* section below.

The alternative to dayhiking is an easy, two-day backpack trip. Stay at Tombstone campground, in a sheltering stand of trees, near a creeklet. An open bench here offers fire pits and a big view. Though the campground is 3.6 km (2.2 mi) shy of Tombstone Lakes, it spares you from wagging all your gear higher and farther. Here's the plan: hike in, pitch your tent, then loop up to Tombstone Lakes and back through Tombstone Pass. Total

Mt. Rae and Elbow River Valley

mileage for day one: 14.6 km (9.1 mi), half of it without your full pack. The next morning, nip up to Rae Lake on your way back to the trailhead.

Because you'll mostly be hiking on a former road, be prepared to share it momentarily with a few mountain bikers and perhaps some equestrians. Uninterrupted tranquility, however, is still possible on this journey. Bikes are prohibited on the spur trails to Rae and Tombstone lakes, and it's a rare biker who hoofs it farther than is necessary to pee in the roadside bushes.

Fact

Before your trip

Be aware that Hwy 40, from Kananaskis Lakes Trail to Highwood Junction, is closed December 1 through June 15.

By Vehicle

From Trans-Canada Hwy 1, drive 62 km (38.4 mi) S on Hwy 40. (Pass the junction with Kananaskis Lakes Trail at 50 km / 31 mi.) Or, from Highwood Pass, drive 5.1 km (3.2 mi) N on Hwy 40. From either approach, turn E into the trailhead parking lot at Elbow Pass day-use area. Elevation: 1963 m (6440 ft).

On Foot

From the middle of the parking lot's E side, ascend the steep, old road through forest. It leads SE, then curves NE. After climbing to 2090 m (6855 ft), the road dips. Reach **Elbow Lake** at 1.3 km (0.8 mi), 2105 m (6905 ft). Strong hikers, eagerly pushing onward, will arrive at the lake in 20 minutes. Those sauntering no farther than the lake might take 40 minutes. There's a campground with 15 tent pads behind the S shore.

Follow the road-trail along the left (W) shore. At the lake's N end, cross a bridged creeklet, then bear left. Proceed generally N on the level road-trail, into an expansive **meadow** dominated by willow but also sustaining yellow buttercup, magenta willow-herb, and white western anemone. Ignore the trail veering right. It climbs 405 m (1328 ft) in 2.7 km (1.7 mi) to unimpressive Rae Glacier.

After hiking 4.3 km (2.7 km) from the trailhead, you can see left (NW) into Piper Creek canyon (Trip 27). Fast hikers will be here roughly an hour after leaving their vehicle, or 35 minutes after leaving the lake's N end. Proceed NE on the road-trail, which now descends slightly. The **Elbow River** is occasionally visible left.

At 5.3 km (3.6 mi), 2000 m (6560 ft), pass the cairned and flagged left fork leading WNW to the Elbow River and Piper Creek canyon. Stay on the road-trail. Fifty paces farther, pass the cairned right fork leading E then SE to Rae Lake (Trip 29). Again, stay on the road-trail, heading NNE. Tombstone Mtn is left (NNW). You'll circle behind its E shoulder to reach the Tombstone Lakes.

At 6.5 km (4 mi), 2006 m (6580 ft), reach a T-junction signed with a **Sheep Valley** trail map that exaggerates your distance from the trailhead. The road-trail left descends to cross a bridge (visible below) spanning the Elbow River. Go that way to reach lower Tombstone Lake in 3 km (1.9 mi). The road-trail right runs generally SE through Sheep Valley, intersecting the trail to Rickert's Pass and Mist Ridge (Trip 35) in 10 km (6.2 mi).

Turn left at the 6.5-km (4-mi) T-junction. Descend a sweeping bend and cross the **Elbow River bridge.** (On your return, you'll see how a brief-but-steep cross-country jaunt will enable you to shortcut this bend.) At 7.1 km (4.4 mi), pass a road forking left to a warden cabin. About five minutes farther, at 7.3 km (4.5 mi), reach **Tombstone campground** on the right.

The tentsites are in a dark stand of trees but within earshot of a creeklet. Nearby is an open bench with fire pits and a fine view of the area. Mt. Rae is S, Elpoca Mtn WSW. For Tombstone Lakes, proceed on the road-trail, past the campground. A couple minutes farther, reach a signed junction at 2000 m (6560 ft). Right (NE) is the Big Elbow trail. For Tombstone Lakes, ascend left (NNW) on the **Little Elbow trail**.

Within 15 minutes, after gaining 37 m (120 ft) in 0.4 km (0.25 mi), reach another junction. The Little Elbow trail (still a road) curves right and ascends steeply N over Tombstone Pass. Fork left here onto an actual **trail** leading NNW, ascending moderately through forest. Horse travel is destroying this trail. It's severely eroded and braided, and horrendously muddy when wet.

Reach the SE shore of **lower Tombstone Lake** at 9.2 km (5.7 mi), 2186 m (7170 ft). Trees curtail your view here, so go left, hop the outlet stream, and follow the rooty trail around the W shore. It forks at the lake's NW corner. Right rounds the N shore. Go left, ascend WNW, and in a few minutes cross a small saddle with a view of **upper Tombstone Lake**. The trail ends just below, on the shore of the upper lake. Embraced by 3035-m (9958-ft), dual-peaked Tombstone Mtn, the upper lake is more scenic than its lower sibling.

Upon returning to the NW corner of the lower lake, you have a choice: (1) Continue retracing your steps all the way to the trailhead. (2) Continue retracing your steps past Tombstone campground, to the signed T-junction above the Elbow River bridge, then extend your dayhike to Rae Lake (Trip 29) as described below. (3) Lengthen and vary your return to Tombstone campground by detouring through Tombstone Pass.

Heading for Tombstone Pass? Don't re-hike the W shore of lower Tombstone Lake. From the lake's NW corner, turn left and round the **N shore**. A gradual ascent leads to a faint junction. Right descends to where you initially arrived at the lower lake's SE shore. Go left and resume ascending, generally N through forest, to a larch-fringed meadowy **draw** at 2273 m (7455 ft).

From the draw, descend N 1.5 km (0.9 mi) to intersect the **Little Elbow trail**—a former road. You've now hiked a total of 11.1 km (6.9 mi). The elevation here is 2125 m (6970 ft). Left on the Little Elbow trail leads 6.8 km (4.2 mi) N to Mount Romulus campground. Go right, initially ascending SE, for Tombstone pass and campground. An unnamed ridge is left (E).

Crest 2238-m (7340-ft) **Tombstone Pass** at 12.5 km (7.8 mi), in a vast, heather-and-grass meadow ringed by larches. To the W, the twin summits of Tombstone Mtn dominate the panorama. The more distant, but still impressive, 3218-m (10,558-ft) Mt. Rae is S. NNW is the ridge dividing the Elbow River's W (Trip 39) and S forks. N, in the distance, is 3053-m (10,017-ft) Fisher Peak.

Proceed SSE on the road-trail. The descent is gradual at first, allowing you to enjoy the view while striding, but it soon steepens sharply. Stay to one side in case bikers charge down from behind you. Bear left on the road-trail where the Tombstone Lakes trail forks right. Bear right where the signed Big Elbow trail forks left. Soon after, the road levels and passes **Tombstone campground** at 14.6 km (9.1 mi). The trailhead, on Hwy 40, is now 7.3 km (4.5 mi) distant. You know the way.

Detour to Rae Lake

From Tombstone campground, retrace your steps to the signed **T-junction** above the Elbow River bridge. Right (W) is the road-trail leading directly back to the trailhead. To detour to Rae Lake, continue straight on the road-trail leading generally SE into Sheep Valley. The following distances start at the T-junction.

In 0.6 km (0.4 mi), near the bend of a hairpin turn, pass a cairned trail on the right. It leads W to intersect the Elbow River road-trail across from Piper Creek canyon. Proceed on the road-trail. At 1.8 km (1.1 mi), just before a **culvert**, turn right onto an actual trail. It ascends generally SW, along the edge of Rae Creek gorge.

Reach **Rae Lake** at 3.2 km (2 mi), 2185 m (7167 ft). Turn left and hop the outlet to extend your detour around Rae Lake's E shore, into the meadow bordering the S shore. Or, to continue as directly as possible, turn right and follow the trail ascending generally NW, above the NE shore.

The trail heading NW gradually climbs out of the lake basin, through lightly forested meadow. It crosses a **shoulder**, then descends—sharply at first but soon gradually—onto a treed slope. The trail diminishes to a route. If you lose it, just keep heading NW, perhaps on game trails. Though the young forest is thick in places, the going is easy.

After exiting the trees, intersect a trail at 4.9 km (3 mi). This is the trail that departed the Sheep Valley road-trail's hairpin turn. Go left (WNW). Descend through a draw and re-enter forest. Intersect the **Elbow River road-trail** at 5.6 km (3.5 mi). Turn left (SW) to reach the trailhead. You're now on familiar ground.

TRIP 29
Rae Lake

LOCATION	Elbow-Sheep Wildland Provincial Park
	Hwy 40, N of Highwood Pass
ROUND TRIP	17.2 km (10.7 mi)
ELEVATION GAIN	432 m (1417 ft)
KEY ELEVATIONS	trailhead 1963 m (6440 ft), lake 2185 m (7167 ft)
HIKING TIME	5 to 6½ hours
DIFFICULTY	easy
MAPS	page 156; Gem Trek *Kananaskis Lakes*

Opinion

Every hiker has unique reasons for striding. Here's one most of us share: discovery. We keep hiking in eager anticipation of discoveries ahead. Some discoveries are personal, others are apparent to all who hike the same trail. En route to Rae Lake, your discoveries will likely include these:

- Elbow Lake is popular not only because it's a mere half-hour from the trailhead but because it's beautiful. And its beauty is unmarred by the sight and sound of others dawdling about the shore.

- Most people hike no farther than Elbow Lake, yet the going is easy and the scenery stupendous in the upper Elbow River Valley, where rolling, sparsely-treed meadowland allows nearly constant views of Elpoca Mtn, Mt. Rae, Tombstone Mtn, and Cougar Mtn.

- Rae Lake is an obscure destination. From the broad trail extending beyond Elbow Lake, you must veer onto an unsigned, bootbeaten route. This discourages visitation, increasing the likelihood of solitude. The result is fertile ground for personal discovery, because silence is the portal to our deeper selves.

Rae Lake adorns Mt. Rae—a big but shy mountain. Its diffident stance, behind the Elk, Opal and front ranges, conceals its majesty. The glimpse you'll attain on this hike, beneath Rae's north ridge, reveals more than is visible from the popular hike into Ptarmigan Cirque (Trip 31) below Rae's south face. Plus, Rae Lake itself—bordered by subalpine meadows, walled in by cliffs—is a climactic sight, unlike Ptarmigan's desolate upper reaches.

For further motivation, read the first three paragraphs of Elbow Lake / Piper Pass (Trip 27). Also read Tombstone Lakes (Trip 28), which describes the advantages of an easy, single-night backpack trip into this area.

photos: *1* Wood lily *2* Calypso orchid *3* Sheep River Valley, *from near Rae Lake* *4* Elephant's head *5* Rae Lake

If dayhiking to Rae Lake, don't be mislead by the mere six hours required to complete the trip. Start early. Allow time to loll near the water's edge, circumambulate the shore, or proceed south behind the lake then ascend southeast onto the 2400-m (7872-ft) ridge forming the cirque's eastern shoulder.

Before your trip

Be aware that Hwy 40, from Kananaskis Lakes Trail to Highwood Junction, is closed December 1 through June 15.

By Vehicle

From Trans-Canada Hwy 1, drive 62 km (38.4 mi) S on Hwy 40. (Pass the junction with Kananaskis Lakes Trail at 50 km / 31 mi.) Or, from Highwood Pass, drive 5.1 km (3.2 mi) N on Hwy 40. From either approach, turn E into the trailhead parking lot at Elbow Pass day-use area. Elevation: 1963 m (6440 ft).

On Foot

From the middle of the parking lot's E side, ascend the steep, old road through forest. It leads SE, then curves NE. Reach **Elbow Lake** at 1.3 km (0.8 mi), 2105 m (6905 ft). Strong hikers will be here in 20 minutes.

Follow the road-trail along the left (W) shore. At the lake's N end, cross a bridged creeklet, then bear left. Proceed generally N on the level road-trail, into an expansive **meadow**. Ignore the trail veering right. It climbs 405 m (1328 ft) in 2.7 km (1.7 mi) to unimpressive Rae Glacier.

After hiking 4.3 km (2.7 km) from the trailhead, you can see left (NW) into Piper Creek canyon (Trip 27). Proceed NE on the road-trail. The **Elbow River** is occasionally visible left.

At 5.3 km (3.6 mi), 2000 m (6560 ft), pass the cairned and flagged left fork leading WNW to the Elbow River and Piper Creek canyon. Stay on the road-trail, heading NNE, but only for another 50 paces. Then abandon the road-trail and turn onto a **cairned right fork**. It leads generally E, then SE to Rae Lake.

Follow the narrow trail through open forest, then up a **grassy draw**. Just beyond and above the draw, reach an unsigned, easy-to-miss right fork at 6 km (3.7 mi), 2037 m (6680 ft). Straight (E) descends to intersect a road; you'll loop back from there after visiting the lake. For now, go right (SE).

The trail diminishes to a route as it rises across the N skirt of **Mt. Rae**. Behind you, Tombstone Pass (N) and Tombstone Mtn (NW) are visible across the valley. Near 2100 m (6888 ft), about ten minutes from the last fork, the route is very faint. If you lose it, just keep heading SE, perhaps on game trails. Though the young forest is thick in places, the going is easy.

About 30 minutes from the last fork, proceed through blowdown to the base of a low **shoulder**. The route reappears here, angling upward, over the shoulder. Ascend to the subalpine meadow atop the shoulder. Here, the route becomes a more discernible trail leading right (S). But before continuing, briefly detour left (E), off-trail, toward a lone larch, where you can glimpse the Sheep Lakes (E) in the valley below.

Elbow River Valley, en route to Rae Lake

Upon returning to the shoulder-top trail, follow it generally S. It dips, then rises into open forest peppered with larch. In a few minutes, you'll be descending SE through lightly forested meadow, with **Rae Lake** visible below.

Reach the lake's **NE shore** at 7.7 km (4.8 mi), 2185 m (7167 ft). Beyond the S shore, a meadow extends into the cirque beneath the N ridge of 3218-m (10,558-ft) Mt. Rae. You can reach it by rounding the lake in either direction. Right, via the thickly forested W shore, is longer. So bear left (SSE), which is also the most efficient way to continue the circuit.

Soon arrive at Rae Lake's **outlet**, where idiots oblivious to *Leave No Trace* guidelines have denuded the shore by camping on it and building multiple firepits. Hop the outlet to detour around the E shore, into the meadow behind the S shore. Or continue the circuit by turning left immediately before the outlet and descending generally NE on a scenic trail above the left (NW) side of **Rae Creek gorge**.

Intersect the **Sheep River Valley road-trail** at 9.1 km (5.6 mi), 2070 m (6788 ft). A few steps to the right, Rae Creek flows through a culvert. Turn left and follow the road-trail NW. At 10.3 km (6.4 mi), 2034 m (6670 ft), near the bend of a **hairpin turn**, abandon the road by turning left (WSW) onto a trail marked by a cairn. It leads generally W, through brushy, rolling terrain.

About fifteen minutes farther, at 11.1 km (6.9 mi), pass an unsigned, easy-to-miss left fork—the route you previously followed across the northern foot of Mt. Rae, to Rae Lake. You're now on familiar ground. Proceed straight (WNW). Descend through a grassy draw and re-enter forest. Intersect the **Elbow River road-trail** at 11.8 km (7.3 mi). Turn left (SW) to return past Elbow Lake and reach the trailhead on **Hwy 40** at 17.2 km (10.7 mi).

TRIP 30
Pocaterra Ridge

LOCATION	Peter Lougheed Provincial Park
	Hwy 40, near Highwood Pass
SHUTTLE TRIP	9.3 km (5.8 mi)
ELEVATION CHANGE	550-m (1804-ft) gain / 875-m (2870-ft) loss
KEY ELEVATIONS	Highwood Pass trailhead 2206 m (7239 ft)
	highpoint 2670 m (8758 ft)
HIKING TIME	5 to 8 hours
DIFFICULTY	moderate
MAP	Gem Trek *Kananaskis Lakes*

Opinion

Nothing you can say
in the wilds
is as important
as what you can hear
if you listen

The challenge is being quiet while hiking with companions, particularly where there's much to exclaim about, such as on Pocaterra Ridge: a supreme skywalk amid great peaks that seem to have gathered 'round to watch *you.*

It begins at Highwood Pass—the highest point in Canada accessible by public road. So within half an hour, you'll burst into the subalpine meadows of Pocaterra Cirque. A steep ascent ensues. You'll clamber briefly, then resume toiling upward. Transcend the first and highest bump, at the south end of the ridgecrest, and away you go. You'll gallop 4 km (2.5 mi), or about two hours, along the mostly alpine crest before dismounting the ridge at its north end.

Exhilarating scenery is constant. Paralleling Pocaterra Ridge, west across a narrow valley, is the spine of the Elk Range. Lower Kananaskis Lake is northwest. Elpoca Mtn, distinguished by steeply-angled sawtooth ridges, is north. Beyond it is Piper Creek canyon (Trip 27) and Tombstone Mtn. Hulking Mt. Rae is east. You can ask more of a ridgewalk, but you'd be greedy. Especially considering this is a convenient one-way trip—a rare indulgence for a hiker. Take advantage of it.

Stride the entire ridge by arranging a vehicle shuttle between the trailheads at each end. You're limited to a single vehicle? A round trip to the third bump on the crest is certainly worthwhile. Better yet, park at the north trailhead, where the trip ends, then hitchhike the short distance to the south trailhead, where the trip begins. You'll snag a ride quickly, especially on a weekend.

Note that the first bump on the crest is a little scrambly—no problem for accomplished hikers, mildly difficult for the unsteady, perhaps

Pocaterra Ridge. Mt. Tyrwhitt distant right.

prohibitive for the acrophobic. From there on, it's a comfortable cruise, though you must regain lost elevation after each inevitable dip. Overall, you'll be coasting slightly downhill. Swooping off the north end of the ridge, the trail eventually withers. Expect a brief thrash near the bottom, just before you pop out of the woods onto the highway.

Athletic hikers can add an additional hour of adventure to the day by detouring from Pocaterra Cirque to Grizzly Col. It's a short, engaging ascent. And the view from the col comprises Grizzly Ridge, part of another wild, mountain dance described below.

Fact

Before your trip
Be aware that Hwy 40, from Kananaskis Lakes Trail to Highwood Junction, is closed December 1 through June 15.

By Vehicle
From Trans-Canada Hwy 1—to reach the S (upper) trailhead, where the **hike begins**—drive 67.4 km (41.8 mi) S on Hwy 40. Or, from Highwood Junction (where Hwys 40, 541 and 940 intersect), drive 37.7 km (23.4 mi) NW on Hwy 40. From either approach, turn W into the Highwood Pass parking lot, at 2206 m (7239 ft).

From Trans-Canada Hwy 1—to reach the N (lower) trailhead, where the **hike ends**—drive 60.6 km (37.6 mi) S on Hwy 40. Or, from the Highwood Pass parking lot, drive 6.8 km (4.2 mi) N on Hwy 40. From either approach, turn E into Little Highwood Pass day-use area, at 1880 m (6166 ft).

On Foot
From the kiosk at the N end of the parking lot, follow the trail NW through willowy meadows. In five minutes, at 0.4 km (0.25 mi), proceed onto the boardwalk. The trail forking right (NE) leads to Ptarmigan Cirque (Trip 31).

After passing benches and interpretive signs, turn off the boardwalk. Follow the path right (WSW) through trees. In one minute, pass a left spur. Bear right (N). Then curve left, drop into a meadowy draw, intersect another trail, and turn right (NW).

About ten minutes along, where the highway is visible, begin a moderate ascent left. The trail is rooty and probably muddy. In another ten minutes, ignore the bootbeaten path ascending left. Proceed on the main trail, descending SW. Soon attain a view SW into Pocaterra Cirque. Pocaterra Ridge begins on the right (N) side of the cirque.

The trail drops through forest, then crosses an avalanche path adorned with cow's parsnip and fuschia fireweed. It undulates over a rockslide and continues through larches. At 2213 m (7260 ft), beside a **creeklet**, begin ascending again. You've now hiked about 40 minutes from the trailhead. Pass a cairn at the W end of a **tarn**. The trail heads W, on grass at the edge of talus.

Reach a large, level meadow in **Pocaterra Cirque** at 2.9 km (1.8 mi), 2285 m (7490 ft). You're now SSE of Little Highwood Pass—the saddle linking Pocaterra Ridge with the spine of the Elk Range. The **trail forks** here at a cairn. Straight (W) continues to the base of Pocaterra Ridge. Left (SW) ascends to Grizzly Col, where snow lingers long. It's worth nipping up there for the view, even if you don't continue beyond. A round-trip detour from Pocaterra Cirque takes 45 minutes to an hour. Upon returning to the cirque, you can resume to Pocaterra Ridge. Skip below for details about Grizzly Col.

Resuming to Pocaterra Ridge, follow the trail NW, toward the grassy slope at the base of a rockslide near the head of Pocaterra Cirque. Choose either of two routes to the S end of the ridgecrest: (1) N, directly up the steep talus slope, with rough sections on black-lichen-covered rocks; or (2) NW, on a moderately ascending path, then N to **Little Highwood Pass** at 2545 m (8348 ft), 4.3 km (2.7 mi). From the pass, turn right (E) for the final, steep, rough ascent to the ridgecrest. The first option is easier, and you'll miss nothing at Little Highwood Pass; it's all visible from the ridge.

From either approach, reach the **S end of Pocaterra Ridge** at 2670 m (8758 ft). This **first bump** is the highest on the ridge. The roughly two-hour ridgewalk along the 4-km (2.5-mi) crest begins here. Follow the bootbeaten path NE, then NNW.

Descend to a 2500-m (8200-ft) saddle, then ascend again. Reach the **second bump** at 2560 m (8400 ft). The Elk Range is left (W) across the canyon. From here on, while hiking the crest, your general direction of travel will be NNW. The ridge dips again, then rises to a **third bump** at 2595 m (8512 ft). Elbow Lake (Trip 27) is visible NNE, just beyond and above Hwy 40.

The ridgecrest drops significantly from the third bump. The path is occasionally along the right side of the crest. Rockfall Lake (shallow, possibly dry) is visible left (W) below you. Trees and boulders clutter the canyon N of it.

Reach a lightly treed **gap** on the crest at 2450 m (8036 ft). Here, a route descends right (SE) initiating a steep, rough, but viable escape to Hwy 40. Proceeding along the ridge, angle right to stay on the NE side. Pass a faint trail descending left.

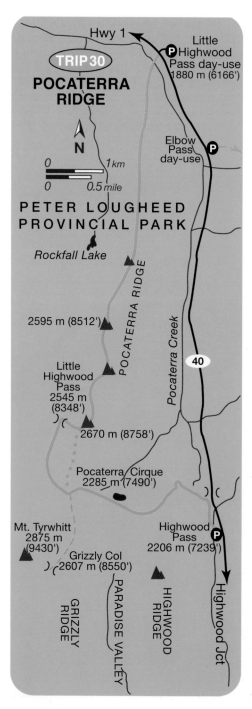

Hwy 1

Little
P Highwood
Pass day-use
1880 m (6166')

TRIP 30

**POCATERRA
RIDGE**

N

Elbow
Pass **P**
day-use

0   1 km

0   0.5 mile

**PETER LOUGHEED
PROVINCIAL PARK**

Rockfall Lake

POCATERRA RIDGE

2595 m (8512')

Pocaterra Creek

Little
Highwood
Pass
2545 m
(8348')

40

2670 m (8758')

Pocaterra Cirque
2285 m (7490')

Mt. Tyrwhitt
2875 m
(9430')

Highwood
Pass
2206 m (7239') **P**

Grizzly Col
2607 m (8550')

Highwood Jct

GRIZZLY
RIDGE

PARADISE VALLEY

HIGHWOOD
RIDGE

Enter a spectacular larch forest at 2380 m (7806 ft). Surmount the **fourth bump**. Visible northwest is Lower Kananaskis Lake. 3030-m (9938-ft) Elpoca Mtn is N. Begin dismounting the ridge.

Continue following the occasionally sketchy path generally N, dropping steeply through open forest, willow, and grass. Your goal, initially visible below, is Little Highwood Pass trailhead parking lot. You'll lose sight of it while descending. Nearing the bottom, bear right. The trail disappears. Rockhop or ford to the N bank of **Pocaterra Creek**. Then thrash onward and upward another few minutes to Hwy 40 and the trailhead immediately N of it. You've hiked 9.3 km (5.8 mi) from Highwood Pass, excluding the Grizzly Col detour.

Grizzly Col

Turn left (SW) at the cairned fork in Pocaterra Cirque. Soon take your pick of paths ascending generally SSE toward the col. Pause at 2440 m (8003 ft), near the base of a talus slope. See the trail angling across the headwall, up to the col? Tag onto it by clambering left (E) up the talus. Then follow the trail right (SSW). Crest 2607-m (8550-ft) **Grizzly Col** about half an hour from, and 322 m (1056 ft) above, Pocaterra Cirque.

Towering above the col's W side is 2875-m (9430-ft) Mt. Tyrwhitt. The unnamed valley

S of the pass descends to Hwy 40. From the col's E side, Grizzly Ridge extends SE. Visible N, well beyond Hwy 40, is Piper Creek canyon, flanked by Elpoca Mtn (left) and Tombstone Mtn (right).

A trail continues on the left (E) side of the col. After contouring SE, it gradually gains 120 m (394 ft) to crest Grizzly Ridge. From there it's possible to proceed cross country and complete a rugged loop. Begin with a sharp descent generally E into Paradise Valley, ascend generally NE over Highwood Ridge, then drop NNE very steeply to the Highwood Pass trailhead parking lot.

Descending Pocaterra Ridge toward Elpoca Mtn

TRIP 31
Ptarmigan Cirque

LOCATION	Peter Lougheed Provincial Park
	Hwy 40, at Highwood Pass
CIRCUIT	4.5 km (2.8 mi)
ELEVATION GAIN	214 m (702 ft)
KEY ELEVATIONS	trailhead 2206 m (7239 ft), highpoint 2420 m (7938 ft)
HIKING TIME	1½ to 2 hours
DIFFICULTY	easy
MAP	Gem Trek *Kananaskis Lakes*

Opinion

Like the trailer for a Hollywood movie, this hike lashes you with fleeting glimpses of drama and adventure. The scenery is thrilling—typical of feature-length hikes in the Canadian Rockies—but cursory. You won't relish a full day's experience here, nor will you pay for it. You'll simply be tantalized, in return for minimal time and effort.

Ptarmigan Cirque is gouged between 3218-m (10,555-ft) Mt. Rae and 2912-m (9551-ft) Mt. Arethusa. After a very brief ascent through forest, the trail enters the cirque and contours meadowy slopes below the soaring peaks. The meadow is a wildflower haven that contrasts sharply with the surrounding austere scree and talus. Aspiring botanists have identified at least 80 species of wildflowers. You'll see yellow glacier lilies here in early July. Dozens of species bloom later, including larkspur, yellow heart-leafed arnica, lavender fleabane, western anemone, alpine forget-me-not, and the ubiquitous Indian paintbrush. In fall, expect to see crimson alpine vegetation, and grass the colour of mustard.

Any time of year, just driving to the trailhead is marvelously scenic. The hike begins at Highwood Pass, the highest point in Canada accessible by public road. En route you'll survey a vast expanse of K-Country, including colossal peaks along the Continental Divide.

Because it begins so high, this trail rockets you into the alpine much faster than most. You'll be there within 30 minutes, and back to your vehicle within two hours. For a longer outing, first hike to Pocaterra Cirque or Grizzly Col. Both are described in Pocaterra Ridge (Trip 30), which shares the same trailhead as Ptarmigan. After enjoying the morning sun in Pocaterra Cirque, catch the afternoon rays in Ptarmigan Cirque. Another short trail nearby, easily combined with this one in half a day, is Little Arethusa (Trip 32).

▲ outlier of
Mt. Rae

**PETER
LOUGHEED
PROVINCIAL
PARK**

TRIP 31

**PTARMIGAN
CIRQUE**

2420 m (7938')

▲ Mt. Arethusa
2912 m (9551')

Hwy 1

Little Arethusa
▲ 2729 m (8950')

TRIP 32

Highwood
Pass

**LITTLE
ARETHUSA** ▲

2206 m (7239')

Storm Mtn
3095 m (10,153')

Pocaterra
Cirque

P

40

N

Storm Creek

0   0.5 km
0   0.3 mile

P 2170 m (7118')

Highwood Jct

Fact

Before your trip

Be aware that Hwy 40, from Kananaskis Lakes Trail to Highwood Junction, is closed December 1 through June 15.

By Vehicle

From Trans-Canada Hwy 1, drive 67.4 km (41.8 mi) S on Hwy 40. Or, from Highwood Junction (where Hwys 40, 541 and 940 intersect), drive 37.7 km (23.4 mi) NW on Hwy 40. From either approach, turn W into the Highwood Pass trailhead parking lot, at 2206 m (7239 ft).

On Foot

From the kiosk at the N end of the parking lot, follow the trail NW through willowy meadows. In four minutes, at 0.4 km (0.25 mi), just before a boardwalk, turn right (NE) at the sign for Ptarmigan Cirque. Cross the **highway**. The trail resumes, heading NE, ascending moderately into subalpine forest.

In about 20 minutes, a right spur offers a very short detour to a viewpoint where you can gaze S, across the highway, at the swooping slopes of Highwood Ridge. At 1.3 km (0.8 mi), 2335 m (7660 ft), reach a **fork**. Go left (N). Right is signed ONE WAY, DO NOT ENTER. It attests to how busy it can be here on weekends. After touring the cirque, you'll loop back to this point

Five minutes farther, break out of trees into the alpine meadow of **Ptarmigan Cirque**. The trail levels, contouring NE on grassy slopes. Mt. Arethusa is ENE across the drainage. At 2.25 km (1.4 mi), reach the head of the loop, on a rocky **terminal moraine**. This is the trail's highpoint: 2420 m (7938 ft).

At the moraine, you can opt to leave the trail and proceed straight (NE), roaming deeper into the desolate cirque. To continue the loop, stay on the trail. It crosses the **creeklet** and curves right.

Watch for hoary marmots on the moraine. They're burrowing rodents: stout-bodied, short-legged, about the size of a cat. Chiefly herbivorous, they have coarse fur, a short bushy tail, and very small ears. Their high-pitched whistle is distinctive, which is why they're also known as whistlers, or whistle pigs.

From the moraine, the trail bends SW beneath Mt. Arethusa. Begin a gradual descent on a rockslide above the creeklet and meadow. Here, where the highway is hidden from view, it's easy to imagine you're deep in the wilderness.

photos: *1 A quick ascent through subalpine forest leads to Ptarmigan Cirque beneath Mt. Rae. 2 Bighorn sheep above Highwood Pass 3 Firewheel*

Hop over the **creeklet** near the mouth of the cirque. Visible SW, across Highwood Pass, is twin-topped Mt. Tyrwhitt. Just N of it is Pocaterra Cirque (Trip 30). Watch for a left spur leading 25 m/yd to a **bench** shaded by trees and overlooking cascades in a gorge.

Shortly after passing the spur, intersect the trail you originally followed into the cirque. Turn left and descend through forest. You're now on familiar ground and will soon reach the highway at Highwood Pass.

TRIP 32
Little Arethusa

LOCATION	Peter Lougheed Provincial Park, SE of Highwood Pass
ROUND TRIP	5.4 km (3.3 mi)
ELEVATION GAIN	559 m (1832 ft)
KEY ELEVATIONS	trailhead 2170 m (7118 ft), summit 2729 m (8950 ft)
HIKING TIME	3 to 4 hours
DIFFICULTY	moderate
MAPS	page 170; Gem Trek *Kananaskis Lakes*

Opinion

You think you see a lot from a car? At 110 kph, you're traveling one kilometre every 33 seconds.

Many people drive through Kananaskis Country and say they've seen it. But appreciating mountains isn't that simple. It's not like wine tasting. It's more like grape crushing. You need to get in the vat and stomp.

An easy yet intriguing place to step in is Little Arethusa.

It's easy because the trailhead is beside Hwy 40, very near Highwood Pass—the highest point in Canada accessible by public road. Moderate effort is quickly rewarded with an engaging panorama.

It's intriguing because this is an entry-level scramble, ideal for hikers seeking a robust romp in which they begin grappling with the terrain.

Though steep, the ascent is on a broad slope covered with scree. Exposure is nil as far as the first summit, but should you decide to bail, that's okay. About halfway up are grassy terraces with gratifying views. You'll peer down into Arethusa Cirque, survey tempestuous Storm Mountain with its distinctive swirling strata, and gaze at Highwood Ridge and the Elk Range.

Attain the first summit and you'll see much more. Beyond the Elk Range is a shark's mouth horizon: row upon row of 3000-m (9840-ft) peaks. For optimal views west across the Continental Divide, ascend before noon. Photographers might want to ascend after 2 p.m., for saturated light on Storm Mtn. Come in autumn and the larches near the mouth of Arethusa Cirque will be electric gold.

En route to Little Arethusa, you'll nip into Arethusa Cirque. Don't bother probing it. Don't even stop there. It's not a worthy objective. Too brushy. Very disappointing compared to nearby, meadowy Ptarmigan Cirque (Trip 31). Besides, you'll survey all of Arethusa Cirque from the shoulder of Little Arethusa.

Arethusa, by the way, was the Greek goddess of springs and fountains. But Little Arethusa is a bone-dry rockpile.

Fact

Before your trip

Be aware that Hwy 40, from Kananaskis Lakes Trail to Highwood Junction, is closed December 1 through June 15.

By Vehicle

From **Trans-Canada Hwy 1**, drive 67.4 km (41.8 mi) S on Hwy 40. Reset your trip odometer to 0 at the Highwood Pass trailhead parking lot. Proceed S another 1.4 km (0.9 mi).

From **Highwood Junction** (where Hwys 40, 541 and 940 intersect), drive NW 36 km (22.3 mi) on Hwy 40.

From **either approach**, turn NE onto the short, unpaved spur entering a clearing immediately S of the guardrail. Park here, just off the highway, at 2170 m (7118 ft).

Ascending Little Arethusa.
Storm Mtn beyond.

On Foot

Walk N through the clearing. About 30 m/yd before the creek, turn right (E). A **cairn** indicates where the trail enters the forest. It climbs moderately above the creek's SE bank, among Englemann spruce and alpine fir. Your general direction of travel is NE, gradually curving E.

In about 15 minutes, at 0.7 km (0.4 mi), 2268 m (7450 ft), the **trail ends** at the creek. This is the mouth of Arethusa Cirque. Little Arethusa is visible left (N). Hop over the **creek** and proceed straight (E) 15 paces. Then turn left (N) and pick up a **faint route** into the larches. Head toward the slope that rises to a terrace beneath Little Arethusa. Presently, cross another fork of the shallow creek. Proceed N, up its W bank.

The route soon disappears. Follow the path of least resistance amid the larches. Several minutes farther, emerge on the left side of a N-S **gully**. Ascend NW, above the gully's left side. Take advantage of steps bootbeaten into the steep, grassy slope. Gain the **terrace** at 2384 m (7820 ft). Having hiked about 30 minutes, you're now in the alpine zone, with no trees between you and Little Arethusa.

Ascend N. Stay between rock (left) and a clutch of krummholz (right). Reach another terrace. Then angle left (NW) up the grassy slope to attain Little Arethusa's **S ridge**, at 2470 m (8100 ft). Decision time. Want to continue climbing on even rougher talus? If not, appreciate the view, then turn back.

Nearby SE is 3095-m (10,153 ft) Storm Mtn, with its distinctive swirling strata. Directly W is the S end of Pocaterra Ridge (Trip 30). Beyond it is the Elk Range. WSW, below the S end of Pocaterra Ridge, is grassy Pocaterra Cirque. Mt. Tyrwhitt rises left of and immediately behind the cirque.

Continue the steep ascent. The loose rock here is just big enough to hamper progress. Patches of smaller, broken rock offer a reprieve. You'll likely follow traces of sheep trail beaten into the talus. At 2.7 km (1.7 mi), 2729 m (8950 ft), step onto the **first summit** of Little Arethusa. The E precipice plunges into the N reaches Arethusa Cirque.

Storm Mtn appears even more impressive. Peaks beyond the Elk Range are now visible. One of the more distinctive is wedge-shaped, 3450-m (11,316-ft) Mt. Joffre, WSW. Others in that vicinity are Mt. Petain and Castlenau Peak. The Royal Group is distant WNW. Even farther is 3406-m (11,172-ft) Mt. Sir Douglas, NW.

Immediately N of the first summit is the 2744-m (9000-ft) second summit of Little Arethusa. The two summits are closely linked by a broken, narrow, precipitous ridge. Only competent climbers should attempt this short, dicey stretch. The second summit grants an aerial view of Ptarmigan Cirque (NW), but the panorama hardly changes. From Little Arethusa's second summit, a razor-sharp ridge continues NE to nearby 2912-m (9551-ft) Mt. Arethusa.

TRIP 33
Mt. Lipsett

LOCATION	Elbow-Sheep Wildland Provincial Park Hwy 40, SE of Highwood Pass
ROUND TRIP	12 km (7.4 mi)
ELEVATION GAIN	705 m (2312 ft)
KEY ELEVATIONS	trailhead 1875 m (6150 ft), summit 2580 m (8465 ft)
HIKING TIME	3½ to 5 hours
DIFFICULTY	moderate
MAP	Gem Trek *Highwood & Cataract Creek*

Opinion

With TVs all but strapped to their heads like feedbags, North Americans gorge nonstop on spectacles, most of which are not real. That's why they lack patience for ordinary life, in which the excellent and the extraordinary are rare, and much is difficult, imperfect, disappointing, or tedious. No wonder most North Americans don't hike. It almost always entails difficulty and tedium. That's certainly true of the Mt. Lipsett approach. But if you stride on, you'll soon relish a genuine spectacle and the fulfillment that comes from having earned it.

Bear in mind, the spectacle atop Mt. Lipsett doesn't compare with the see-forever, 360° vistas afforded by higher summits nearer the Great Divide. Calling Lipsett a "mountain" strains the definition. By Canadian Rockies standards, it's just a big hill. The western half of the panorama extends across the Highwood River headwaters to distant peaks of the Divide. And the eastern half of the panorama is blocked by 3138-m (10,295-ft) Mist Mtn (Trip 34). But the Patagonian immensity and austerity of Mist Mtn is awesome at such close range. And the rest of the view is enriched by the liberating experience of walking Lipsett's lengthy alpine summit ridge without a single pesky tree imposing its will over yours.

The wilderness you'll survey from atop Lipsett is most scenic in late fall, when larches add a splash of gold to the forest, and a dusting of snow highlights the crags above Running Rain Lake (south-southwest). Lipsett is also a good choice in fall because it's a relatively short trip. You can hike it during the warmest part of the day—11 a.m. to 3 p.m.— avoiding the damp chill of early morning and the plummeting cold of evening.

What's tedious about the hike? The initial hour or so is on a sketchy trail, then an overgrown road. They meander inefficiently through forest that is neither beautiful to behold nor generous with views. It's especially dull a second time, on the return. That's why it's preferable to hike Mt. Lipsett as a one-way shuttle trip rather than a round trip.

By not retracing the meandering, forested ascent, you'll reduce your total distance to 9 km (5.6 mi), and you'll slash the day's tedium by 50%.

Ascending Mt. Lipsett

Hiking one-way, however, requires a cross-country descent from the summit, southwest to Hwy 40. It's extremely steep, and it ends with a 20-minute bushwhack.

Casual hikers will find this a challenge, perhaps an overwhelming one. They shouldn't attempt it. Strong, experienced hikers will find it spices the trip with a pinch of adventure yet poses no serious obstacle. They should yell "Wahoo!" and go for it. Hitchhiking the short distance back to the trailhead can be easy. But if your party has two vehicles, arrange a shuttle as described in the *By Vehicle* directions below.

Fact

Before your trip

Be aware that Hwy 40, from Kananaskis Lakes Trail to Highwood Junction, is closed December 1 through June 14.

By Vehicle

Follow directions for Trip 34 to the Mist Mountain trailhead—a large, grassy clearing between the highway and the forest—at 1875 m (6150 ft).

If you intend to make this a one-way shuttle trip, and your party has two vehicles, park the second one about 9 km (5.6 mi) S of Highwood Pass, or 4 km (2.5 mi) W of the trailhead. That's roughly where your cross-country descent should end.

On Foot

Start hiking at the W end of the clearing. Ascend N to the forest edge. Look for a **rusted pole** at the NW corner of the clearing. Follow the sketchy trail that departs near the pole. It leads N into forest.

In about four minutes, reach an overgrown road. Don't turn onto the road. Stay on the trail, continuing directly across the road, ascending NW. Soon ascend steeply N, just left of a **stream gorge**. A few minutes farther, the trail curves left (WSW), away from the gorge.

About 20 minutes from the trailhead, ignore the game path forking left (NW). The trail is faint here, but stay on it by bearing right and curving N. One minute farther, however, go left (W) onto a gently ascending **old road**.

About 45 minutes from the trailhead, the road-trail makes a **hairpin turn** right (SE) at 2065 m (6773 ft). Scattered alpine larches here are gold in late September. In thinning forest, attain glimpses across the valley to the rounded ridges of the Elk Range. Mt. Odlum is SW. Mt. Loomis is S.

Ascend left (W). Views continue. Ten minutes farther, the trail broadens and curves NNE. Mist Mtn looms ahead. Mt. Lipsett is visible left (NW)

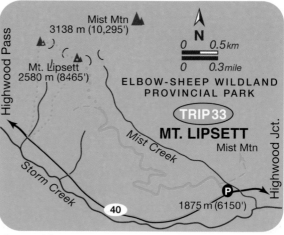

through trees. About 1½ hours from the trailhead, the trail exits subalpine forest and surges into the **alpine zone**.

Proceed NW. Enjoy a brief, level respite on a SW-facing slope. Within 15 minutes, you'll see the trail ahead curving left (NW). It ends soon in that direction and will only divert you from

your goal. So abandon the trail here and continue **cross-country**: straight, ascending moderately, up the fall line.

At 6 km (3.7 mi) ascend just right of the summit and reach the top of 2580-m (8465-ft) **Mt. Lipsett**. The much higher and more dramatic peak a mere 1.2 km (.75 mi) NE is 3138-m (10,295-m) Mist Mtn. Highwood Pass is NW. Rugged peaks of the Great Divide are S, beyond the Elk Range.

You now have three options: (1) Retrace your steps to the trailhead. (2) Descend generally SW, cross-country, to Hwy 40, then either hitchhike or drive your shuttle vehicle back to the trailhead. (3) Descend NW to a saddle, ascend to Mt. Lipsett's outlier (slightly lower than the summit but affording a better vantage of Highwood Pass), then either (a) retrace your steps to the trailhead, or (b) descend generally S, cross-country, to Hwy 40, where you'll either hitchhike or drive your shuttle vehicle back to the trailhead.

Before choosing, look downslope (SW) from the summit. Are you certain you'll be comfortable on such a steep, trail-less descent to the highway? If you're hesitant, don't be foolish; option one is for you. If you're confident and eager, however, you'll enjoy options two or three, and you'll spare yourself a tediously gradual descent on the trail you just hiked. Option three simply takes about a half hour longer than option two.

Directions for options two and three? They're unnecessary for anyone who's capable, and they might entice those who aren't, so our guidance ends here. If you're up to the challenge, you'll grok the way. That's part of the fun. Below treeline, just maintain your downhill course until you intersect the highway. We found game trails helpful in the dense forest. The approximately 3-km (1.8-mi) descent to the highway (from either the summit or the outlier) takes about 45 minutes. When you hit pavement, the trailhead is left (SE).

In the unlikely event that you fail to catch a ride back to the trailhead, no worries. It's only a 4-km (2.5-mi) walk, and a pleasantly scenic one at that. Besides, if you don't catch a ride, it's probably because there were few vehicles, which means your walk will be peaceful.

TRIP 34

Mist Mountain

LOCATION	Elbow-Sheep Wildland Provincial Park
	Hwy 40, SE of Highwood Pass
ROUND TRIP	11 km (6.8 mi)
ELEVATION GAIN	1263 m (4143 ft)
KEY ELEVATIONS	trailhead 1875 m (6150 ft), summit 3138 m (10,295 ft)
HIKING TIME	6 to 7 hours
DIFFICULTY	challenging scramble
MAP	Gem Trek *Highwood & Cataract Creek*

Opinion

Silence. It's rarely cited as a reason to climb a mountain, but it's an increasingly valid one as our world grows louder. Because intrusive, irritating sound can damage more than your hearing. It contributes to rising blood pressure, declining productivity, and higher serum-cholesterol levels. Studies show that incessant noise makes people less caring, less communicative, less reflective; more apt to feel helpless and powerless. Even routine hospital noise impedes healing.

In search of silence, head for Mist Mountain. The arduous ascent deters all but the hardiest of local hikers and scramblers, so you'll likely be alone, subjected only to the sound of your panting, gasping breath, and the clink of your boots on steep, shifting scree. Up top, bathed in serenity, you can watch the Rockies flowing to the horizon like ragged tidal waves.

Just don't underestimate the difficulty of this adventure, or overrate your mountaineering competence, or miscalculate the suffering involved. Mist Mtn sifts the intrepid from the casual. For about an hour—after the scrambling begins in earnest, until you've dropped your pack on the summit ridge—it's pure trudgery. The scree is so loose, the incline so steep, you'll need Sisyphian endurance. Step up, slide back. Step up, slide back. Step up, slide back.

We include it in this book of premier trips because of the challenge and accomplishment it offers as the highest K-Country peak south of Highwood Pass. And because there are two places en route where, should you decide the summit will outstrip your desire or ability, you can stop and still feel glad you came. The first is about an hour up, on an unnamed, grassy, alpine pass. The second is about two hours up, on top of a prominent rock rib, still below the Mist Mtn cirque, but high enough where you'll have sampled the trials and joys of the scramble.

After grappling with Mist Mtn, you'll fully appreciate it upon subsequent sightings. It's visible from Raspberry Ridge (Trip 55), from Mt. Burke (Trip 56), even from Hwy 40 while driving northwest out of Highwood Junction.

True to its name, the mountain seems to summon mist, clouds, rain. So plan this trip for a day when you're assured of a flawless, blue sky. If the weather threatens to turn, hike elsewhere. Minus its panoramic reward, Mist Mtn—silent though it might be—is just a rock quarry, and you're sentenced to hard labour.

Fact

Before your trip

Be aware that Hwy 40, from Kananaskis Lakes Trail to Highwood Junction, is closed December 1 through June 15.

By Vehicle

From **Trans-Canada Hwy 1**, drive S on Hwy 40. Crest 2206-m (7239-ft) Highwood Pass at 67 km (41.5 mi). Reset your trip odometer to 0 here—not at the parking lot, which is 0.4 km (0.25 mi) farther. In another 13 km (8.1 mi) turn left (N) into a large, grassy clearing between the highway and the forest.

Ascending Mist Mtn

Or start at **Highwood Junction**, where Hwys 40, 541 and 940 intersect. (It's 43 km / 26.7 mi SW of Longview; 31 km / 19.2 mi NW of where Hwy 532 joins Hwy 940.) Set your trip odometer to 0. Drive NW on Hwy 40. At **20.2 km (12.5 mi)** pass Mist Creek day-use area on the left. At **21.2 km (13.1 mi)** cross the signed bridge over Mist Creek. At **24.8 km (15.4 mi)** turn right (N) into a large, grassy clearing between the highway and the forest.

From **either approach**, park near the W end of the clearing, at 1875 m (6150 ft).

On Foot

Hike NNE. A short, gentle ascent leads to the forest edge. Ignore the orange metal post. Follow the remains of an old road N through trees. Boulders block vehicle entrance. In a few minutes reach a T-junction at 1890 m (6199 ft). Turn right (E) on the grassy, former highway. Follow it generally ENE through thick brush and young trees.

About 15 minutes from the trailhead, look for a **cairned path** crossing the road. Immediately beyond, hikers have placed logs across the road to discourage you from proceeding in that direction. The path ascends left (N) and descends right (S). It's clearly more substantial than the game trails you've passed thus far. Go left, up the hillside, into an opening in the

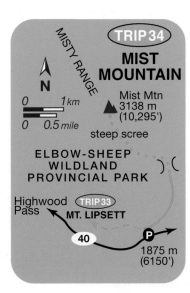

forest. Right descends to the highway but deteriorates into a bushwhack and dumps you at the wrong end of the clearing.

Ascend steeply for twelve minutes. The path levels briefly at 1997 m (6550 ft). About 30 minutes from the trailhead, reach a **fork**. Bear right, curving (NE). To prevent you from ascending straight (NW), hikers have blocked that option with rocks and logs.

The right fork descends slightly and contours. Berry bushes thrive here. Within five minutes, at 2024 m (6640 ft), attain the trip's first view. Ahead is the wide, V-shaped, **grassy draw** you'll be ascending. NW, above you, are rocky cliffs on Mist Mtn's SE-curving arm.

Keep hiking N to the obvious, alpine pass. Follow a faint bootbeaten path through the grass. Re-entering trees, the tread is more distinct. Cross willowy slopes. Step over or around wildflowers growing in the little-used path: powder-blue alpine forget-me-nots, and bright-yellow buttercups. Reach the **nameless col** at 3 km (1.9 mi), 2301 m (7547 ft), about an hour from the trailhead.

Piercing the pass, continue left (NW) around a knob, into the next drainage. Contour across loose, very steep talus. After maintaining your elevation, angle upward where you're comfortable doing so. Clamber onto the prominent **rock rib**. It affords the easiest, most enjoyable route up the drainage. Magenta willow-herb thrives here. At about 2410 m (7900 ft), hop over the meltwater stream. Above the stream's N bank, ascend W, then NW on heather and rock.

Pick your way, gradually curving NW, into the **cirque** embraced by the arms of Mist Mtn. What begins as a moderately ascending boulder romp soon turns grim as you encounter ever-steepening scree. Either keep slogging up the shifting rock, or scramble onto the airier but more solid spine to the left. Whichever you choose, your goal is N. Crest the **summit ridge** at 3050 m (10,000 ft). Conquistadors will be here about 2 hours from the pass, 3 hours from the trailhead.

After a well-earned rest, turn right for the final, short push, generally E. Compared to the steep scree you just vanquished, the crest of the summit ridge is a relief. The angle of ascent eases; the rock is more stable underfoot. Step onto the 3138-m (10,295-ft) **summit of Mist Mtn** after hiking and scrambling a total of 5.5 km (3.4 mi). If you're here within 3½ hours of leaving the trailhead, you deserve a medal for exceptional fitness and determination. You'll see that a previous visitor was honoured with a plaque after he was smote by lightning. It's a sobering admonition to mind the weather during your summit festivities.

The Mist Mtn panorama is vast. Listed here are but a few notable highlights. The Elk Range is SW and W. See the gleaming white expanse farther W? That's Petain Glacier (Trip 26). Mt. Assiniboine is NW. Storm Mtn, NNW, anchors the other end of the Misty Range. Misty Basin is N, at the head of Mist Creek valley. Mist Ridge (Trip 35) forms the valley's far wall, NE. Three-peaked Odlum Ridge is nearby SSE. The austere Highwood Range is SE.

Because you can glissade down the scree in a fraction of the time it took to climb, it's possible to reach your vehicle 2½ hours after departing the summit of Mist Mtn.

TRIP 35
Mist Ridge

LOCATION	Elbow-Sheep Wildland Provincial Park Hwy 40, SE of Highwood Pass
ROUND TRIP	14.8-km (9.2-mi) minimum round trip to ridgecrest, 23-km (14.3-mi) circuit, 4-km (2.5-mi) round-trip detour on Storm Mtn ridge
ELEVATION GAIN	716 m (2348 ft) to ridgecrest, 1058 m (3470 ft) on circuit, 238 m (781 ft) on Storm Mtn ridge detour
KEY ELEVATIONS	trailhead 1765 m (5789 ft), Mist Ridge S summit 2424 m (7951 ft), Mist Ridge N summit 2515 m (8249 ft) Rickert's Pass 2341 m (7678 ft), Storm Mtn ridge high- point 2579 m (8459 ft)
HIKING TIME	up to 7-hour round trip, 7 to 8 hours for circuit 1 hour for Storm Mtn ridge detour
DIFFICULTY	moderate to challenging, depending on distance
MAP	Gem Trek *Highwood & Cataract Creek*

Opinion

We know it's considered rude to ask someone his or her age. But when we cross paths with a hiker many years our senior, and he or she is a paragon of vitality, we'll ask anyway.

They're never offended. They graciously accept our query as a compliment. And sometimes their answers are enlightening.

One aged hiker's response was especially memorable because it began with a long, penetrating gaze during which he intuited we were really seeking advice, not his exact age.

"The thing is to just keep rolling," he said.

We've shortened his counsel to a one-word mantra: Momentum. It summarizes the means to a long, athletic life.

Maintaining momentum in the abruptly vertical Rocky Mountains, however, is relentlessly challenging except in a few, special places, like Mist Ridge.

Here, momentum is easily attained and continually rewarded. You can roll along the gentle, alpine ridgecrest for hours, seemingly afloat in 360° scenery.

To the east, you'll overlook Cliff Creek valley. On the west side is Mist Creek valley, whose far wall is a stupendous massif anchored at each end by a goliath: Mist Mtn (south, Trip 34), Storm Mtn (north).

Mist Ridge (not to be confused with Mist Mtn) ranks among Kananaskis Country's premier ridgewalks. The others are Northover Ridge (Trip 24) and Pocaterra Ridge (Trip 30). Northover is much longer than Mist and is

severely rigourous. Pocaterra is shorter than Mist but has more demanding sections. Most hikers will prefer Mist.

An advantage of Mist Ridge is that it's in a rain shadow. When grim weather descends upon K-Country, perseverance might be rewarded at Mist. We've hiked here in sunshine while rain pounded the Great Divide near Kananaskis Lakes.

After a normal winter, Mist Ridge should be snow-free by late June. The slopes can be green and floral by early July. The wildflower display is a sprite's delight: scorpionweed, fleabane, wild blue flax, plumed aven, alpine forget-me-not, Jacob's ladder, moss campion, rock jasmine.

Surmounting the S summit of Mist Ridge—where actual ridgewalking begins—takes about two hours, but it's pleasantly varied and doesn't qualify as "steep." Beyond, the 4-km (2.5-mi) ridgecrest poses only moderate ups and downs, requires no scrambling, and is never exposed.

Relaxed, eyes-up striding allows you to gorge on the panorama. Libation for the feast, however, is in short supply. A stream crossing about an hour from the trailhead will be your last opportunity to refill waterbottles until you drop off the ridge, into Mist Creek valley, homeward bound. So haul more water than you think you'll need.

You'll cross several tributary streams in Mist Creek valley. All are reliable water sources. So much for excitement on this leg of the journey. It's just a plod through disenchanted forest. Fires raged here long ago. Today, trees again deprive hikers of scenery. A couple meadows offer brief scenic respites, but that's all.

Nor will you see Mist Creek. *Missed Creek* is more like it. The trail stays well away. But you could see a bear. You'll likely see bearberry jam (scat). This is grizzly habitat. Making noise to warn bruins of your presence is the best way to prevent an encounter.

In defense of the Mist Creek valley trail, it does allow a circuit. Hiking all of Mist Ridge out-and-back would be more strenuous due to repeat elevation gain. And the Mist Creek valley trail is mercifully level, granting a speedy exit. From Rickert's Pass, where you depart the ridge, it's possible to zoom to the trailhead in three hours.

Also consider that, from Rickert's Pass, a short but very rewarding detour is possible onto Storm Mtn ridge. It adds a grand finale to the day but makes for a very long hike. So point your boots at Mist Ridge shortly after the summer solstice (June 21). Get an early-morning start. And bring your headlamp—just in case.

Despite the invitation of a circuit and the appeal of the Storm Mtn ridge climax, most hikers do not descend from the north summit of Mist Ridge to Rickert's Pass. They keep to the crest of Mist Ridge, cruising it in both directions. Momentum purists—forward ever, backward never—power through the entire circuit in as little as seven hours.

Either way, enjoy your roll.

Fact

Before your trip

Be aware that Hwy 40, from Kananaskis Lakes Trail to Highwood Junction, is closed December 1 through June 14.

By Vehicle

From **Trans-Canada Hwy 1**, drive S on Hwy 40. Crest 2206-m (7236-ft) Highwood Pass at 67 km (41.5 mi). Reset your trip odometer to 0 here—not at the parking lot, which is 0.4 km (0.25 mi) farther. Proceed S another 17.5 km (10.9 mi).

From **Highwood Junction** drive NW 20.2 km (12.5 mi) on Hwy 40. (Highwood Junction is where Hwys 40, 541 and 940 intersect. It's 43 km / 26.7 mi SW of Longview; 31 km / 19.2 mi NW of where Hwy 532 joins Hwy 940.)

From **either approach**, turn W into the trailhead parking lot at Mist Creek day-use area. Elevation: 1765 m (5789 ft).

On Foot

The signed trail departs the N end of the parking lot. Follow it across the **highway**. Pierce a stand of trees. Bear right (E) on a grassy roadbed. Soon turn left and hike up-valley, generally NNW, on a trail that was obviously once a road.

A gradual ascent leads to a **junction** at 2 km (1.2 mi), 1890 m (6199 ft), about 25 minutes from the trailhead. Left (NW) is the circuit return through Mist Creek valley from the far end of the ridge. For now go right (N).

At 3.7 km (2.3 mi), 2107 m (6911 ft), after hiking about an hour, bear left (E) where an abandoned road ascends right (SW). Descend, rockhop a **stream**, bear left, then immediately curve right.

Enter the subalpine zone. Veer sharp left on a trail ascending into a meadowy **saddle** at 5.4 km (3.3 mi), 2225 m (7298 ft), about 1½ hours from the trailhead.

Go left briefly before turning right (N) to resume ascending the road. It switchbacks left (SW) then curves right (NW) around the **S end of Mist Ridge**.

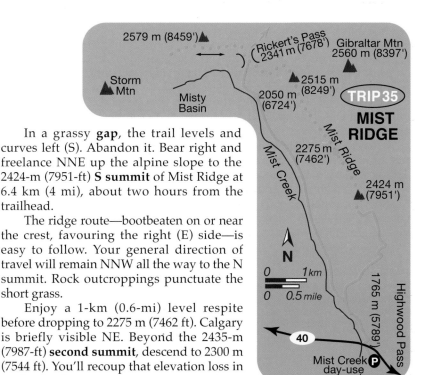

2579 m (8459')▲

Rickert's Pass
2341 m (7678')

Gibraltar Mtn
2560 m (8397')▲

▲ Storm
Mtn

Misty
Basin

▲ 2515 m
(8249')

2050 m
(6724')

TRIP 35

**MIST
RIDGE**

2275 m
(7462')

Mist Creek

Mist Ridge

2424 m
▲ (7951')

N

0   1 km

0   0.5 mile

1765 m (5789')

Highwood Pass

40

Mist Creek Ⓟ
day-use

In a grassy **gap**, the trail levels and curves left (S). Abandon it. Bear right and freelance NNE up the alpine slope to the 2424-m (7951-ft) **S summit** of Mist Ridge at 6.4 km (4 mi), about two hours from the trailhead.

The ridge route—bootbeaten on or near the crest, favouring the right (E) side—is easy to follow. Your general direction of travel will remain NNW all the way to the N summit. Rock outcroppings punctuate the short grass.

Enjoy a 1-km (0.6-mi) level respite before dropping to 2275 m (7462 ft). Calgary is briefly visible NE. Beyond the 2435-m (7987-ft) **second summit**, descend to 2300 m (7544 ft). You'll recoup that elevation loss in moderate steps.

Approaching the N summit, contour at 2482 m (8141 ft), just below the crest, on its left (W) side. Tranquil, pastoral Misty Basin is visible left (WNW), beneath Storm Mtn. The route descends the left (W) side of the 2515-m (8249-ft) **N summit**—highest point on Mist Ridge.

Reach a 2400-m (7872-ft) saddle overlooking forested Sheep River Valley (N). After following the route around the left (S) side of a rocky knob, you can then survey the route up Storm Mtn ridge (ahead, NW). It's a bootbeaten path initially traversing the face of a pyramidal peaklet—the farthest right (easternmost) summit on Storm Mtn ridge.

Whether proceeding up Storm Mtn ridge or heading home via the circuit, you must drop to **Rickert's Pass**: lowest point on Mist Ridge, about four hours from the trailhead.

Reach a **junction in the pass** at 12.7 km (7.9 mi), 2341 m (7678 ft), immediately before a rocky outcrop. Left (S) switchbacks into forest, then follows the floor of Mist Creek valley back to the trailhead. Right (NE), through a cleft, is the Rickert's Creek trail descending to intersect the Sheep River trail. Ahead (NW) is the path continuing onto Storm Mtn ridge.

The Storm Mtn ridge path angles left (W) below the first summit. About 2 km (1.2 mi) from the pass (30 minutes if you can ignite your booster rockets) top out at 2579 m (8459 ft) on the **middle summit of Storm Mtn ridge**. It's a superb vantage. Burns Creek canyon is N. The creek's source, Burns Lake, is NW. Above and beyond the lake are Mt. Arethusa and Mt. Rae. Sheep River

Valley is NE. Mist Creek valley is SSE. Misty Basin is S. Above and beyond it is Mist Mtn at the S end of the Misty Range. Storm Mtn looms WSW.

After retracing the route to Rickert's Pass junction, descend right (S) on the **Mist Creek trail**. At treeline, it immediately switchbacks right (NW), dropping into the forest.

Once the trail levels on the **valley floor**, your general direction of travel will remain SSE. The rate of descent is barely perceptible. Rockhop several streams where you can refill water bottles.

Cross a large, **willowy meadow**. Proceed through a forest of lodgepole pine and Englemann spruce. Cross another **willowy meadow**. The last obstacle—a sharp drop into a creek drainage, and a stiff climb out—seems a perverse punishment near the end of such a long day.

Reach a **junction** at 21 km (13 mi), 1890 m (6199 ft). If you've been marching, you'll arrive here about three hours from the pass. You're now on familiar ground. Bear right to vanquish the final 2 km (1.2 mi) to the trailhead.

Lyall's saxifrage

TRIP 36
Picklejar Lakes

LOCATION	Elbow-Sheep Wildland Provincial Park Hwy 40, SE of Highwood Pass
ROUND TRIP	9 km (5.6 mi)
ELEVATION GAIN	474 m (1555 ft)
KEY ELEVATIONS	trailhead 1729 m (5670 ft), first lake 2160 m (7085 ft) third lake 2183 m (7160 ft)
HIKING TIME	3 to 5 hours
DIFFICULTY	moderate (due only to short, steep, final approach)
MAP	Gem Trek *Highwood & Cataract Creek*

Opinion

Lakes are to hikers what sticks are to dogs. No matter how far God tosses one out there in the woods, we'll chase it down and find it.

Our infatuation with lakes, though obvious, is not easy to explain. Is it because, standing on the shore of a backcountry lake, we can admire the surrounding mountains? Is it because lakes are a diversion, inviting us to swim or fish? Is it simply because lakes serve as destinations by affording a definitive sense of arrival?

There's a deeper reason why we love lakes. It's because they're still. We live complex, frenetic lives. Even the forests we hike through are visually busy. But lakes are islands of stillness. Reaching a lake at trail's end has the effect of a tranquilizer dart. Staring at a lake is profoundly calming.

Our eyes dive into the water. The sight alone refreshes us. It douses the fire of thought. Slakes our thirst for tranquility. Whether they're as clear as the mountain air or an ineffable shade of blue-green, lakes soothe us. And who these days doesn't need a little soothing?

For that reason, the trail to Picklejar Lakes is among the most popular in Kananaskis Country. It quickly leads to four, small lakes stairstepping into a cirque in the desolate Highwood Range. On a sunny day, the Picklejars contrast dramatically with the subalpine greenery and stark gray cliffs surrounding them. The second lake—deep, crystalline, frigid—tempts proud Canadians to demonstrate a cultural conceit: tolerance of cold. A quick dunk might be invigorating, if the weather's hot. You first.

Fact

Before your trip

Be aware that Hwy 40, from Kananaskis Lakes Trail to Highwood Junction, is closed December 1 through June 15.

First Picklejar Lake

By Vehicle

From **Trans-Canada Hwy 1**, drive S on Hwy 40. Just after cresting 2206-m (7239-ft) Highwood Pass, watch for the trailhead parking lot (right / SW) at 67.4 km (41.8 mi.) Reset your trip odometer to 0 here. Proceed S another 19.7 km (12.2 mi). Do not stop at Picklejar Creek day-use area.

From **Highwood Junction**, drive 17.1 km (10.6 mi) NW on Hwy 40. (Highwood Junction is where Hwys 40, 541 and 940 intersect. It's 43 km / 26.7 mi SW of Longview; 31 km / 19.2 mi NW of where Hwy 532 joins Hwy 940.)

From **either approach**, turn W into the trailhead parking lot at Lantern Creek day-use area. Elevation: 1729 m (5670 ft).

On Foot

Lantern Creek, not Picklejar Creek, offers the best access to Picklejar Lakes. From the parking lot, walk left (N) along the highway. Just past Lantern Creek, cross to the **right (E) side of the highway**. Pick up the trail curving NE into aspen and conifers above the creek's NW bank. Begin a vigourous ascent.

In 20 minutes, reach a viewpoint on a **grassy slope** at 1878 m (6160 ft). Ahead, you can see the trail vaulting to a pass. Continue traversing E. You're high above the creek, which is audible but not visible. The mountains you're entering are among the Highwood Range.

At 1966 m (6450 ft), about 40 minutes from the trailhead, cross a **creeklet** and turn left (N), climbing more grassy slopes. Though the ascent steepens abruptly, there are no switchbacks. Seeking stable footing, hikers have strayed widely. Result: a **broad, denuded swath** affording almost no traction. Toil upward. Descending is even worse.

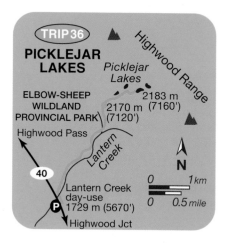

TRIP 36 ▲

PICKLEJAR LAKES

Highwood Range

Picklejar Lakes

ELBOW-SHEEP
WILDLAND
PROVINCIAL PARK

Highwood Pass

2183 m
2170 m (7160')
(7120') ▲

Lantern Creek

N

40

0   1 km

0   0.5 mile

Lantern Creek
day-use
1729 m (5670')

P

Highwood Jct

Having gained a new appreciation for labour-saving, switchbacking trails, crest a 2137-m (7010-ft) **pass**. Strong hikers arrive here one hour after leaving the trailhead. Ahead (N) is a sharp drop into forest. Turn right (E) and resume ascending steeply on a slightly less eroded, grassy slope.

Attain views. Mist Mtn is WNW. The S end of Mist Ridge is NW. **Top out** at 2170 m (7120 ft). The airy trail, now descending on shale, grants an overview of the first lake. You might also spy a trail in the forested valley below (left / NW). It leads to Picklejar Creek. Exiting that way is not recommended.

Reach the shallow **first lake** at 4.2 km (2.6 mi), 2160 m (7085 ft). Campsites are across the outlet stream, in trees, above the N shore. Follow the S-shore trail through grass, toward the inlet stream. It briefly climbs, then drops to the smaller **second lake**—five minutes from the first. An arresting, battleship-like peak rises above it. The trail veers right (S) and ascends. Five minutes farther, reach the deep, **third lake** at 2183 m (7160 ft). The trail ends here.

Round the third lake on either side. A route skirts the N shore, then ascends through trees and over rock slabs. Another route crosses a rockslide to the S and continues across scree. Whichever you choose, reach the shallow **fourth lake** at 4.5 km (2.8 mi), 2149 m (7050 ft). A rock-and-grass spur right (S) of the SW shore offers a view of both the third and fourth lakes. Beyond the fourth lake is a talus bowl topped by banded cliffs.

Fourth Picklejar Lake

TRIP 37

Talus Lake

LOCATION	Hwy 66, SW of Bragg Creek
ROUND TRIP	20.8 km (12.9 mi) cycling, plus 10 km (6.2 mi) hiking
ELEVATION GAIN	207 m (680 ft) cycling, plus 405 m (1328 ft) hiking
KEY ELEVATIONS	trailhead 1610 m (5280 ft), lake 2223 m (7290 ft)
HIKING TIME	2½ hours cycling, plus 4 to 5 hours hiking
DIFFICULTY	moderate
MAPS	Gem Trek *Bragg Creek and Elbow Falls*
	Gem Trek *Kananaskis Lakes*

Opinion

Perhaps modern life is a disaster. That would explain why so many people lack mental and physical vigour. Apathy is a common reaction to disasters. It was widespread among survivors of the Hiroshima bombing. The Japanese called it *burabura*, or *do-nothing sickness*. It can rapidly lead to physical deterioration if not countered. So here's an anti-apathy trip. Not just a hike, but a bike-and-hike. Your goal is a resplendent, teal lake adorning a craggy, austerely handsome Front-Range cirque. It's a hot day? The creeks are running? Plunge into an inviting bedrock pool en route, thus completing your own, vigourous, semi-Iron-Man afternoon: bike, hike, and swim.

The journey begins on the Little Elbow trail—a rocky road initiating a 38-km (23.6-mi) loop popular with mountainbikers. You, however, will pedal only the first stretch, to Mt. Romulus backcountry campground. After stashing your steed, you'll march up an unofficial, infrequently hiked trail. Though not indicated on most maps, the trail is evident on the ground, easy to follow until it approaches the Forks, where you must be mindful.

The Front Range sizzles when summer cooks. Some find the hot, dry atmosphere soothing, especially if inclined to dip in the aforementioned Talus Creek pools about 45 minutes up the trail. Otherwise, save this trip for early summer, cloudy weather, or autumn. Any time of year, you'll be exploring a world of scree, talus, rocks and boulders. After climbing through open forest you won't burst into meadows. A few hardy wildflowers will nevertheless brighten the way: purple asters, shrubby cinquefoil with yellow flowers, and white, exotic-looking, fringed grass-of-Parnassus. Upon reaching Talus Lake, the depth and clarity of the water might tempt you to dive in. Talk about vigourous. Even on a day of record-setting heat, the water will be numbingly cold.

Before coming solely to visit Talus Lake, consider that two other trips in this book—West Fork Little Elbow River (Trip 39), and Paradise Pass (Trip 38)—entail cycling to Mt. Romulus campground. If you can muster three days, bring your tent and establish a basecamp at Romulus. Devote day one

Talus Lake

to Talus Lake, the shortest of the three excursions. On day two, trek all the way to Piper Pass via the West Fork Little Elbow. On day three, hike to Paradise Pass, then saddle up and ride out.

For peace of mind, bring a cable and lock to secure your bike to a tree trunk. You'll likely want to wear a helmet, cycling shorts, gloves, and perhaps cycling shoes. Cache those along with your bike while you're hiking.

Fact

Before your trip

Be aware that Hwy 66, from Elbow Falls to the trailhead, is closed December 1 through May 15.

By Vehicle

Follow the directions for Forgetmenot Ridge (Trip 50) to the end of Hwy 66, about an hour SW of Calgary. Park just beyond the Elbow River campground entrance, in the small pullout on the right, at 33 km (20.5 mi), 1610 m (5280 ft). If the pullout is full, return to the spacious lot just outside the campground entrance.

By Bike

Your goal is Mt. Romulus backcountry campground, 10.4 km (6.5 mi) SW of the trailhead. Though you'll be on an old road the entire way, it undulates frequently and gains 207 m (680 ft). Moderately strong cyclists will do it in 1½ hours. The return, largely downhill, takes only about an hour.

From either the pullout or the parking lot, ascend the campground entrance road SW. As it curves W, stay on the main road, continually bearing left where right spurs access campsites. Go around a couple metal gates, or through them if open. Vehicles are prohibited beyond a final trailhead parking lot that might also be gated.

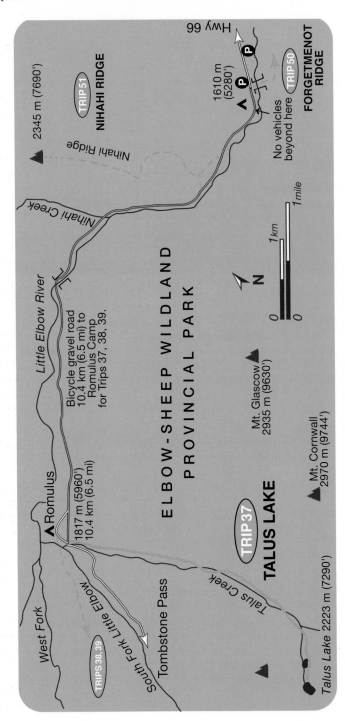

In a couple minutes, pass a sign for Nihahi Ridge and Little Elbow trail. Cross a cattleguard. About ten minutes along, pass a trail forking right (NW) into the forest; it also climbs to Nihahi Ridge (Trip 51). Keep following the road. It curves NW now, on the Little Elbow River's N bank.

About 15 minutes along, cross the stony bed of **Nihahi Creek** (likely shallow or dry). A signed trail forks right, probing the creek canyon upstream (NNW). Keep following the road. Two minutes farther, cross a bridge to the Little Elbow River's S bank. The road now leads SW, climbing a long, steep hill to 1755 m (5756 ft).

After cycling about an hour, pass a bench at a viewpoint on the left. Mt. Remus (cliffbands) is NNW, across the valley. Left of it (NW) is Mt. Romulus (brown scree slopes). Soon cross a tributary streambed.

Pass a road forking right (W)—the first entrance to Mt. Romulus campground—after cycling nearly 1½ hours. Proceed SW on the main road. A few minutes farther, at 1817 m (5960 ft), immediately before the **confluence of Talus Creek and South Fork Little Elbow River**, another road forks right (N). This is the second entrance to Mt. Romulus campground. The main road left climbs S over Tombstone Pass.

If your goal is Talus Lake, stop cycling here. Stash your bike, plus any cycling gear you won't need, in the forest—left (SE) of the road, E of the Talus Creek drainage.

If your goal is the West Fork Little Elbow (Trip 39) or Paradise Pass (Trip 38), turn right (N) onto the campground's second entrance road. In two minutes, immediately before entering the campground, reach a four-way junction. Ahead (N) are the campsites. Right (E) is the first entrance road. Left (W) is the road you'll hike to either destination after stashing your bike. It quickly crosses the South Fork, then leads SW, up the West Fork valley.

On Foot

The unsigned Talus Lake trail forks left (SSE) from the main road. Look for it opposite the campground's second entrance, E of Talus Creek, W of the Mt. Romulus campground sign.

Follow the trail across stony flats. In a few minutes, it climbs a steep, dirt bank, at the edge of pines. E, across Talus Creek gorge, you can see the road that ascends to Tombstone Pass. Soon dip into a mossy gully. Your general direction of travel is SE. The trail undulates above the E wall of the creek gorge.

After about 20 minutes and little elevation gain, the trail descends a gentle ridge over stony ground, through pine and Engelmann spruce. Cross a bedrock stream gully. After a short, rough ascent, Talus Creek is visible and audible. The trail again undulates.

At 1930 m (6330 ft), cross another stream gorge with bedrock pools (possibly dry). A little farther, after hiking about 45 minutes, arrive at the E bank of **Talus Creek**. It too has large bedrock pools—inviting on a hot day. Just 15 m/yd upstream, the trail crosses to the W bank. In another minute, it re-crosses to the E bank and continues generally SE. Ahead, the canyon opens. The long wall of Mt. Cornwall is left (E).

At 2.5 km (1.6 mi), 1915 m (6280 ft), immediately before a tributary stream joins Talus Creek, the trail climbs steeply left on scree, out of the drainage. The ascent eases on a terrace above the tributary's E bank. The trail heads S, then turns right (W), crosses the tiny tributary and enters trees. After swerving S again, it leads through open forest broken by grassy clearings.

Beyond the clearings, the trail curves right (W) and drops sharply to Talus Creek. Rockhop to the NW bank. Head upstream. Follow a shallow depression beside trees, about 3 m/yd from the bedrock creekbed. In two minutes, where the tread is faint, go 5 m/yd right. Pick up a cairned route for the remaining short distance to **the forks**, at 3.7 km (2.3 mi), 2088 m (6850 ft).

Proceed WSW on a rocky route. A blocky peak (S) divides the two upper forks of Talus Creek. The route enters the SW fork, right of the peak. Cairns offer guidance among giant boulders and rock heaps. Go through a dry gully. The faint route leads just below and right of the largest, cabin-size boulder visible ahead (W). Ascend among boulders, then on grass, toward the distant cirque. Cross another dry creekbed and ascend its left bank. Reach a **shallow lakelet** at 2162 m (7090 ft).

A path rounds the lakelet's SE side. Tag onto a trail ascending across the scree slope above a cascade in the gorge. Pass through tight krummholz. About 15 minutes from the lakelet, overcome the headwall. The NE shore of **Talus Lake** is 10 m/yd below, at 2223 m (7290 ft). You've hiked 5 km (3 mi) from Mt. Romulus campground.

The teal lake is in a cirque whose walls are talus slopes rising to sheer cliffs. A grassy bench is left, above the lake. The view NE, out of the cirque, is dominated by Mt. Cornwall.

Nearing Paradise Pass (Trip 38)

TRIP 38
Paradise Pass

LOCATION	Elbow-Sheep Wildland Provincial Park
	Hwy 66, SW of Bragg Creek
ROUND TRIP	20.8 km (13 mi) cycling, plus 17.4 km (10.8 mi) hiking
ELEVATION GAIN	207 m (680 ft) cycling, plus 787 m (2580 ft) hiking
KEY ELEVATIONS	trailhead 1610 m (5280 ft), pass 2576 m (8450 ft)
TRAVEL TIME	2½ hours cycling, plus 7 to 8 hours hiking
DIFFICULTY	moderate
MAPS	Gem Trek *Bragg Creek and Elbow Falls*
	Gem Trek *Kananaskis Lakes*

Opinion

Easy is flavourless. Relaxation is forgettable. So here's a spicy, strenuous journey. The destination, Paradise Pass, is accurately named. It's sublime but remote. To get there and back in a day, you'll need your mountain bike.

After a scenically motivating, 1½-hour ride on a rocky, undulating road, hitch your mechanical horse to a tree near Mt. Romulus backcountry campground. For peace of mind, use a cable and lock. Your helmet, cycling shorts, gloves and shoes? Cache those nearby. Then begin hiking.

You'll still be on a former road, but one succumbing to entropy. Often narrow and overgrown, it's actually a wide trail. Plus it offers frequent views of the beautiful, steep-walled, mountain valley you're piercing. So you won't grouse about what's underfoot.

The final leg, on undeveloped trail, is where the ascent begins in earnest. The grade isn't Olympic, just athletic. You'll escape the trees and enter subalpine meadows in 20 minutes. From there on, the terrain is inspiring: rolling alplands ringed by the Opal Range, The Ripsaw, and Tombstone Mountain.

After cresting Paradise Pass, the trail descends north, skirts Evan-Thomas Lake (visible from the pass), and curves northeast to intersect the North Fork Little Elbow River trail at Evan-Thomas Pass. Left (north-northwest) leads to Hwy 40. Right (southeast) loops back to Mt. Romulus campground. But the loop scenery is lacklustre. Returning the way you came is more engaging, as well as shorter.

Before coming solely to visit Paradise Pass, consider that two other trips in this book—West Fork Little Elbow River (Trip 39), and Talus Lake (Trip 37)—entail cycling to Mt. Romulus campground. If you can muster three days, bring your tent and establish a basecamp at Romulus. Devote day one to Talus Lake, the shortest of the three excursions. On day two, trek all the way to Piper Pass via the West Fork Little Elbow. On day three, hike to Paradise Pass, then saddle up and ride out.

Mounts Hood and Packenham, from Paradise Pass trail

Another option is repacking on the morning of day two and moving your camp 5 km (3.1 mi) farther southwest, into the West Fork valley, just past where the West Fork and Paradise Pass trails split. That will save you from repeating the 9.4-km (5.8-mi) round trip between Mt. Romulus campground and the trail split. Hiking that in-and-out stretch only once, however, requires you to do it bearing a full load, rather than twice with just a daypack. A lonelier, more scenic campsite up the West Fork valley on night two tilts the scales in favour of moving camp.

Fact

Before your trip

Be aware that Hwy 66, from Elbow Falls to the trailhead, is closed December 1 through May 15.

By Vehicle

Follow the directions for Forgetmenot Ridge (Trip 50) to the end of Hwy 66, about an hour SW of Calgary. Park just beyond the Elbow River campground entrance, in the small pullout on the right, at 33 km (20.5 mi), 1610 m (5280 ft). If the pullout is full, return to the spacious lot just outside the campground entrance.

By Bike

Follow the directions for Talus Lake (Trip 37). Turn right (N) onto the Mt. Romulus backcountry campground's second entrance road, at 1817 m (5960 ft). In two minutes, immediately before entering the campground, reach a four-way junction. Ahead (N) are the campsites. Right (E) is the first entrance road. Left (W) is the road you'll hike to Paradise Pass after stashing your bike. It quickly crosses the South Fork Little Elbow River, then leads SW, up the West Fork valley.

On Foot

From the four-way junction immediately S of Mt. Romulus backcountry campground, take the road leading W. In a couple minutes, either ford the **South Fork Little Elbow River** or cross it on a footlog. Follow the road SW, ascending steeply through a corridor of trees.

You're entering the **West Fork Little Elbow River valley**. In about 15 minutes, where the road crests, pause before descending. Look W. You'll see where the route to Paradise Pass climbs right (NW) behind a massive ridge. That's also where the main West Fork valley (Trip 39) veers S to Piper Pass.

Continue generally SW on the road. The valley's towering cliff walls are frequently visible. At 1820 m (5970 ft), about 20 minutes along, the road intersects the **river**. Don't ford. Instead, look left. You'll find a trail traverses the steep forest above the S bank, allowing you to bypass not only the first ford but a second one just upstream. In a couple minutes, drop back to the road, bear left, and resume up-valley.

At 1878 m (6160 ft), after hiking about an hour, reach a broad, rocky **channel**. It's probably shallow, possibly dry. Hike in it, angling left. Resume on the road a couple minutes upstream.

Ascend to a minor **fork** at about 1¼ hours. Ignore the overgrown bench (left). Bear right, descend toward the river, then turn left (upstream). Hike through the rough, washed-out **gully** to regain the trail just ahead.

Within another five minutes, the road passes a **campsite** on the left and intersects the river. Either ford or rockhop to proceed SW.

About seven minutes farther, reach a cairn in a **tiny clearing** at 1933 m (6340 ft). The overgrown road ends here. You've hiked 4.7 km (2.9 mi) from Mt. Romulus campground.

About 15 paces beyond the cairn, the **Paradise Pass trail** forks right (NW). The West Fork Little Elbow trail veers left, immediately crosses a creek, then leads S to Piper Pass.

The Paradise Pass trail soon splits. Right is easier. The paths rejoin shortly. A steep ascent on slippery dirt grants a superb view S, up the West Fork.

At a moderate grade, the trail leads W, then NW. At 2064 m (6770 ft), about 20 minutes from the road's end cairn, the grade eases on grassy, bushy, subalpine slopes.

About 35 minutes up, drop into a willowy draw with a creeklet. Then stay left on the main trail. Descend through tight trees to a reliable **creek** at 2159 m (7080 ft). It's a steep, slippery ascent out. The trail begins switchbacking in meadows. You'll see willow-herb, yarrow (fern-like leaves), and stands of krummholz (stunted trees).

At 2257 m (7403 ft), about an hour up, the trail curves N on a grassy ridge. Mounts Hood and Packenham punctuate the Opal Range, left (W). Proceed along the edge of a small but impressive stream gorge. Arrive in **Paradise Basin**.

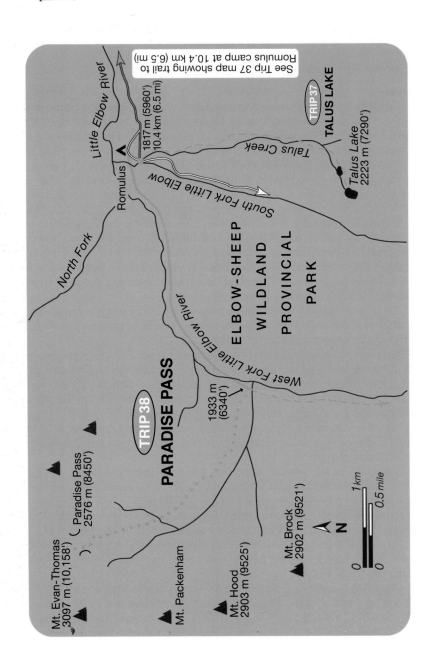

See Trip 37 map showing trail to
Romulus camp at 10.4 km (6.5 mi)

TALUS LAKE

TRIP 37

Talus Lake
2223 m (7290')

Talus Creek

Little Elbow River

Romulus

North Fork

1817 m (5960')
10.4 km (6.5 mi)

South Fork Little Elbow

ELBOW-SHEEP
WILDLAND
PROVINCIAL
PARK

West Fork Little Elbow River

TRIP 38

PARADISE PASS

1933 m
(6340')

Paradise Pass
2576 m (8450')

Mt. Evan-Thomas
3097 m (10,158')

Mt. Packenham

Mt. Hood
2903 m (9525')

Mt. Brock
2902 m (9521')

N

0   1 km
0   0.5 mile

Continue N across grassy meadow for 10 to 15 minutes before ascending the final scree slope to the pass. Right (E) is a cirque beneath the striking peaks of The Ripsaw—unlabeled on most maps.

Reach 2576-m (8450-ft) **Paradise Pass** about 1½ hours from the road's end cairn. You've hiked 8.7 km (5.4 mi) from Mt. Romulus campground.

WNW of the pass is 3097-m (10,158-ft) Mt. Evan-Thomas. N of it, the Opals diminish to a grassy ridge. NW, below the pass, is forested Evan Thomas Lake. Looking SSW, down the E wall of the Opal Range, you can see through Piper Pass (Trips 27 and 39) to Rae Glacier on Mt. Rae.

scarlet gilia

TRIP 39
West Fork Little Elbow River

LOCATION	Elbow-Sheep Wildland Provincial Park
	Hwy 66, SW of Bragg Creek
ROUND TRIP	20.8 km (13 mi) cycling, plus 22 km (13.6 mi) hiking
ELEVATION GAIN	207 m (680 ft) cycling, plus 990 m (3247 ft) hiking
KEY ELEVATIONS	trailhead 1610 m (5280 ft), Piper Pass 2580 m (8462 ft)
TRAVEL TIME	2½ hours cycling, plus 8 to 9 hours hiking
DIFFICULTY	moderate
MAPS	Gem Trek *Bragg Creek and Elbow Falls*
	Gem Trek *Kananaskis Lakes*

Opinion

The farther out on a limb you go, the more exhilarating it feels coming back in. And Piper Pass via the West Fork Little Elbow River valley is definitely way out there. It's a positively Homeric journey if you pull it off in a single day. Mostly because of the marathon distance. But also because the sketchy route probing the upper West Fork valley requires navigational competence. And because the final ascent to the pass demands that you climb like a yak on a headwall so steep and rocky that even a yak would balk. You're swift as a Yeti pursued by photographers? A daytrip is possible. Start early on a bombproof-blue mid-summer day. Pack your headlamp in case of a late return. You'll be thrilled by the scenery, elated by the accomplishment. You're a mere mortal hiker? Keep reading. There are advantages, in addition to common sense, for making this a multi-day adventure.

The journey begins with a scenically motivating, 1½-hour bike ride on a rocky, undulating, old road. You'll tether your two-wheeled pony at Mt. Romulus backcountry campground. For peace of mind, secure it to a tree using a cable and lock. You'll likely want to wear a helmet, cycling shorts, gloves, and perhaps cycling shoes. Stash those along with your bike.

Then begin hiking. You'll still be on an old road, but one succumbing to entropy. Often narrow and overgrown, it feels more like a wide trail. Besides, it offers frequent views of the beautiful, cliff-sided, mountain valley you're piercing. So you won't grumble about what's underfoot.

From road's end, you'll veer into the secluded, upper West Fork valley. In the shadow of the worship-worthy Opal Range, an undeveloped trail glides across meadows, fades while climbing through subalpine forest, then zings into the alpine zone. Here the terrain turns feral, all but bearing its teeth. Steep grassy slopes give way to a riot of rock. The valley's upper reaches could have been dynamited from the constricting walls. Novices unnerved by this chaotic basin and the headwall's terrifying, vertical

The Opal Range and West Fork Little Elbow River Valley

appearance should turn back at the tarn, justifiably proud of their achievement. Pushing onward and upward calls for strength and confidence. It's not even a scramble, but the severe grade keeps the scree and talus unsteady. Experienced mountain freaks will revel in the challenge.

Piper Pass is a lonely, scenic perch among lofty, jagged peaks. It affords stirring views north and south. You'll see the trail continuing through Piper Creek basin, into Piper Creek canyon (Trip 27). Having previously attained Piper Pass via that southern approach should not discourage you from returning from the north, via the West Fork valley. Only atop the pass will the scenery be familiar. If traversing the pass on a backpack circuit appeals to you, read *Opinion* paragraphs six and seven in Trip 27.

Before coming solely to explore the West Fork Little Elbow River valley, consider that two other trips in this book—Paradise Pass (Trip 38), and Talus Lake (Trip 37)—entail cycling to Mt. Romulus campground. If you can muster three days, bring your tent and establish a basecamp at Romulus. Devote day one to Talus Lake, the shortest of the three excursions. On day two, trek all the way to Piper Pass via the West Fork Little Elbow. On day three, hike to Paradise Pass, then saddle up and ride out.

Another option is repacking on the morning of day two and moving your camp 5 km (3.1 mi) farther southwest, into the West Fork valley, just past where the West Fork and Paradise Pass trails split. That will save you from repeating the 9.4-km (5.8-mi) round trip between Mt. Romulus campground and the trail split. Hiking that in-and-out stretch only once, however, requires you to do it bearing a full load, rather than twice with just a daypack. A lonelier, more scenic campsite up the West Fork valley on night two tilts the scales in favour of moving camp.

Fact

Before your trip
Be aware that Hwy 66, from Elbow Falls to the trailhead, is closed December 1 through May 15.

By Vehicle
Follow the directions for Forgetmenot Ridge (Trip 50) to the end of Hwy 66, about an hour SW of Calgary. Park just beyond the Elbow River campground entrance, in the small pullout on the right, at 33 km (20.5 mi), 1610 m (5280 ft). If the pullout is full, return to the spacious lot just outside the campground entrance.

By Bike
Follow the directions for Talus Lake (Trip 37). Turn right (N) onto the Mt. Romulus backcountry campground's second entrance road, at 1817 m (5960 ft). In two minutes, immediately before entering the campground, reach a four-way junction. Ahead (N) are the campsites. Right (E) is the first entrance road. Left (W) is the road you'll hike up the West Fork Little Elbow River valley after stashing your bike. It quickly crosses the South Fork Little Elbow River, then leads SW.

West Fork Little Elbow River Valley.
Piper Pass is the lowpoint on the skyline.

On Foot

Follow the directions for Paradise Pass (Trip 38). In about 1½ hours, reach a cairn in a **tiny clearing** at 1933 m (6340 ft). The overgrown road ends here. You've hiked 4.7 km (2.9 mi) from Mt. Romulus campground.

About 15 paces beyond the cairn, the trail to Paradise Pass forks right (NW). For Piper Pass, turn left (SW) and immediately hop over a creek.

Proceed on a **trail** that's distinct but narrow due to encroaching tree branches. It leads S through forest and is relatively level. About 20 minutes from the road's end cairn, arrive at a spacious meadow granting a view S into the upper West Fork valley, nearly to its end. The Opal Range forms the valley's right (W) wall. The N ridge of Tombstone Mtn forms the left (E) wall.

Ahead is the **West Fork Little Elbow River**—actually a stream at this point. The trail, mucky in places, proceeds S, following the river upstream, into and across the meadow. Expect to hop the river a couple times.

Approaching the S end of the meadow, note when the trail re-enters **forest**. About seven minutes farther, you'll encounter a **fork**. Proceed left (SSE). Right (SW) soon ends in a rocky wash-out among the trees.

The trail, having dwindled to a **route**, soon begins climbing. Where the grade steepens dramatically, and the route all but disappears, abandon it. Do not traverse south for long. Ascend east among the trees. Soon reach the edge of a steep-walled **ravine**—about 45 minutes from the last fork.

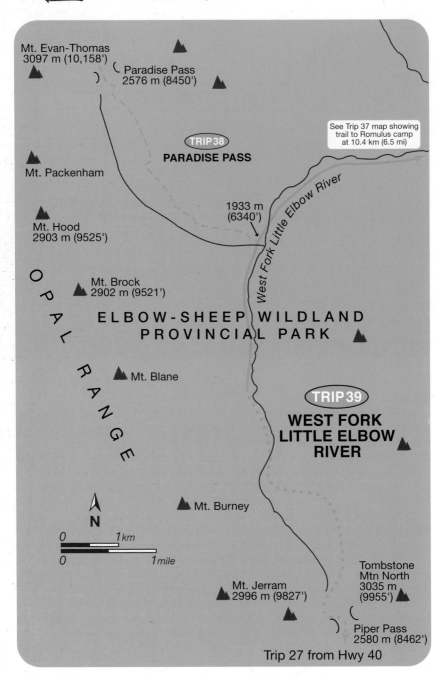

Mt. Evan-Thomas
3097 m (10,158')

Paradise Pass
2576 m (8450')

See Trip 37 map showing
trail to Romulus camp
at 10.4 km (6.5 mi)

TRIP 38
PARADISE PASS

Mt. Packenham

1933 m
(6340')

West Fork Little Elbow River

Mt. Hood
2903 m (9525')

Mt. Brock
2902 m (9521')

O P A L   R A N G E

E L B O W - S H E E P   W I L D L A N D
P R O V I N C I A L   P A R K

Mt. Blane

TRIP 39
**WEST FORK
LITTLE ELBOW
RIVER**

N

Mt. Burney

0   1 km
0   1 mile

Mt. Jerram
2996 m (9827')

Tombstone
Mtn North
3035 m
(9955')

Piper Pass
2580 m (8462')

Trip 27 from Hwy 40

photos: *1 Approaching West Fork Little Elbow River Valley 2 White camas 3 Piper Pass*

1

2

3

Continue SE along the edge of the ravine, into the **alpine zone**. Grass soon gives way to rock, so take a break here and appreciate your accomplishment. Piper Pass, visible S, is now clearly within reach yet still appears insurmountably steep.

Resume by contouring S into the **barren basin**. Skirt a **tarn**. Approach the **headwall**. You've now hiked about 2½ hours from the road's end cairn.

The **final ascent route**, created and maintained by animals, is rarely trod by humans. It's perceptible, but arduously steep and rough, on loose, awkward talus and scree. It climbs through charcoal-coloured rock, then cream, then chocolate.

Begin toiling upward on the far right (W) side of the upper basin. Ascend generally S, then angle left (SE). Crest 2580-m (8462-ft) **Piper Pass** at the low edge of the chocolate rock, 11 km (6.8 mi) from Mt. Romulus campground.

The pass is flanked by 3035-m (9955-ft) Tombstone Mtn (left / NE), and 2996-m (9827-ft) Mt. Jerram (right / WNW). SSE, on the horizon, is 3218-m (10,558-ft) Mt. Rae and its tiny glacier. The S approach to Piper Pass (Trip 27) is via Piper Creek canyon. The upper reaches of that trail are visible below, in Piper Creek basin.

photos page 207: *1 Wasootch Ridge (Trip 46)* *2 Jumpingpound Ridge (Trip 48)* *3 Old Baldy Ridge (Trip 47)*

Fairholme Range, from Canmore

Shoulder-Season Trips

TRIP 40
Grotto Canyon

LOCATION	Bow Valley Wildland Provincial Park
	Hwy 1A, ESE of Canmore
ROUND TRIP	4 km (2.5 mi) to 7 km (4.3 mi)
ELEVATION GAIN	100 m (328 ft) to 235 m (771 ft)
KEY ELEVATIONS	trailhead 1300 m (4264 ft)
	canyon forks 1395 m (4576 ft)
	canyon forested beyond 1535 m (5035 ft)
HIKING TIME	2 to 3 hours
DIFFICULTY	easy to moderate
MAP	Gem Trek *Best of Canmore*

Opinion

The difference between ascending a mountain and probing a canyon is the difference between the ego and the id: mountains talk, canyons listen.

Mountains are the earth's extroverts. Canyons are their opposite, the introverts. Each elicits a hiking experience that mirrors the topography. Attaining a summit is celebratory. "Wahoo!" you say, "We made it!" Standing in the depths of a canyon is meditative. "Whoa" you whisper, "This is cool."

That's not to say canyons aren't fun. They are. The fun is simply less exuberant, more cerebral. Besides, due to their lower elevations, canyon floors allow snow-and-ice-free hiking earlier in spring and later in fall than do mountain trails.

So, in you go, rather than up. An ideal place to do it is Grotto Canyon, southeast of Canmore.

Bring the whole family to investigate this deep, narrow gash in the front range. The canyon is so skinny, it stirs children's desire to peek around the next bend. They imagine themselves on a journey into the bowels of the earth.

Grotto Creek—usually a mere trickle—provides gentle, soothing water music. Climbers are fond of the canyon's sheer, solid walls and will likely divert your attention for a few minutes. But if you look closely, you'll see something more interesting: a pictograph panel created 1,000 years ago by a Native artist.

With little ones in tow, turn around where the canyon forks, about 40 minutes from the trailhead. This steep-sided sanctum is an arresting natural cathedral that compels people to speak in hushed, respectful tones.

The narrows end just past the fork. Hikers who've come for exertion and exploration can ramble and rock-hop another 4 km (2.5 mi) up the canyon's broader, boulder-strewn west fork, where the creek is usually dry.

photos: *1 Grotto Canyon 2 & 3 1,000-year-old rock art in Grotto Canyon*

Fact

By Vehicle

From **Calgary**, drive E on Hwy 1. About 8 km (5 mi) after passing Deadman's Flats, take the Hwy 1A exit for Canmore. At the stop sign, turn left onto Bow Valley Trail (Hwy 1A). Shortly beyond, where Elk Run Blvd forks left, reset your trip odometer to 0 and proceed straight on Bow Valley Trail (Hwy 1A).

From downtown **Canmore**, drive E on Main (8th) Street. At the T-junction (traffic lights), turn right onto Railway Ave. Follow it across the train tracks and through the intersection (traffic lights) with Bow Valley Trail. You're now on Benchlands Trail. Cross over Hwy 1. After a long ascent, fork right, onto Elk Run Blvd. Immediately cross the bridge over Cougar Creek. Proceed S on Elk Run Blvd to the T-junction with Bow Valley Trail (Hwy 1A). Reset your trip odometer to 0 and turn left onto Bow Valley Trail (Hwy 1A).

From **either approach**, at 9.8 km (6.1 mi) turn left into the Grotto Pond picnic-area parking lot. Elevation 1300 m (4264 ft).

On Foot

The signed Grotto Creek trail departs the W side of the parking lot. Follow it generally SW. Wherever confusion is possible, directional signs keep you on course. Soon pass the **Baymag plant**, which produces magnesium-oxide.

At 1 km (0.6 mi), having hiked about 15 minutes, the mouth of Grotto Canyon is visible ahead. There's a **bench** on the left here, atop a mound that affords a surprisingly good view of the Bow Valley.

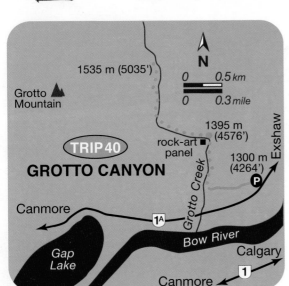

1535 m (5035')

Grotto Mountain

N

0 ———— 0.5 km

0 ———— 0.3 mile

1395 m (4576')

rock-art panel

Grotto Creek

Exshaw

1300 m (4264')

TRIP 40

GROTTO CANYON

Canmore

1A

Bow River

Gap Lake

Calgary

Canmore

1

Pigeon Mountain is visible SSE. Right of it (SSW) is enormous Mt. Lougheed. West Wind Pass (Trip 4) is the prominent gap SW. Right of the pass are the Three Sisters (Trip 1), with Little Sister in front.

Immediately below the bench, curve right (N). Ignore the hiker sign and the trail ascending left (WNW) beyond it. Enter the **canyon mouth**. Simply follow the rocky creek-bed N. Noise from the Baymag plant is now inaudible.

About 25 minutes from the trailhead, the **canyon narrows** and the walls steepen. Grotto Canyon is popular with sport climbers. You'll likely see them. If not, you can see the routes they climb by looking for the bolts they've drilled into the rock.

Where the creekbed curves around a wall jutting out from the left—about 35 minutes from the trailhead—stop. On that wall is a **rock-art panel** created by Natives about 1,000 years ago. The pictographs were painted in red ochre. They're 1.67 m (5.5 ft) above the canyon floor. They cover a space of about 1 m (3.3 ft) high by 1.5 m (4.9 ft) wide. Close examination will reveal a string of five warriors, a buffalo, a horned figure, and a canoe.

Just three minutes past the rock art, the **canyon forks**. The elevation here is 1395 m (4576 ft). You're now about 40 minutes from the trailhead. The right fork is impassable to hikers due to a cliff graced with a small cascade. But the left (W) fork beckons. Carry on.

The canyon remains narrow for only a short distance. The creekbed, strewn with larger boulders, becomes rougher. Continue at least ten minutes to where the **canyon broadens** and the view expands. You can peer into the canyon's upper reaches and admire the craggy ridges of Grotto Mountain above the left (SW) wall. Soon pass several **hoodoos** (pillars formed when the surrounding earth eroded away).

Stretches of discernible route, bootbeaten into the rock-and-gravel creek banks, occasionally allow comfortably striding. But up-canyon progress often requires you to boulder-hop back and forth across the deepening creekbed. At least the elevation gain is insignificant.

At 3 km (1.9 mi), 1535 m (5035 ft)—about 45 minutes from the fork, or 1½ hours from the trailhead—even ambitious hikers might want to turn around. The **canyon is forested** from here on, so views diminish and bushwhacking is necessary.

TRIP 41

Mt. Yamnuska

LOCATION	Bow Valley Wildland Provincial Park NW of where Hwy 40 departs Hwy 1
DISTANCE	7-km (4.3-mi) round trip to NE ridge 9.8-km (6.1-mi) circuit across summit
ELEVATION GAIN	515 m (1689 ft) to NE ridge 875 m (2870 ft) to summit
KEY ELEVATIONS	trailhead 1365 m (4477 ft), NE ridge 1880 m (6166 ft) summit 2240 m (7347 ft)
HIKING TIME	2-hour round trip to NE ridge 5-hour circuit across summit
DIFFICULTY	easy to ridge, challenging to summit
MAP	Gem Trek *Canmore & Kananaskis Village*

Opinion

"I have a surprise for you," the Earth says.

She said that to us every time we glanced at Mt. Yamnuska while driving Hwy 1 east of Canmore. But we weren't listening. We ignored the mountain for years.

"Yam," as it's locally known, is on the prairie's edge, a mere 48-minute drive from northwest Calgary. It's a minor peak that, when viewed from a distance, is dwarfed by the main range of the Rockies.

Geopolitically, this little crag is of no significance. Three-quarters of it, including the summit, are outside the protection of any park boundaries.

But Yam is among Alberta's most popular hiking and climbing destinations. On many weekends the carpark is full, and people are clambering all over the mountain, assailing it from every angle.

Yam's popularity was a key reason Kathy and I avoided it. We assumed it would be too crowded to be enjoyable.

Surprise #1: It's bigger than it looks from the highway—big enough that, the first time we hiked Yam, we didn't realize there was a busload of kids up there until we returned to the trailhead.

Yam's proximity to the highway was another reason we shunned it. We figured the traffic noise would be annoying.

Surprise #2: It's farther from the highway than it appears. Despite Kathy's super-hero auditory powers, she was unperturbed by the highway.

We also kept blowing off Yam because we rarely climb. Yam's reputation flourishes among climbers. Its sheer southeast face gives the impression that if you're not on a rope there's little to explore.

Surprise #3: Every aspect of the mountain is fascinating, from its forested lower skirts, to its hidden, northwest slopes. It offers scenically rewarding shoulder-season hiking for all: stumblers, striders, and scramblers.

Diversity makes anyplace more intriguing—city or forest. Here, the trail pierces a lively mix of pine, aspen, and stout fir. And the airy canopy is wildflower-friendly. Magenta-and-yellow shooting stars, lavender clematis, and purple violets are among the blossoms you'll likely see here in early summer.

Without overtaxing winter-wilted muscles, the trail quickly lofts you to views of Nakoda Lodge on Chief Hector Lake, and the big mountains stretching from Canmore into Kananaskis Country. Eventually it crests Yam's northeast ridge, overlooking a lonely valley ringed by husky peaks.

Most people stop there, break out their tuna sandwiches and Kettle Chips, appreciate the lofty perch, then head home gratified. Strong, experienced hikers (and a few unsuspecting naifs wearing tennis shoes) proceed to the summit.

Though 80% of the remaining journey is on a distinct trail, 18% is merely a route, and 2% entails scrambling. In one place, a fixed cable aids your passage across a cliff. The next horizontal 50 m (55 yd) require you to mountain-goat it along narrow, exposed ledges. Beyond that, you'll simply be hiking steep terrain.

You're confident? Don't stop on the northeast ridge. The summit panorama is spectacular. From there, you can descend Yam's southwest slope, traverse beneath the southeast face, enjoy an exuberant glissade (sliding descent) on a long scree slope, and complete a circuit.

But if you continue, stay safe. Trust the wise voice within. If you feel deeply hesitant, turn back. Don't push beyond your comfort zone. The surprises along the Mt. Yamnuska circuit will wait until you're ready for them.

Fact

By Vehicle

From **Calgary**, drive W on Hwy 1. Take exit 114, signed for Bow Valley Provincial Park and Exshaw. Proceed N on Hwy 1X.

From **Canmore**, drive E on Hwy 1. Take exit 114, signed for Bow Valley Provincial Park and Exshaw. Turn left at the stop sign, cross over Hwy 1, and proceed N on Hwy 1X.

From **either approach**, soon cross the bridge over the Bow River. Hwy 1X then bends left (W) to intersect Hwy 1A. Turn right (N) onto Hwy 1A and in 2 km (1.2 mi) turn left (NW) onto the unpaved road signed for Yamnuska. Enter the trailhead parking lot 300 m (328 yd) farther. Elevation: 1365 m (4477 ft).

On Foot

Depart the W end of the parking lot, beside the kiosk. The trail soon crosses a **road** and heads generally NW. Watch for shooting stars in the trailside grass.

A short ascent leads to a **signed junction** at 1 km (0.6 mi), 1465 m (4805 ft). Ahead (W) is the trail you'll return on if you hike the circuit. For now, go right (N). Look for clematis (a climbing vine) and violets among the aspen.

photos: *1 & 3 The crux, two hours from the trailhead 2 Final ascent of Mt. Yamnuska 4 & 5 Glissading down the mammoth scree slope*

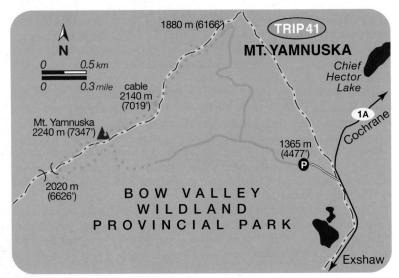

After a level respite, resume ascending. The grade eases near 1630 m (5346 ft), about 40 minutes from the trailhead. Ignore the steep left spur. Bear right (ENE) along the edge of the slope. Switchback left (W) at 1730 m (5674 ft), where a stone arrow points the way.

About an hour from the trailhead, crest Yam's **NE ridge** at 3.5 km (2.2 mi), 1880 m (6166 ft). The easy hiking ends here, above CMC (Calgary Mountain Club) Valley, but below Yam's craggy upper reaches.

Continuing? Ascend SW into the **prominent crack**. It's easier than it appears to hoist yourself through and gain a view of the terrain leading to the summit. If what you see rattles you, about face. If you're up to the challenge, you'll recognize the route without guidance. It ascends generally SW, mostly across scree and talus.

At 2140 m (7019 ft), about two hours from the trailhead, reach the crux: a **fixed cable spanning a cliff**, followed by 50 m (55 yd) of mildly exposed, horizontal scrambling on ledges. The challenge is more mental than physical. Footholds are solid throughout. Soon resume hiking.

Three hours from the trailhead, step onto the 2240-m (7347-ft) **summit** of Mt. Yamnuska at 5.5 km (3.4 mi). You'll want a topo map to identify all the peaks spanning the horizon from W to S.

The circuit (easier than reversing the ascent) poses no serious obstacles. Resume by descending SW to a 2020-m (6626-ft) **saddle** at 6.3 km (3.9 mi). Upper CMC Valley is visible right (N). Turn left (S) and continue descending.

Curve ENE. Contour across Yam's **SE face** at 1800 m (5904 ft). Pass above a short scree slope. Ten minutes farther, at 7.1 km (4.4 mi), reach a **mammoth scree slope**. Turn right (SE) and glissade down. Woo hoo!

The trees funnel you to a **trail** at 7.5 km (4.7 mi), 1670 m (5478 ft). After emptying the pebbles from your boots, go left (ESE). Pass beneath a **cascade**. At 8.8 km (5.5 mi), reach the **signed junction** where you began the circuit. Right leads ten minutes to the trailhead.

Contouring trail on southeast side of Mt. Yamnuska

TRIP 42

Grassi Lakes

LOCATION	Bow Valley Wildland Provincial Park immediately SW of Canmore
ROUND TRIP	3.8 km (2.4 mi) to lakes plus 0.2 km (0.1 mi) to rock art
ELEVATION GAIN	155 m (508 ft) to lakes, plus 25 m (82 ft) to rock art
KEY ELEVATIONS	trailhead 1430 m (4690 ft) lower Grassi Lake 1585 m (5200 ft)
HIKING TIME	1 to 3 hours
DIFFICULTY	easy
MAP	Gem Trek *Best of Canmore*

Opinion

Lawrence Grassi is one of our heroes. Some might call him a *role model*, but that would suggest they could emulate him, which is highly doubtful.

Grassi climbed the Canadian Rockies like a yak, was the first to solo Mt. Assiniboine, built the most exquisite trails in the range, accomplished herculean feats like hauling firewood up sheer scree slopes to alpine huts, and occasionally carried injured climbers down to civilization on his back. Definitely a hero.

If you ever stay at the Elizabeth Parker Hut, near Lake O'Hara in Yoho National Park, check out the cast-iron stove. It arrived there—long before a road pierced that wilderness enclave—atop Grassi's burly shoulders.

But you don't have to go that far to admire his heroics. Simply come to Canmore and hike the town's most cherished trail. Built by the great mountain man, it leads to a destination named in his honour: the Grassi Lakes.

Grassi immigrated to Canada from Italy in 1912 at the age of 22. He laboured for the Canadian Pacific Railway, then mined coal in Canmore. During a 1924 miners' strike, rather than hang out at the union hall, he engineered the trail you're now reading about. He later became a mountain guide and national-park warden.

All of Grassi's trails evince old-world craftsmanship and artistry. This one, though short and easy, passes several benches en route. It ascends gradually through forest, darts up stone stairs beside splashy cascades, and affords an aerial view of Canmore and the Bow Valley.

The Grassi Lakes—mere ponds, linked by a short stream spanned by a folkloric bridge—are cupped in a petrified coral reef. They're fed by a thermal sulphur spring through a fault line below. The gin-clear water is vibrantly tinted in shades of blue and green à la Claude Monet.

So despite their diminutive size, the twin lakes are beautiful. The setting is impressive too: a narrow gap between the soaring walls of Ha Ling Peak and Mt. Rundle. The vertical rock, riddled with holes, was dubbed *the Golf Course* by local climbers. Benches at both lakes invite you to sit and watch them defy gravity.

Above the second lake is a rock-art panel (red-ochre pictographs) created by Natives about 1,000 years ago. The paintings are faint, puzzling, except for a small, human figure—affectionately known as *Canmore Man*—holding a hoop in his raised fist.

photos: **1** *Cascades below Grassi Lakes* **2** *Grassi Lakes* **3** *Stone stairs built by Lawrence Grassi*

Fact

By Vehicle

In Canmore, drive W on Main (8th) Street. Turn left onto 8th Avenue. Follow it over the Bow River bridge. At the T-junction, turn left onto Three Sisters Drive. Ascend, soon forking right onto Smith-Dorrien / Spray Trail (Hwy 742). Pass the Canmore Nordic Centre and reset your trip odometer to 0. Pavement ends at 1.2 km (0.7 mi), but immediately before, at 1.1 km (0.7 mi), turn left onto Ken Ritchey Way (signed *No Exit*) and descend, still on pavement. At 1.6 km (1 mi) bear right into the trailhead parking lot. Elevation: 1430 m (4690 ft).

On Foot

The trail departs the right (NW) side of the parking lot, between the kiosk and the toilets. Follow it left (W), past the picnic tables. Immediately ahead is a gate preventing vehicle access; proceed beyond it.

In a couple minutes reach a **signed fork**. Ignore the labels *easy* and *difficult*. You'll gain precisely the same elevation either way. Go left (WSW) on the **trail**. It ascends sharply near the end but is very scenic. Right (WNW) is a former road—gradual the whole way but viewless.

About ten minutes up the trail, at 1510 m (4953 ft), the grade steepens. Pass the first **bench**, hop several creeklets, and attain views of the reservoir below, Canmore beyond.

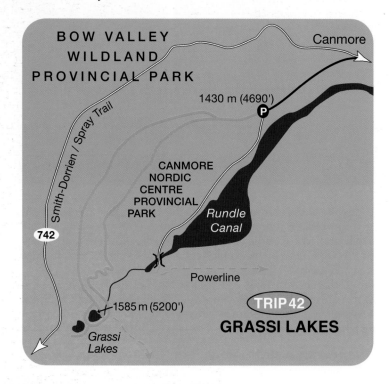

Imagine Lawrence Grassi in that bustling town, where, until just before his death in 1980, he lived in a humble, plumbing-less cabin whose only appliance was a coal-burning stove.

Reach the **first cascade overlook** about 15 minutes from the trailhead. Here the trail curves right (SW). It soon splits (right is easier) but the forks rejoin just above. Bear left (SSW) beneath a prominent outcrop. Climb the **stone stairs**.

At 1560 m (5117 ft) is another **bench and a plaque** commemorating Grassi. Visible ENE, across the Bow Valley, is Cougar Creek canyon between Mt. Lady Macdonald (left) and Grotto Mtn (right).

Pass the **third bench** at 1580 m (5182 ft). A bit farther is a **footlog** spanning the lakes' **outlet stream**, which feeds the waterfall below. Cross to the SE bank. A bedrock rib leads to a gravel clearing.

Ignore the left fork ascending SE toward a huge, silver, utility pipe. Go right (W) one minute to a **junction** near the E corner of **lower Grassi Lake**, at 1.8 km (1.1 mi), 1585 m (5200 ft). At a brisk pace, you'll arrive here within 30 minutes.

Right (NW) is the former road—an optional return route to the trailhead. For now, go left (WSW) along the lower lake's S shore. Pass yet another **bench**.

A **bridge** across the **short creek** between the lakes allows you to circle the lower lake. For now, go left around the SE shore of upper Grassi Lake. Pass one more **bench**. Sport-climbing routes festoon the surrounding walls.

Continue up the trail, generally W. **Stairs** temper the abrupt ascent. About five minutes above the upper lake, look right (N) for a **huge, trailside boulder** with a distinctly overhanging ledge. Beneath that ledge is the aforementioned Native rock art.

Grassi Lakes outlet stream

TRIP 43
Mt. Rundle, South Summit

LOCATION	Spray Valley Provincial Park, Hwy 742 W edge of Canmore
ROUND TRIP	4 km (2.5 mi) to bench, 5.2 km (3.2 mi) to summit
ELEVATION GAIN	612 m (2007 ft) to bench, 852 m (2795 ft) to summit
KEY ELEVATIONS	trailhead 1688 m (5535 ft), bench 2300 m (7544 ft) summit 2540 m (8331 ft)
HIKING TIME	3 hours for bench, 4 to 5 hours for summit
DIFFICULTY	moderate to bench, challenging to summit
MAPS	page 224; Gem Trek *Best of Canmore*

Opinion

Life: if you do it right, it's exhausting. Remember that truth when you arrive in Canmore, gaze up at the skyline-dominating wedge you're about to ascend, and your knees buckle. Because the south summit of Mt. Rundle affords a panorama and sense of achievement that more than compensate for the rigourous ascent.

The mountain's south summit is just one end of a hulking massif—so lengthy it also looms above Banff townsite. That's where the true summit is: farther north. But the south summit is an easier goal, more quickly attained, and competitively scenic.

The trail to the north summit is a viewless slog most of the way. The trail to the south summit is instantly captivating. Glimpses of big scenery quickly widen into sweeping vistas.

The immediate surroundings also vie for your attention. Multiple routes engage you in a kind of terrestrial tic-tac-toe. Loose rock on steep inclines calls for secure boot placement.

About halfway, you might wonder if the mountain ever relents. It does. Below the summit, a grassy, nearly-level bench invites you to drop your pack, relax, and gaze at the peak-studded horizon.

In summer, the bench is a flowery oasis in a stoney realm. Many people stop here, recline, nibble on lunch, devour the scenery, then descend, pleased with their accomplishment.

Resuming the ascent poses one challenge: a short burst of light scrambling through rockbands guarding the summit. Some hikers do it without using their hands, others grab rocks to steady themselves.

If you summit, you'll see distant giants, including Mt. Temple, near Lake Louise, and Mt. Assiniboine. To the south is a mountainous collage: chunky peaks pasted one on top of the next. And the aerial perspective of Canmore and the Bow Valley is engrossing.

Fact

By Vehicle

In **Canmore**, drive W on Main (8th) Street. Turn left onto 8th Avenue. Follow it over the Bow River bridge. At the T-junction, turn left onto Three Sisters Drive. Ascend, soon forking right onto Smith-Dorrien / Spray Trail (Hwy 742). Pass the Canmore Nordic Centre and reset your trip odometer to 0. Pavement ends at 1.2 km (0.7 mi). The road levels in Whiteman's Gap—a pass between Ha Ling (left / E) and the S summit of Mt. Rundle (right / N). Proceed along the W side of Whiteman's Pond. Slow down. At 5 km (3.1 mi), 1688 m (5535 ft), park in the pullout on the left (E), at the S end of the pond, in front of a rock outcrop.

From **northern K-Country**, drive N on Smith-Dorrien / Spray Trail (Hwy 742). Reset your trip odometer to 0 at the Goat Creek trailhead parking lot (left / W). Ascend N into Whiteman's Gap. At 0.4 km (0.2 mi), 1688 m (5535 ft), park in the pullout on the right (E), at the S end of Whiteman's Pond, just after a rock outcrop.

photos: *1 The Mt. Rundle trail ascends above Whiteman's Pond. 2 Mt. Rundle's south summit, from Rundle Canal, Canmore 3 Ascending to Mt. Rundle summit block*

On Foot

The trail departs the W side of the road, about 50 paces N of the pullout. It initially leads N, left of the double telephone-pole stanchion.

After veering left, begin switchbacking, ascending steeply into the trees, heading generally SW. Here on the lower reaches of the mountain, the trail is distinct and easy to follow.

Soon curve right (N). With only incidental variation, this will remain your general direction of travel until near the summit. The aggressive grade eases occasionally but only briefly.

You'll face more ambiguity the higher you go, because the trail splinters and braids. In general, bear right (closer to the sheer SE face) until you've surmounted treeline and worked your way above rocky slopes to a broad, grassy, nearly-level **bench** at 2300 m (7544 ft). Punctuated by a prominent cairn, it's just below a scattering of stunted trees. The view from here is immense.

The final push to the summit block entails light scrambling on loose rock and narrow ledges. But there's no actual exposure. It's very steep but not sheer. If you go, remember that your sense of confidence and comfort is usually an accurate measure of your safety. Should you feel anxious or hesitant, turn back.

Proceeding? Stand near the prominent cairn and look up at the summit block. You'll see a peaklet NNW. Directly below it is a **tan rockband**. Immediately below that is a **black rockband**. A route pounded into the talus will lead you there. Then angle right, between those rockbands.

You'll be above the rockbands after ten minutes of scrambling. Resume hiking on another path pummeled into the talus by previous summiteers. Crest the **summit ridge** a mere three minutes farther. Suddenly you're peering down the other side of the mountain. Bear right, clamber over a couple head-high ledges, and Mt. Rundle's 2540-m (8331-ft) **S summit** is yours.

The Bow Valley is ESE. Mt. Temple is NW, towering above Lake Louise. Mt. Assiniboine is SW. Mt. Rundle's soaring buttresses—accessible only to climbers—rake the sky NNW.

After returning to the bench, remember to bear left on the remaining descent. Hugging the sheer SE face will help you keep to the main trail.

On Mt. Rundle's summit ridge

TRIP 44
Ha Ling Peak

LOCATION	Bow Valley Wildland Provincial Park
	Hwy 742, SW of Canmore
ROUND TRIP	5.4 km (3.3 mi)
ELEVATION GAIN	741 m (2476 ft)
KEY ELEVATIONS	trailhead 1666 m (5463 ft), summit 2407 m (7897 ft)
HIKING TIME	1½ to 4 hours
DIFFICULTY	moderate
MAP	Gem Trek *Best of Canmore*

Opinion

Before Canmore shapeshifted into a luxe resort village, it was a gritty coal-mining town. Back then, residents burrowed into the mountains. Today they clamber over them: the south summit of Mt. Rundle (Trip 43), Mt. Lady Macdonald (Trip 45), Middle Sister (Trip 1), and especially Ha Ling. The trailheads are all within a ten-minute drive of Main Street. But Ha Ling—the incisor jutting skyward from Canmore's southwest corner—is the most clambered over of the bunch, because it's the least arduous ascent.

Local outdoor athletes train here, bounding up to the summit in 50 minutes or less, careening back down in under 30. Those figures, however, attest only to the vigour of Canmore's elite, not to the ease of this hike. The Ha Ling trail begins switchbacking steeply through forest, then surges past treeline onto very steep talus and scree, where it fades to a route. Imagine a mix of ball bearings, marbles, and billiard balls on a 45° incline. Bring your trekking poles for added purchase on the way up, extra shock absorption on the way down, and more stability throughout.

How long will it take you to get up and down Ha Ling? That depends on your experience and ability. A woman we know who's retired, rarely hikes, and suffers from asthma, was keen to summit this striking mountain that she gazes up at every day from her Canmore home. Neighbours who are strong hikers offered to guide her. It took four hours up, but she made it. On top, deeply moved by the tremendous panorama and the thrill of accomplishment, she wept.

Allow yourself at least 45 minutes on the summit, to peer at Canmore far below and stare at the Canadian Rockies in every direction. And step cautiously up there. The crest of the mountain ends abruptly at the sheer northeast face.

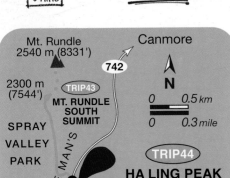

Fact

By Vehicle

In **Canmore**, drive W on Main (8th) Street. Turn left onto 8th Avenue. Follow it over the Bow River bridge. At the T-junction, turn left onto Three Sisters Drive. Ascend, soon forking right onto Smith-Dorrien / Spray Trail (Hwy 742). Pass the Canmore Nordic Centre and reset your trip odometer to 0. Pavement ends at 1.2 km (0.7 mi). The road levels in Whiteman's Gap—a pass between Ha Ling (left / E) and the S summit of Mt. Rundle (right / N). Proceed along the W side of Whiteman's Pond. The road then descends S. At 5.4 km (3.4 mi), where the road is again level, turn right (W) into the Goat Creek trailhead parking lot. Elevation: 1666 m (5463 ft).

On Foot

From the Goat Creek trailhead parking lot, go left (N) about 80 paces on Hwy 742. Turn right onto the gated service road and ascend S. At the top of the hill, cross the **bridged canal**. The easy-to-follow trail starts behind the **shed**, initially ascending SE into forest. Switchbacks lead generally ENE. After gaining 400 m (1312 ft) in about 20 to 30 minutes, you'll see the Goat Range (SW) through thinning forest.

At 2.3 km (1.4 mi), 2275 m (7462 ft), you're near treeline, just below the col between Ha Ling Peak (left / N) and 2444-m (8016-ft) Miners Peak (ahead / ESE). Consider detouring to Miners Peak on the return. For now, follow the route steeply left (N). It zigzags through talus on this final pitch to your now visible goal.

Reach Ha Ling's **summit** cairn at 2.7 km (1.7 mi), 2407 m (7897 ft). The entire route to the S summit of Mt. Rundle (Trip 43) is visible NW. Left of and beyond Rundle is Mt. Temple—distant but recognizable. The Goat Range is SW. Canmore sprawls below you (NE) in the Bow Valley. The Fairholme Range, walling in the valley's far side, is cleaved by Cougar Creek canyon. Mt. Lady Macdonald (Trip 45) is left (N) of the canyon, Grotto Mtn is right (S).

photos: *1 Canmore and Fairholme Range, from Ha Ling summit ridge 2 Ha Ling, from Quarry Lake, Canmore 3 Topping out on Ha Ling*

TRIP 45
Mt. Lady Macdonald

LOCATION	Bow Valley Wildland Provincial Park NE of Canmore
ROUND TRIP	6.6 km (4.1 mi) to shoulder 7.6 km (4.7 mi) to summit ridge
ELEVATION GAIN	917 m (3008 ft) to shoulder 1117 m (3664 ft) to summit ridge
KEY ELEVATIONS	trailhead 1383 m (4535 ft) shoulder 2300 m (7544 ft) summit ridge 2500 m (8200 ft)
HIKING TIME	4½ to 7 hours for shoulder 5½ to 8 hours for summit ridge
DIFFICULTY	moderate
MAP	Gem Trek *Best of Canmore*

Opinion

True Canadians love a snow-laden winter and all the sliding, gliding sports it allows. But come March, even the hardiest of us are sick of slush and ice and long to walk the earth again. In Canmore, we're tantalized, even tormented, by the sight of Mt. Lady Macdonald, whose sun-blasted southwest slope turns brown and advertises "spring!" long before winter has actually lost its grip on the Bow Valley. And year after year we're teased into charging up Lady Mac too soon, only to discover the trail's upper half remains thickly glazed and slick as a salesman. But the mountain usually sheds its frozen patina by April, so it's still among the earliest available shoulder-season hikes in this book, as well as one of the most challenging and rewarding.

Sticklers know Lady Mac is in the Fairholme Range, well outside even the loosest definition of K-Country. It's in this book nevertheless, because northeast Canmore is fastened like a barnacle to Lady Mac's lower slopes; the hike is immensely popular with locals as well as visitors; and the mountain is just across the valley from Mt. Rundle (Trip 43), Ha Ling Peak (Trip 44), Three Sisters Pass (Trip 3), Middle Sister (Trip 1), and West Wind Pass (Trip 4), all of which can legitimately claim to be K-Country residents.

It's ironic that Lady Mac's early availability is due in part to its steep incline. While it gives the entire slope good sun exposure, and causes snowmelt to run off rather than pool, it makes this an excruciating first hike of the season for anyone whose fitness level has slipped over the winter. Expect a muscle-straining ascent and joint-pounding descent. The lady is merciless. She'll generously reward you, however, with inspiring views. Within 30 minutes you'll overlook Cougar Creek canyon and survey much of the Bow Valley and its west-wall peaks. Chief among them is Mt.

Ascending Mt. Lady Macdonald.
Mt. Rundle is across the Bow Valley.

Rundle—a fantastically crenulated, fortress-like mountain stretching all the way from Canmore to Banff townsite. It's an awesome spectacle, especially from the aerial vantage of Lady Mac.

Though you can abandon the ascent midway up and feel compensated for your effort, try to reach level ground atop Lady Mac's 2300-m (7544-ft) south shoulder. It's a 2½-hour dash if you're swift, a 3½ hour plod if you're slow. Here, at 3.3 km (2 mi), you can lounge on the wooden platform intended to serve as a helipad for an aborted tourism venture. Nearby is the foundation for what would have been a teahouse unless Canmorites had said "no way!" Imagine helicopter flights constantly shuttling tourists between downtown and Lady Mac. The noise would have persecuted residents below. And the crowds would have been a pox on the mountain. What remains of the absurd teahouse is still a blight, but think of it as an encouraging symbol: sanity does occasionally prevail over destructive development.

The trail ends on the shoulder, so most hikers turn back there. But an obvious route, bootbeaten into the scree, continues beyond. It climbs 200 m (656 ft) in 0.5 km (0.3 mi) to Lady Mac's summit ridge. If you want more exercise, a heightened sense of adventure, and a bit better panorama, go for it. From the ridgecrest, you'll see the summit of Lady Mac farther north, at the end of a long, alarmingly sheer arête. Unless you're a fearless, black-belt scrambler, spare yourself the risk.

Before setting out for Lady Mac, fully hydrate yourself and pack a couple litres of water per person. It can get hot up there, you'll be working hard, and you'll encounter no water other than perhaps trickling snowmelt.

Wondering about the peak's aristocratic moniker? It was named in honour of Lady Susan Macdonald, wife of Canada's first prime minister, Sir John Macdonald. While iconoclasts rightfully resent the tradition of proffering mountains as tokens and demeaning them with irrational names

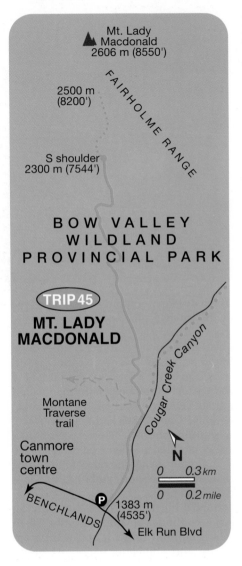

Mt. Lady
Macdonald
2606 m (8550')

2500 m
(8200')

FAIRHOLME RANGE

S shoulder
2300 m (7544')

BOW VALLEY
WILDLAND
PROVINCIAL PARK

TRIP 45
MT. LADY
MACDONALD

Cougar Creek Canyon

Montane
Traverse
trail

Canmore
town
centre

N

0   0.3 km
0   0.2 mile

BENCHLANDS

P   1383 m
(4535')

Elk Run Blvd

that serve only to feed politicians' voracious egos, at least Lady Susan showed some enthusiasm for the Canadian Rockies. While traveling by train from Lake Louise to Golden via Kicking Horse Canyon, she rode—despite Sir John's adamant objection—in front of the locomotive, on the cow catcher, so she could better appreciate the stirring scenery.

Fact

By Vehicle

From **Calgary**, drive W on Trans-Canada Hwy 1. Take Exit 91, signed for Canmore and Hwy 1A. After curving to the stop sign, set your trip odometer to 0, and turn left (E) onto Bow Valley Trail / Hwy 1A. At 0.5 km (0.3 mi), turn left (N) onto Elk Run Blvd. Proceed uphill. At 1.8 km (1.1 mi), immediately after crossing the bridge over Cougar Creek, turn right into the paved parking lot, at 1383 m (4535 ft).

From **Canmore**, at the intersection of Railway Avenue and Bow Valley Trail, drive NE over the Trans-Canada Hwy. Proceed uphill on Benchlands Trail into east Canmore. It curves right (SE). Pass the store and café at Cougar Crossing, on the right. Just beyond, where the road forks near the eagle sculpture, bear right (S) onto Elk Run Blvd. Then immediately turn left into the paved parking lot. It's just before the bridge over Cougar Creek, at 1383 m (4535 ft).

On Foot

Follow the paved path NNE, between fenced backyards (left) and the deep Cougar Creek drainage (right). The creek is usually dry here, except for a brief, spring flood.

The shoulder of Mt. Lady Macdonald (upper center), just below the summit

Pavement soon ends. Proceed on smooth, packed dirt, then a broad, rocky path. Mt. Lady Macdonald is visible directly ahead (N). Grotto Mtn is E, beyond the creek.

Reach a signed junction within seven minutes. The Montane Traverse trail forks left (NW) into forest. Continue straight (NNE) along the creek. One minute farther, go left onto an unsigned trail. Two minutes farther, reach a signed junction at 1.1 km (0.6 mi). Right follows the creek upstream (NE). Go left (N) onto the Lady Macdonald trail and ascend out of the canyon.

About 20 minutes from the trailhead, ignore a faint left fork. Bear right. Ignore other sketchy spurs ahead. Keep to the obvious main trail, which ascends generally N.

At 1555 m (5100 ft), you can gaze out of the pine-and-fir forest, across the Bow Valley. Ha Ling Peak (Trip 44) is SW. Mt. Rundle (Trip 43) is W. Cascade Mtn is NW. A bit higher, you can appreciate the Three Sisters (Trip 1) to the S, and Mt. Lougheed SSE. After hiking 25 minutes from the trailhead, attain a view ENE deep into Cougar Creek canyon.

The forest is gradually opening. At 1848 m (6060 ft) pass an inviting **stone bench** that seats three. The trail proceeds along the edge of the slope, ascends a rockslide, then switchbacks up through boulders before briefly re-entering forest. At a chaotic **boulder pile**, the way forward is less evident. Slow down, look for cairns, and notice where hikers' boots have left dirt prints on the rock surfaces.

Trail soon resumes, with a short steep pitch leading to a sharp, **revelatory bend** at 2114 m (6934 ft). Mt. Lady Macdonald's summit ridge, and the level shoulder just below it, are now visible ahead (N). The view also extends NW, across the mountain's SW face, and up the Bow Valley.

After a tight switchback, you might find the trail is again, momentarily, hard to discern. Stay left, out on the edge of the slope, then ascend through a couple, huge boulders to where obvious tread resumes. Traverse right (WSW) back toward the mountain's S side. The trail climbs gradually, then vaults steeply to the brink of a precipitous slope that plunges into Cougar Creek canyon. Turn left (N) here for the final approach.

Reach level ground atop the mountain's **S shoulder** at 3.3 km (2 mi), 2300 m (7544 ft). Strong hikers will be here 2½ hours after departing the trailhead and will complete the descent in 2 hours. Slow hikers will arrive in 3½ hours and will take nearly as long to descend.

The shoulder bears two structures. One is the foundation of a teahouse abandoned long before completion. Nearby is a spacious wooden platform that would have been the helipad for teahouse-bound passengers but now serves a more exalted purpose: comfortable sprawl space for hikers in need of a rest.

In addition to the nearby landmark mountains previously mentioned, many more are visible from the shoulder of Mt. Lady Macdonald. The western horizon reveals Banff National Park's peak-studded southern reaches.

Pushing on to the summit ridge? Though only 0.5 km (0.3 mi) farther, it's 200 m (656 ft) higher, so it's a significant slog. But the route, as well as the ridgecrest, are visible from the shoulder. It poses no obstacle other than steepness. Allow perhaps another hour to tag the crest, marvel at its vertiginous E face, and return to the shoulder.

From where you'll attain the **summit ridge**, it's a very challenging, 0.5-km (0.3-mi) scramble N along the crest to Mt. Lady Macdonald's 2606-m (8550-ft) summit. All but samurai mountaineers will be gripped by the exposure and should turn back.

Mt. Lady Macdonald, from Main Street, Canmore

TRIP 46
Wasootch Ridge

LOCATION	Elbow-Sheep Wildland Provincial Park
	Hwy 40, S of Barrier Lake
ROUND TRIP	11 km (6.8 mi) to trail's end cairn
ELEVATION GAIN	1010 m (3315 ft)
KEY ELEVATIONS	trailhead 1433 m (4700 ft)
	trail's end cairn 2130 m (6986 ft)
HIKING TIME	4 to 6 hours
DIFFICULTY	moderate
MAP	Gem Trek *Canmore and Kananaskis Village*

Opinion

Ridges have ruffles. Though hikers persist in imagining themselves striding effortlessly along horizontal crests, the reality is that most ridges are severely serrated. In the craggy Canadian Rockies, ridges tend to plunge, swoop and soar as crazily as stunt pilots at an air show. So Wasootch Ridge is peculiar. Once the trail launches you steeply onto the crest, the few ups and downs are mellow all the way to trail's end. Yet views are nearly constant, and the scenery is remarkably stirring for a ridge whose front-range location makes it hikeably snow-free in spring and fall.

You'll soon be peering down into Wasootch and Porcupine creek canyons, and up at the long, north tentacle of Mt. McDougall. The venerable peaks west of Kananaskis Village will also compete for your attention. Among the trees you'll brush past along the crest are limber pines—gnarled, twisted beings who appear to be patience and tenacity incarnate. Wildflowers also grace the ridge. Look for lavendar Jacob's ladder, moss campion, rock jasmine (tiny, white, with yellow centre), red roseroot, sawwort (dark-purple strands, thistle-like), purple saxifrage, and white mountain avens.

The trail on Wasootch Ridge was constructed by nothing more than continued foot traffic over the years, but you'll find it a competent hiking guide. It leads to a big cairn, one kilometer shy of the high point. Most ridgewalkers turn around at the cairn rather than scramble the rest of the suddenly intimidating ridge. The cairn is a fine place to relax, empty your boots, wiggle your toes in the breeze, and sip your Platypus full of lemonade. Remember: the ridge is dry. Pack more liquid than you think you'll need.

Fact

By Vehicle

From **Trans-Canada Hwy 1**, drive S on Hwy 40. Slow down after crossing signed Porcupine Creek. At 17 km (10.6 mi) turn left for Wasootch Creek day-use area.

Mt. Lorette, from Wasootch Ridge

From the turnoff to **Kananaskis Village**, drive N on Hwy 40. Slow down after crossing signed Wasootch Creek. At 23.1 km (14.3 mi) turn right for Wasootch Creek day-use area.

From **either approach**, proceed 0.7 km (0.4 mi) to the road's end parking lot, at 1433 m (4700 ft).

On Foot

The trail departs the middle of the parking lot's E side. Ignore the signed, level trail going left (NNE) to Baldy Pass. Just beyond the signpost, go right (SE) behind a few spruce trees to a small, gravel clearing. Ignore the game path (right). Between the two incorrect options, the Wasootch Ridge trail immediately rockets up-slope, ENE.

The initial ascent is very steep. It's soon apparent that the trail is heading SE. This will remain your general direction of travel to the end of the ridge. Within three minutes, at 1483 m (4865 ft), rock slabs afford a view

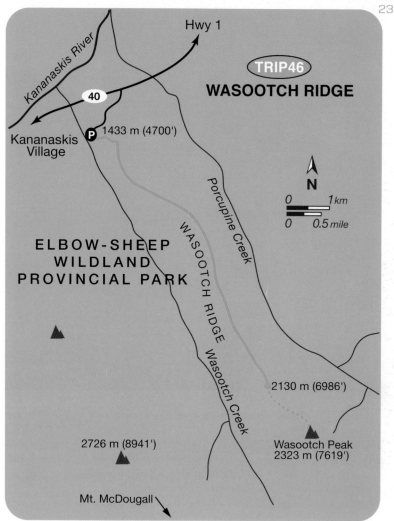

WASOOTCH RIDGE

Kananaskis River

Hwy 1

40

Kananaskis Village

P 1433 m (4700')

Porcupine Creek

N

0   1 km

0   0.5 mile

ELBOW-SHEEP WILDLAND PROVINCIAL PARK

WASOOTCH RIDGE

Wasootch Creek

2130 m (6986')

2726 m (8941')

Wasootch Peak 2323 m (7619')

Mt. McDougall

W to Mt. Allan (Trip 16) and NW to Mt. Lorette. Where no trail is apparent, proceed S across the slabs. Within 12 m/yd, turn sharp left (E), pick up the trail again, and resume the taxing ascent.

Near 1555 m (5100 ft) the grade eases in young, open forest along the ridgecrest. Mount Baldy is visible left (NNE). The trail favours the right (W) side of the crest. Inspiring views continue.

About 30 minutes from the trailhead, mature trees restrict vision but grant shade. The trail veers left near a cairn at 1723 m (5650 ft), where a faint right fork is crudely blocked off.

Within 40 minutes, attain a view SSE up Wasootch Creek canyon. Much of the ridge is visible ahead. The canyon's right (W) wall is the long, N arm of 2726-m (8941-ft) Mt. McDougall. After a short drop, the trail rises into the open. Where it fades near 1829 m (6000 ft), look left (higher). It resumes near the crest, with views into Porcupine Creek canyon (left / E).

Overall the ascent remains moderate. Your upward progress, however, is occasionally interrupted where the trail descends off minor summits before climbing to successively higher ones. Where the crest narrows, briefly follow a ledge on the right side before clambering around the left. Later, where the ridge broadens in the subalpine zone, the trail is less distinct, but the way forward remains obvious.

At 5.5 km (3.4 mi), 2130 m (6986 ft), reach **trail's end** on a rounded summit topped by a substantial cairn. Hiking time from the trailhead: about 2¼ hours. Mounts Sparrowhawk (Trip 6) and Bogart are visible W. The quadruple summits of Mt. Lougheed are WNW. Mt. Rundle (Trip 43) is NW, beyond Skogan Pass.

Moss campion

Most of the ridge is now behind you. The remaining 1 km (0.6 mi) is only partially visible, but it's evident that pressing onward poses significantly more challenge. Proceed only if you're a capable scrambler who doesn't need guidance. Another 40 minutes of vigorous, occasionally hands-on effort is necessary to attain the **final summit** on Wasootch Ridge, at 6.5 km (4 mi), 2323 m (7619 ft).

TRIP 47
Old Baldy Ridge

LOCATION	Elbow-Sheep Wildland Provincial Park
	Hwy 40, SE of Kananaskis Village
ROUND TRIP	16 km (10 mi)
ELEVATION GAIN	854 m (2802 ft)
KEY ELEVATIONS	trailhead 1520 m (4986 ft), ridge 2374 m (7788 ft)
HIKING TIME	5 to 6 hours
DIFFICULTY	moderate
MAP	Gem Trek *Canmore and Kananaskis Village*

Opinion

You are a sensual creature. Your nose can catch the scent of berries in a forest, so you won't starve. Your ears can detect the distant snap of a twig, granting you a head start on a predator. Your eyes can leap far ahead of your feet, helping you bound across boulders without falling. But modern life—motionless work, cubicles, recycled air, artificial light—deprives your senses.

What we all need, every spring, is a retreat. A celebration of our sensuality and a reminder to cultivate it. For many of us, early-season hiking serves that purpose. In K-Country, an ideal retreat destination is Old Baldy Ridge.

An urbanite friend joined us here one June. Though the need to resuscitate our senses was unspoken, he obviously felt it. The hike exhilarated him. He jubilantly flung off his clothes and padded barefoot across Old Baldy Ridge, every pore gorging on the experience.

Prairie crocus, or pasque flowers, on Old Baldy Ridge in early June

The ridge is nondescript, neither craggy nor tall. It has forested flanks, a blunt top, and an overshadowing neighbour: 2826-m (9270-ft) Old Baldy Mtn. Motorists plying Hwy 40 ignore the ridge, gazing instead at Mt. Lorette, Mt. Allan (Trip 16), Mt. Kidd, The Wedge, and other singular peaks nearby.

But Old Baldy Ridge is a fine grandstand from which to gaze upon those and other monumental mountains. The ridgetop is broad and, true to its name, treeless—perfect for napping, picnicking, dancing, or walking barefoot. Clothing optional, we've observed. Just remember there's not a scrap of shade up there, and even brief, UV-ray exposure can burn winter-white skin. Our friend suggests sunscreen. We prefer a hat, long sleeves, and pants.

Though the trip begins on an old road, it leads to an engaging, rugged trail—streamside for about an hour. Where it briefly deteriorates to a slender, bootbeaten route climbing the gully wall, acrophobes might be unnerved. A luxuriant, subalpine gorge beckons beyond, and the hiking is again easy. Over-the-shoulder views of The Fortress and The Wedge reward upward progress.

The final, grassy-slope ascent is steep, but by then the scenic reward is evident and inspiring. On a clear, calm day, arrival atop the ridge can be euphoric. So it's best to carefully select your companions for this retreat, in case they're inspired to make a scenic contribution to the ridgecrest panorama.

If you don't visit Old Baldy Ridge in early summer, wait until fall. It's a premier shoulder-season trip, available sooner and later than others of similar elevation in central and north K-Country. Even in November, the stream you'll follow part way can still be flowing heartily. Late July to mid-September, however, choose another trip.

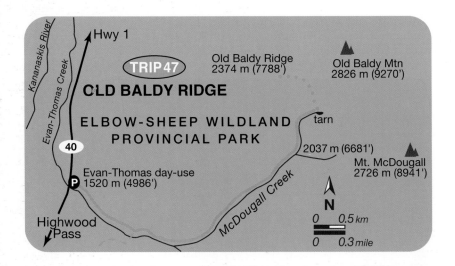

The meadowy cirque beneath Old Baldy Mtn (left)

Wood lily

Fact

By Vehicle

From **Trans-Canada Hwy 1**, drive 27.2 km (16.9 mi) S on Hwy 40. Or, from Highwood Pass, drive 40 km (24.8 mi) N on Hwy 40. From either approach, turn E into the signed Evan-Thomas trailhead parking lot, at 1520 m (4986 ft). It's 0.4 km (0.25 mi) north of the bridge over Evan Thomas Creek.

On Foot

On the S side of the parking lot, right of the outhouse, begin on an unpaved, former road: the **Evan-Thomas Creek trail**. Immediately reach a T-junction. Turn left (SE).

At 1.7 km (1.1 mi), about 20 minutes from the trailhead, reach a T-junction with the Wedge Connector from the S. Right is overgrown. Bear left (ENE), still on road/trail, ascending gradually.

About five minutes later, the road curves right (SSW) and begins descending. In another 40 m/yd look for a **cairned trail** forking left into the trees. It departs the road at 1605 m (5266 ft), above and before a creek. Hike the rough, narrow trail SSE, then E, ascending gently through a pleasant forest of fir and big spruce. You're now following the left (N) bank of **McDougall Creek**, gradually curving NE, upstream, into the drainage. A few, easy, creek crossings ensue.

At 1750 m (5740 ft), about 50 minutes from the trailhead, the drainage narrows into a **gorge**. The path deteriorates on the eroding slope above the creek. Some stretches are just 25 cm (10 in) wide, next to a precipice. If you're surefooted, it's not an obstacle. Only when muddy or icy might it slow a capable hiker or deter others.

Beyond, the forest is more open, mixed with dwarf aspen. About one hour in, at 1825 m (5988 ft), the narrow **valley opens**. Old Baldy Mtn is visible ahead (NE). Your goal is the ridge SW of it. The Fortress and The Wedge are visible behind you. The trail continues ascending above the creek's NW bank.

Cross a minor **rockslide**, then negotiate several more, narrow sections. Entering forest in the upper drainage, the trail returns to more comfortable terrain. At 5.8 km (3.6 mi), 2037 m (6681 ft)—less than two hours for strong hikers—arrive where the creek's right (E) fork drops to the confluence in a series of cascades and pools. Follow the **left fork, curving N**, ascending moderately toward the hill of chunky rock. The swirling slopes of 2726-m (8941-ft) Mt McDougall are visible right (SE).

Progressing up the grassy, flowery draw, hop the stream several times. The trail curves right (E) and climbs into trees. Cross a boggy meadow to a seasonal **tarn**. You're now at the **mouth of a cirque** walled-in by Old Baldy Mtn (N) and Mt. McDougall (SE).

Proceed across the meadow and rockslide. Ascend past a tall cairn to the grassy, rocky **shelf** beneath a short outcrop (left / NNW). Aim for the next cairn above (NNE). A faint route leads left of a **giant spruce** to a small gully. Ascend NNW on the right side of the **gully**. Above, cross back to the gully's left side.

At 2374 m (7788 ft) top-out on the rounded crest of **Old Baldy Ridge**, beneath 2826-m (9270-ft) Old Baldy Mtn (right, ENE). Follow the ridge left until the impressive view completely unfolds.

Mt. Collembola and Mt. Allan are visible NW. Mt. Lougheed's four sharp peaks are left of Allan. Mt. Kidd is WSW. The Fortress is SW. The Wedge is left of it, nearby SW. Mt. Joffre is distant S.

Wildflowers adorn the ridgecrest in early summer. Look for baby-blue alpine forget-me-not, red Indian paintbrush, yellow succulent stonecrop, and magenta shooting star.

Old Baldy Mtn, from Old Baldy Ridge

TRIP 48
Jumpingpound Ridge

LOCATION	Powderface Trail, S of Hwy 68
SHUTTLE TRIP	17 km (10.5 mi) one way
ELEVATION CHANGE	640-m (2100-ft) gain / 976-m (3200-ft) loss
KEY ELEVATIONS	Jumpingpound trailhead 1835 m (6020 ft)
	Jumpingpound Mtn 2225 m (7300 ft)
	ridge lowpoint 1945 m (6380 ft)
	Dawson trailhead 1500 m (4920 ft)
HIKING TIME	6 to 8 hours
DIFFICULTY	easy
MAP	Gem Trek *Bragg Creek and Elbow Falls*

Opinion

Dogs have to be walked. It's just universally understood that if you don't walk your dog, you're a negligent pet owner. So the statement "Gotta take the dog for a walk" clears your path of other obligations.

Saying "Gotta take my partner for a walk," however, doesn't elicit the same response. Not even close. Instead, you get raised eyebrows, concern, pity—all based on the assumption your spouse is an invalid.

How odd. Walking is tonic for relationships. Hiking—shared adventure—can be as therapeutic as marriage counseling, spurring couples' awareness of their deep bond by requiring them to rely on it and giving them time to savour it.

Only on the trail do we (Craig and Kathy) escape the locust-like swarm of details that devours us at home and work. Suddenly life is simple, fun, beautiful, and once again we relax into our love.

Yet it's not partner walking that's the national pastime. It's dog walking: being awkwardly tugged along behind a leash, stopping for an embarrassing butt sniff or humiliating poop scoop.

This must change. So here's one of Kananaskis Country's easiest, most convenient trails: a blessedly undemanding, scenically captivating, foothill ridgewalk available spring through fall. A mere hour from the city, the path will quickly loft you and your partner above the trees, where you can amble in harmony for most of a day.

Jumpingpound Ridge is popular with mountainbikers, but hiking is equally rewarding here. The broad, level, grassy ridgecrest often allows effortless striding. The views are vast—out across the prairie and deep into the Rockies' front range. Wildflowers, including moss campion, alpine forget-me-not, and rock jasmine, are abundant.

photos: **1** *Shooting stars abound on Jumpingpound Ridge in early summer* **2** *Shooting Star* **3** *Jumpingpound Ridge* **4** *Prairie Crocus* **5** *Gentian*

Jumpingpound Ridge can be hikeably snowfree as early as mid-May, when the Powderface Trail access-road opens. It's also a viable autumn destination through late October.

Ideally, at least two couples in two vehicles should arrange a shuttle, allowing both to complete the entire ridgewalk. Lacking a second vehicle, hitchhike between the trailheads; it's easy on weekends.

Given only half a day, Jumpingpound is still worth hiking because you can bail off the ridge early, to the Lusk Pass trailhead, where your total distance will be just 9.4 km (5.8 mi). This abbreviated trip still grants you, and your partner of course, 2.5 km (1.6 mi) of scenic ridgewalking. It also requires a shorter shuttle or hitch between trailheads.

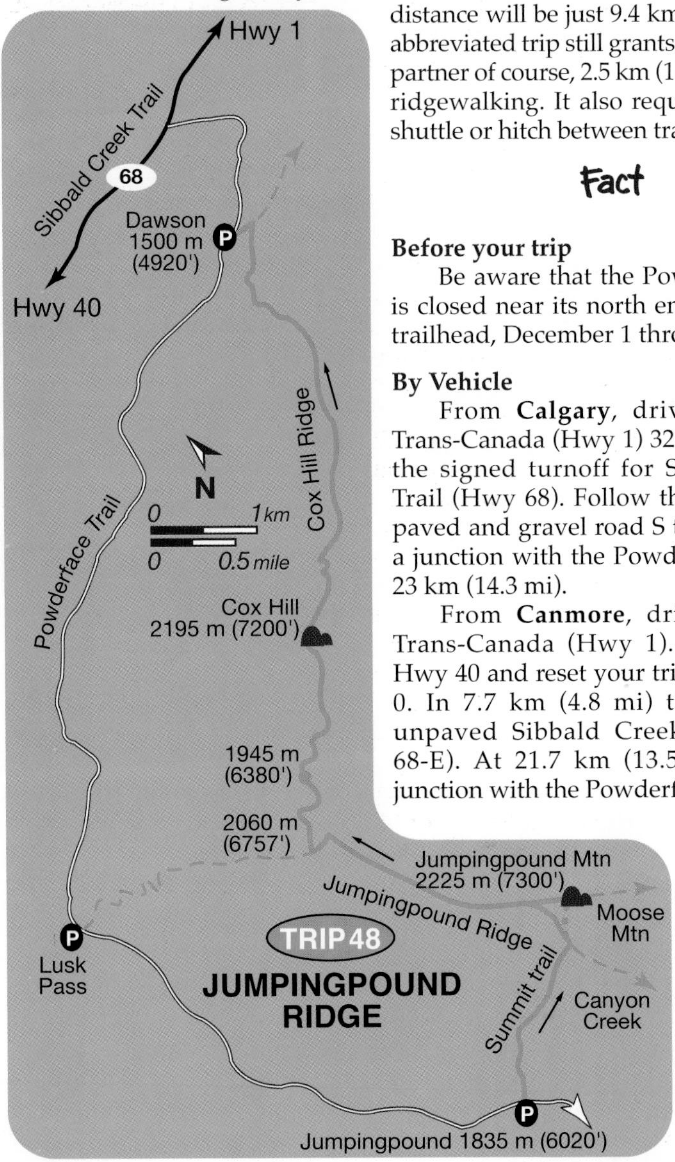

Fact

Before your trip

Be aware that the Powderface Trail is closed near its north end, at Dawson trailhead, December 1 through May 15.

By Vehicle

From **Calgary**, drive W on the Trans-Canada (Hwy 1) 32 km (19 mi) to the signed turnoff for Sibbald Creek Trail (Hwy 68). Follow this alternating paved and gravel road S then W. Reach a junction with the Powderface Trail in 23 km (14.3 mi).

From **Canmore**, drive E on the Trans-Canada (Hwy 1). Turn S onto Hwy 40 and reset your trip odometer to 0. In 7.7 km (4.8 mi) turn left onto unpaved Sibbald Creek Trail (Hwy 68-E). At 21.7 km (13.5 mi) reach a junction with the Powderface Trail.

From **either approach**, reset your trip odometer to 0 and drive S on the Powderface Trail. In 3 km (1.9 mi) turn left into **Dawson trailhead**, at 1500 m (4920 ft). Park here, whether arranging a shuttle or hitchhiking, then continue SW to **Jumpingpound trailhead** at 16.7 km (10.4 mi), 1835 m (6020 ft). Park in the small pullout on the right (SW) side of the road.

On Foot

The Jumpingpound Summit trail starts on the NE side of the road. Predominantly used by hikers, it's the most direct access to the ridgecrest. Equestrians favour the slightly longer access via Lusk Pass. Most mountainbikers begin at the S trailhead, just N of Canyon Creek.

Enter spruce forest and begin ascending NE—your general direction of travel until cresting the ridge. The well-engineered, moderately graded, switchbacking trail crosses several footbridges. At 1982 m (6500 ft) the ascent eases. Six minutes farther, a short spur leads SE to a **bench** overlooking Elbow River Valley (SW). The main trail steepens.

At 2.5 km (1.6 mi), 2135 m (7003 ft), top out on the **ridgecrest** and intersect Jumpingpound Ridge trail at a **signed junction**. Right descends the forested crest S toward Canyon Creek. Turn left and curve N through open forest. In a few minutes, bear right at a signed fork. Keep ascending the grassy slope NE toward Jumpingpound Mtn.

Summit 2225-m (7300-ft) **Jumpingpound Mtn** at 3.3 km (2 mi). Fast hikers will arrive here one hour after leaving the trailhead. The panorama includes Cox Hill to the N, Moose Mtn ESE, and the Fisher Range SW. Keep reading to resume the one-way ridgewalk. If you're hiking only a round trip, consider a short detour toward Moose Mtn (skip below for directions) before retracing your steps to the trailhead.

From Jumpingpound Mtn, resume the ridgewalk by bearing right (NW) and descending briefly. This shortcut is on a different trail than the one you ascended. Gradually curve NNW across the broad, nearly level, grassy ridgecrest. About half an hour beyond Jumpingpound Mtn, re-enter forest at 2160 m (7085 ft). The trail then contours just below the crest, on the right (E) side. A moderate descent ensues. You're still heading NNE.

At 5.9 km (3.7 mi), 2060 m (6757 ft), within one hour of leaving Jumpingpound Mtn, arrive at a **signed junction**. Go right (NE) to continue the ridgewalk. Left (NW) descends 3.5 km (2.2 mi) to the Powderface Trail at Lusk Pass. If you exit that way, your total hiking distance will be 9.4 km (5.8 mi) when you reach the road. On weekends, it should be easy to hitchhike S, back to the Jumpingpound trailhead.

Continuing the ridgewalk, the trail heads NE and briefly ascends. It then drops through open, rocky terrain and plunges into forest. At 1945 m (6380 ft), the **lowpoint** of the trip, the trail begins climbing again. The ascent is initially steep but soon eases. Burst out of the trees onto grass at 2110 m (6921 ft).

The trail ascends NE then N, rolling onto the broad, flat, 2195-m (7200-ft) summit of **Cox Hill** at 9 km (5.6 mi). Looking S, you can survey much of the ridgewalk you've completed thus far. Numerous peaks are visible in the distance. NW are Mounts Kidd, Bogart and Sparrowhawk. N is Mt. Yamnuska, whose sheer cliffs attract rockclimbers. The prairie is NE.

Depart Cox Hill NE. The trail enters krummholz (stunted trees) then drops steeply into open, lodgepole-pine forest. A few short ascents remain, but you're generally descending now. Near the valley bottom, the trail passes a viewpoint where you can cool your brakes while gazing at the forested foothills.

After rounding the base of a clearcut, reach level ground and proceed E. Turn left at a signed junction, cross a footbridge over a creeklet, and arrive at **Dawson trailhead**. Elevation: 1500 m (4920 ft). You've hiked 17 km (10.5 mi) from Jumpingpound trailhead.

Toward Moose Mtn

If you're hiking only a round trip, you might want to venture toward Moose Mtn before retracing your steps to the trailhead. From the summit of **Jumpingpound Mtn**, look ESE. That's Moose Mtn, crowned with a fire lookout. The first 25 minutes in that direction is easy and rewarding, so allow 45 minutes for this extension.

Departing the Jumpingpound summit, follow the trail leading NE. After a shallow dip, rise over the **first bump** at 2195 m (7200 ft), about 15 minutes from the summit. After a faint section of trail, drop to 2127 m (6977 ft) at 20 minutes. Ascend to a meadowy, **second bump** at 2182 m (7157 ft), about 25 minutes from the summit.

Atop the second bump, it's apparent that continuing to Moose Mtn involves significant elevation change and a discouraging road walk. So its

best to end this foray atop the second bump, which affords a broad perspective of the Front Range. Visible NNW is Mt. Yamnuska (Trip 41), with its distinctive, scree-slope glissade paths. NW is Mt. Loughheed, with Mt. Rundle (Trip 43) immediately right of it.

Prairie crocus

TRIP 49
Upper Kananaskis Lake

LOCATION	Peter Lougheed Provincial Park S of Hwy 40/742 junction
LOOP	14.9 km (9.2 mi)
ELEVATION GAIN	negligible
KEY ELEVATIONS	trailhead and lakeshore 1725 m (5658 ft)
HIKING TIME	4½ to 6 hours
DIFFICULTY	easy
MAP	Gem Trek *Kananaskis Lakes*

Opinion

After washing a down sleeping bag (labour best avoided as long as possible), put it in a clothes dryer on low heat. When the bag's no longer sodden, add clean tennis balls to the dryer. The balls jostle apart the clumps of wet down and fluff them up.

Walking does for people what tennis balls do for wet down bags. When our thoughts lie heavy in our brains like sodden clumps, walking jostles them apart and fluffs them up, because it quickly exposes us to the surprising, random, unfiltered.

It helps to walk in new places, of course, among fresh stimuli. Natural surroundings are preferable. Long is good. Loops are best. The trail circling Upper Kananaskis Lake is a mental tennis-ball par excellence.

The lake is ringed by big mountains rising abruptly from the water's edge. But the trail clings tenaciously to the shore, gaining little elevation. So while the loop is long, it's relatively easy. Views across the lake are frequent and impressive. And you can hike here in shoulder season.

Because Trips 20 through 25 also begin at Upper Kananaskis Lake, and all grant alpine-zone access, the lakeshore trail is often ignored, as it should be in summer. But when the high country is snowbound, striding here feels like a gift. It's worth a try in early May, though you might encounter icy patches. And it usually remains a viable option through mid-November. Even when snow-covered, the trail is distinct, easy to follow. And as long as the snow is only inches deep, strong hikers can maintain a 4-kph (2.5-mph) pace without snowshoes.

Hiking the loop clockwise, as described below, has two important advantages: (1) It allows you to assess the snow-depth sooner, before you're committed to completing the entire trip. (2) If it gets dark before you finish, or someone in your party tires, you can eliminate the final 5.6 km (3.5 mi) by hitchhiking from the North Interlakes day-use area, to your vehicle at the Upper Lake day-use area. Bear in mind, however, this east-shore leg is mostly *on* the water, passes several beaches, and affords the best views. Try not to miss it.

Upper Kananaskis Lake, from above north shore. Mt. Sarrail left, Mt. Lyautey right.

As for snow, the initial south-shore leg will likely have less than the west shore. So if the snow seems too deep during the first 45 minutes, don't expect conditions to improve until you reach the north shore. The sunnier north and east shores should have the least snow.

Fact

By Vehicle

Follow the directions for Rawson Lake (Trip 25) to the Upper Lake day-use area, on the SE shore of Upper Kananaskis Lake. Park at the far S end of the unpaved lot, at 13.4 km (8.3 mi), near the trailhead sign for Kananaskis and Rawson lakes. Elevation: 1725 m (5658 ft).

On Foot

The wide trail leads SW around the shore of Kananaskis Lake. Breaks in the forest grant views. Curve W within 15 minutes. Mt. Indefatigable (Trip 20) is visible NNW, across the lake.

At 1.2 km (0.75 mi), just past the bridge over **Sarrail Creek falls**, the signed Rawson Lake trail forks left (SE). Bear right (W) and continue following the Upper Kananaskis Lake shoreline.

After curving NW, pass a faint left fork at 5.2 km (3.2 mi). It leads SW to Hidden lake. Proceed straight on the main trail, which now climbs above Upper Kananaskis Lake's W shore. In May or November, the snowpack will likely be heavier here than elsewhere around the lake, because Mt. Lyautey (left / W) blocks the afternoon sun.

Cross a bridge over the **Upper Kananaskis River** at 6.8 km (4.2 mi). Immediately downstream, Lower Kananaskis Falls tumbles over tiered ledges into a large pool. On the river's N bank, the trail veers right (NE). Soon enter a field of angular boulders. Mt. Indefatigable is ahead (NE). Left (W) is Mt. Putnik. Behind you (SW) is Mt. Lyautey.

At 7.6 km (4.7 mi), 1740 m (5707 ft), pass a right (S) spur to **Point campground**. It has 20 tentsites with tables, fire pits, and bear-proof food storage. Proceed N on the main trail among more boulders.

At 8.8 km (5.5 mi) bear right where left ascends 100 m (110 yd) N to intersect the Three Isle Lake trail (Trip 23), which is a broad, rocky, fire road at that point. The lower, lakeshore trail affords more pleasant hiking because it's dirt, often covered with pine needles. Through the trees, Mounts Sarrail and Foch are visible right (S).

Intersect the Three Isle Lake trail at 10.2 km (6.3 mi) and bear right (E). At 10.7 km (6.6 mi), the trail ascending Mt. Indefatigable forks left. Proceed straight (E). At 11 km (6.8 mi), curve right and cross the **spillway bridge**. Follow the trail SE atop the dam.

Just before the paved **North Interlakes parking lot**, reach the trailhead **kiosk**. Turn right here and continue SW on the lakeshore trail, which for a brief stretch is just 6 m (20 ft) above the water. It soon drops to lake level, curving S then SE. Pass a couple pebble beaches where deadfall has collected.

Approaching a small peninsula, the trail curves left (NE), rounds a cove, then turns SE again and passes the **White Spruce parking area**.

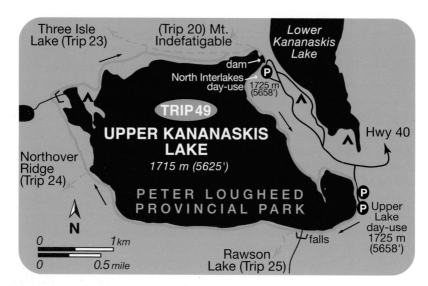

Three Isle
Lake (Trip 23)

(Trip 20) Mt.
Indefatigable

Lower
Kananaskis
Lake

dam

North Interlakes
day-use

P
1725 m
(5658')

TRIP 49

**UPPER KANANASKIS
LAKE**

1715 m (5625')

Hwy 40

Northover
Ridge
(Trip 24)

**PETER LOUGHEED
PROVINCIAL PARK**

P
P Upper
Lake
day-use
1725 m
(5658')

N

0   1 km
0   0.5 mile

falls

Rawson
Lake (Trip 25)

Continue on a wide, gravel-topped dam. Beyond, cross the pavement and proceed over a small footbridge.

Arrive at the N, paved end of the **Upper Lake day-use area**. Instead of walking through the long parking lot, go right. Resume on the lakeshore trail. Follow it S, past the picnic area. Reach the trailhead where your vehicle is parked—at the far, unpaved end of the lot—at 14.9 km (9.2 mi).

Kananaskis Lake, from above northwest shore. Mt. Sarrail right.

TRIP 50
Forgetmenot Ridge

LOCATION	Don Getty Wildland Provincial Park end of Hwy 66
ROUND TRIP	14 km (8.7 mi)
ELEVATION GAIN	715 m (2345 ft)
KEY ELEVATIONS	trailhead 1610 m (5280 ft) Forgetmenot Mtn 2330 m (7642 ft)
HIKING TIME	5 to 7 hours
DIFFICULTY	easy
MAP	Gem Trek *Bragg Creek and Elbow Falls*

Opinion

Legend holds that a courting couple admired a cluster of tiny, light-blue flowers beside a raging river. While picking them for his love, the man tumbled into the whitewater and was swept away. He tossed the flowers to her, calling his last words: "Forget me not!" This dainty flower, known as alpine forget-me-not, is a delight to behold. Its striking beauty is unforgettable. Many hikers consider it symbolic of their most memorable mountain experiences.

The rounded crest of Forgetmenot Ridge offers fulfilling yet relatively easy hiking. And, true to its name, the dryas-covered ridge burgeons with wildflowers June through early August. Look for cobalt gentian; pink-purple sweet vetch; purplish-blue harebells; purple dwarf larkspur; fuzzy, pale-yellow sulphur plant; succulent, deep-red stonecrop; white mountain-avens; purple-tipped, grey-fluffed sawwort; red-pink pods of inflated oxytropis; yellow cinquefoil; purple scorpionweed; and bluish-purple aster.

Views rapidly expand on the steep initial ascent. Then you'll enjoy a scenic, 3-km (1.9-mi), alpine cruise. High above Elbow River Valley, you'll parallel the Front Range—impressive opening act for the headlining main range farther west. You'll also overlook the foothills swelling from the east.

Eager hikers training for an adventurous summer should besiege Forgetmenot Ridge in June. It will likely be snow-free then, while nearby peaks are still dramatically snow-laden. You can also hike here in October. The season is rapidly closing then, so venturing above treeline feels like sneaking in after hours.

Fact

Before your trip

Be aware that Hwy 66, from Elbow Falls to the trailhead, is closed December 1 through May 15.

By Vehicle

From Calgary, drive W on Trans-Canada Hwy 1. About 15 minutes beyond the city outskirts, exit right, following signs for Bragg Creek.

Vetch, Forgetmenot Ridge, mid-June

Proceed on Hwy 22, S then SW. Upon reaching the 3-way junction at the hamlet of Bragg Creek, reset your trip odometer to 0.

0 km (0 mi)
Bear left (S), following signs for Turner Valley and Elbow Falls.

3.3 km (2 mi)
Reach the junction of Hwy 22 and Hwy 66. Turn right (W) onto Hwy 66 (Elbow Falls Trail) and proceed generally SW into K-Country.

22 km (13.6 mi)
Pass a left fork that quickly leads to Elbow Falls. The view is worth a brief detour.

31 km (19.2 mi)
Go left. The unpaved road straight ahead is the Powderface Trail.

32 km (19.8 mi)
Pass Forgetmenot Pond day-use area on the left. The N end of Forgetmenot Ridge rises behind it (SE).

32.3 km (20 mi)
Pass a spacious parking lot on the left. Proceed straight, through the Little Elbow River campground entrance.

33 km (20.5 mi)
Reach a small pullout on the right, at 1610 m (5280 ft). Park here for Forgetmenot Ridge, Nihahi Ridge (Trip 51), Talus Lake (Trip 37), West Fork Little Elbow River (Trip 39), or Paradise Pass (Trip 38). If the pullout is full, return to the spacious lot just outside the campground entrance.

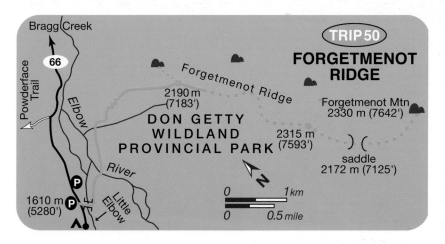

FORGETMENOT RIDGE

Bragg Creek

66

Powderface Trail

Elbow

Forgetmenot Ridge

2190 m (7183')

DON GETTY
WILDLAND
PROVINCIAL PARK

2315 m (7593')

Forgetmenot Mtn 2330 m (7642')

saddle
2172 m (7125')

River

Little Elbow

P

1610 m P (5280')

0   1 km
0   0.5 mile

On Foot

From the small pullout, cross the road, head generally ESE, then cross the pink **suspension bridge** over Little Elbow River. From the spacious parking lot, follow the wide gravel path SW 0.6 km (0.4 mi) along the river, then turn left and cross the suspension bridge. The bridge is the zero-point for distances.

Having crossed the bridge to the SE bank, drop back to the river. Pass a road forking right. Stay on the trail near the river. Five minutes beyond the bridge, follow the trail right, into forest. Soon reach a four-way, map-signed junction. Go left (E) on the **Wildhorse Trail**. Straight (S) is signed for Big Elbow, Threepoint, and Tombstone. Shrubby cinquefoil with yellow flowers brightens the ground cover. In a few minutes, cross a horse trail.

At 1 km (0.6 mi), cross the broad, stony channels of the **Elbow River**. In May, you might encounter only a trickle here. During summer, the water can be so high that crossing is dangerous. By fall, the river subsides underground, perhaps leaving the channels dry. On the E bank, continue NE on the wide dirt trail.

At 1.8 km (1.1 mi), just past a tiny, **unnamed creek** (probably dry), turn right at a cairn onto a narrow, rough trail ascending ENE through forest above the creek drainage. At 3 km (1.9 mi) the trail heads NE and continues ascending, though less steeply, near the left (W) edge of a NW-jutting spur of Forgetmenot Ridge. After a brief level reprieve on the spur, go right (SSE) at a flagged fork. Visible NNW, across the Elbow River Valley, is Powderface Ridge rising above the Powderface Trail. Nihahi Ridge (Trip 51) is NW. Mt. Remus is W.

The steep ascent continues on scree among scattered trees. Choose any of the bootbeaten paths. They stay close to together, heading generally SE. All fade before reaching a saddle. Cairns indicate the route heading SE through open forest. At 2128 m (6980 ft), about two hours from the trailhead, reach **grassy slopes** just beneath the ridge.

Continuing the now gentle ascent, pass a chaotic display of limestone karst. A bootbeaten path pierces a stand of trees before surmounting the **crest of Forgetmenot Ridge** at 4 km (2.5 mi), 2190 m (7183 ft). Fix this point in mind for your descent. A clump of rocks serves as a landmark.

2

3

4

Forgetmenot's N end is left, rising to 2240 m (7347 ft). Go right and follow the trail-less ridge S, contouring near 2204 m (7230 ft). The Front Range is visible W, across Big Elbow River valley. Starting at the N end of the range you can identify a lower, unnamed peak, then 2935-m (9629-ft) Mt. Glasgow. Just S of that, and slightly higher, is Mt. Cornwall. Next is Outlaw Peak. Just E of that is Banded Peak. On the NW horizon are mountains beyond Hwy 1.

At 5 km (3 mi) a NE-jutting arm of Forgetmenot Ridge invites exploration. It rises to 2256 m (7400 ft). But first continue SSE along the main ridge. While returning, you can decide if you have time and energy for the detour. On the main ridge you'll be closer to the bigger Front Range peaks rather than the foothills.

The ridge gently descends SSW. Drop to 2186 m (7170 ft) in a grassy, willowy saddle between shoulders. At 5.6 km (3.5 mi) the ridge veers W, rising 55 m (180 ft) to a **rocky knoll**. From the knoll's W edge, the ridge heads S. Choose the smoothest route through shattered rocks near the W side of the ridge. Abundant clearcuts fragment the forest below: SE, E, and NE. Desolate Moose Mtn is visible way N.

Proceed SSE, over dryas and rock slabs, past scattered trees. Reach the 2315-m (7593-ft) **summit of Forgetmenot Ridge** at 7 km (4.3 mi). Three Point Mtn is visible SSW. Beyond it, SW, is 2863-m (9393-ft) Cougar Mtn. This section of the ridge is covered with black-lichen-splotched rock. Most dayhikers will want to turn around here.

Beyond the summit, the ridge dives 143 m (470 ft) to a saddle above the headwaters of Howard Creek and linked to Forgetmenot Mtn. It's an easy, grassy descent to the 2172-m (7125-ft) **saddle**, but there the hiking is tedious, over rough rock. The ascent resumes SE, again mostly on grass. Top out on 2330-m (7642-ft) **Forgetmenot Mtn** at 9.6 km (6 mi). The view extends S of Threepoint Mtn and Mt. Rose to larger Bluerock Mtn. E of that is small Mt. Ware (Trip 52), a shoulder-season destination near Sheep River Provincial Park.

Return to where you first crested Forgetmenot Ridge. Descend from the landmark clump of rocks. Aiming for Forgetmenot Pond, go W toward trees. Flagging indicates where to enter the trees. The path then leads NW along the spur jutting toward Powderface Trail. Continuing the descent, stay right of most trees. Maintain a course that would split Powderface Ridge and Forgetmenot Pond. But don't feel compelled to follow these directions precisely. Your goal is simply to get down the way you came up. Upon intersecting the Wildhorse Trail, turn left (SW) and parallel the Elbow River. You're now on familiar ground.

If your vehicle is in the spacious parking lot just outside the campground entrance, consider a shortcut. Instead of hiking all the way back to the suspension bridge, leave the trail shortly after crossing the Elbow River's broad, stony channels. Angle right (NW). Hike cross-country, ford the Little Elbow River, and shortly beyond you'll hit the parking lot—about half an hour sooner than via the trail.

photos: *1 Forgetmenot Ridge, from near its south end* **2** *Fording the Elbow River, to begin ascending Forgetmenot Ridge* **3** *Alpine forget-me-not* **4** *Larkspur*

TRIP 51
Nihahi Ridge

LOCATION	Hwy 66, SW of Bragg Creek
ROUND TRIP	10 km (6.2 mi)
ELEVATION GAIN	735 m (2410 ft)
KEY ELEVATIONS	trailhead 1610 m (5280 ft), S summit 2345 m (7690 ft)
HIKING TIME	3 to 4 hours
DIFFICULTY	challenging
MAP	Gem Trek *Bragg Creek and Elbow Falls*

Opinion

You measure happiness with an altimeter? If so, you want the Rockies under your boots as early and late in the hiking season as possible. An exciting place to do that is Nihahi Ridge.

Southwest of Calgary, Nihahi is where the Rockies begin. To the east are foothills and prairie. To the west, the topography erupts. Straddling the crest of Nihahi Ridge in early June, you'll see the snow-mantled peaks beyond. Or come in October, when icy flourishes again accentuate the mountains' stature, yet the ridge itself is not yet white.

The first hour of this short trip is a cheery hike on an adequate but increasingly steep trail. During the final half hour to the ridge's south summit, however, you'll tussle with the rocky, airy cliffs that the Stoney Indian word *Nihahi* describes. Light scrambling is necessary. At least one member of your party should be a strong, patient mountain goat who can assist and reassure the inexperienced.

Many hikers surmount Nihahi without previously scrambling anything but eggs. If you're wary but willing, give it a go. You can attain inspiring views without endangering yourself. Just turn around before the ridge outstrips your desire and ability. Beyond the south summit, the ridge is a tightrope walk that only skilled scramblers should attempt.

Fact

Before your trip

Be aware that Hwy 66, from Elbow Falls to the trailhead, is closed December 1 through May 15.

By Vehicle

Follow the directions for Forgetmenot Ridge (Trip 50) to the end of Hwy 66, about one hour SW of Calgary. Park just beyond the Elbow River

photos: *1 Ascending Nihahi Ridge 2 Scrambling onto Nihahi Ridge*

1

2

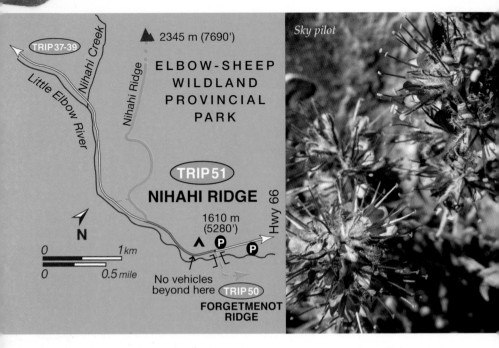

Sky pilot

2345 m (7690')

ELBOW-SHEEP WILDLAND PROVINCIAL PARK

Nihahi Creek

Nihahi Ridge

Little Elbow River

TRIP 37-39

TRIP 51

NIHAHI RIDGE

1610 m (5280')

Hwy 66

N

0 ——— 1 km
0 ——— 0.5 mile

No vehicles beyond here TRIP 50

FORGETMENOT RIDGE

---

campground entrance, in the small pullout on the right, at 33 km (20.5 mi), 1610 m (5280 ft). If the pullout is full, return to the spacious lot just outside the campground entrance.

On Foot

From either the pullout or the parking lot, ascend the campground entrance road SW. As it curves right (W), stay on the main road, continually bearing left where right spurs access campsites. Proceed beyond a couple metal **gates** barring vehicle traffic.

This road is the approach to Talus Lake (Trip 37), Paradise Pass (Trip 38), and West Fork Little Elbow River (Trip 39), but you'll be departing it soon. Pass a sign for Nihahi Ridge and Little Elbow trail. Cross a cattleguard. About five minutes beyond the final gate, follow a **signed trail** forking right (NW) to Nihahi Ridge. Enter forest and begin a gentle ascent. A couple minutes in, go left. About five minutes farther, reach a **fork**. Go right and ascend N, again following a sign for Nihahi Ridge.

At 1720 m (5642 ft), Nihahi Ridge is visible NW. Also attain views SW to Mounts Glasgow and Cornwall. About half an hour from the trailhead pullout, enter stunted, **open forest** and grassy **meadows**. After a brief, shallow descent, the stiff climb resumes NW. The trail curves left (W, then SW) beneath rock bands, before veering right (N) to ascend the ridgecrest.

Reach a **fork** at 1845 m (6050 ft). Go right, ascending N. Mounts Romulus and Remus are visible W, above the Little Elbow River Valley (Trips 37, 38, and 39). About 15 minutes farther, proceed up the open, rocky slope. At 2090 m (6855 ft), about an hour from the trailhead, the dirt trail is severely steep and scoured. It affords minimal traction. At least you're now on the E side of the crest, sheltered from the often fierce W wind.

At 2170 m (7118 ft) several routes lead upward. Left is the quickest ascent to the trail just right of the crest. Then go right one minute farther to the more gradual ascent along the escarpment beneath the crest. Choose either of two sections of trail that soon rejoin before ending beneath a short **scree gully** on the left. You've hiked 1⅓ hours from the trailhead pullout. You must now grapple with challenging terrain to reach the trip's climax.

Scramble 5 m (16 ft) up the vertical gully, then go left (NW) to regain the **ridgecrest**. Continue on scree at a gentle grade for about ten minutes. Reach vertical rock slabs at 2293 m (7520 ft). What might appear to be a difficult scramble actually isn't—if you go left, around the chunky rocks.

Like steps, stone blocks allow you to work though a break in the craggy escarpment to 2310 m (7577 ft). Proceed NW along the crest another five minutes to reach the **S summit of Nihahi Ridge** at 4 km (2.5 mi), 2345 m (7690 ft). Total hiking time: about 1½ hours.

Powderface Ridge is visible NE, across Ford Creek valley. Forgetmenot Ridge is SE. Mt. Remus is WSW, and Mt. Fullerton is N of it. The massif comprising Mounts Glasgow and Cornwall, as well as Outlaw and Banded peaks, is SSW.

The crest of Nihahi Ridge, composed of angular rock slabs, is precipitously narrow. The right (E) side is vertical. The left (W) side is only slightly less sheer. All but advanced scramblers should turn around at the S summit. The N summit of Nihahi Ridge is 7 km (4.3 mi) NW.

Elbow Falls

TRIP 52
Mt. Ware

LOCATION	between Bluerock Wildland and Sheep River provincial parks, Hwy 542, W of Turner Valley
ROUND TRIP	17.4 km (10.8 mi)
ELEVATION GAIN	524 m (1719 ft)
KEY ELEVATIONS	trailhead 1600 m (5248 ft), summit 2124 m (6969 ft)
HIKING TIME	5½ to 7 hours
DIFFICULTY	easy
MAP	Gem Trek *Bragg Creek and Elbow Falls*

Opinion

Sheep River country is equestrian heaven. The rolling, forested foothills tax hikers' patience more than their vitality. But that's what you need in shoulder season, so you can stride instead of mush through slush. And this trip leads you above the equine zone, onto the trail-less slopes of Mt. Ware for vistas unhindered by trees, and tranquility seldom interrupted.

Numerous trails wiggle through Sheep River country. This is the most rewarding because it accesses one of the area's few, true mountains. Nothing overshadows Mt. Ware, so its sun-pummeled slopes promise you a snow-free ascent perhaps by late May. From the summit, you'll admire the Front Range—a stirring sight in May, June, or October, when snow lends definition to the peaks.

The approach to the mountain is engaging. You'll hike through a coniferous forest broken by meadows and stands of aspen. The aspen—lime in spring, gold in fall—contrast vibrantly with the dominant evergreens. Within an hour of the trailhead, you'll pass a cascade where Gorge Creek glides over smooth bedrock. The final ascent of Mt. Ware is cross-country, but the terrain and vegetation are amicable, the routefinding straightforward.

Because this is a low-elevation trail, it's hikeable as early as May, as late as November. Avoid it late June through August, or risk baking your brains to liquid. Besides, summer is prime time for exploring higher and deeper in the vastly more exciting, main range.

Yet another reason to hike Mt. Ware is the drive from Turner Valley. The quiet highway swoops out of the prairie, toward the Rockies, granting constant views of the aspen-cloaked foothills. The beauty spikes in late September, when the aspen leaves are so brilliant yellow they appear to have absorbed every ray of summer sunshine. Either before or after the hike, you can also visit nearby Sheep River Falls—an unheralded K-Country marvel.

photos: *1 On Mt. Ware's north slope 2 Aspen in Sheep River country 3 Indian paintbrush*

Between the trailhead and the base of Mt. Ware, expect to encounter mountainbikers, horseback riders, and cattle. Yes, road apples and cowpies are part of the scenery. And, true to its name, Sheep River country is home to flocks of bighorn sheep, which contribute to the annual, spring outbreak of ticks. Be wary whenever you sit, and check your dark, secret recesses after the hike.

Fact

Before your trip
Be aware that Hwy 546, from just W of the Sheep River ranger station to the Gorge Creek trailhead, is closed December 1 through May 15.

By Vehicle
From Calgary, drive S on Hwy 2. Take Hwy 2A direct to Okotoks. Drive S through Okotoks, then go W on Hwy 7, to the town of Black Diamond. Reset your trip odometer to 0 at the junction of Hwys 7 and 22.

0 km (0 mi)
Starting W on Hwy 22 from Black Diamond to Turner Valley.

4 km (2.5 mi)
In Turner Valley, proceed straight W on Sunset Blvd (Hwy 546), where Hwy 22 goes right (N) to Millarville.

4.9 km (3 mi)
Bear right to continue W on Hwy 546. Soon pass a sign stating that Bluerock Wildland Provincial Park is 35 km (21.7 mi) ahead.

19.3 km (12 mi)
Enter Kananaskis Country.

22.4 km (13.9 mi)
Pass the Sheep River ranger station (right).

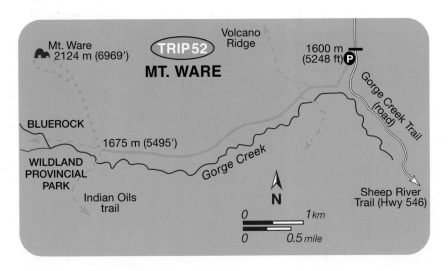

25.8 km (16 mi)
Enter Sheep River Provincial Park.

33.5 km (20.8 mi)
Turn right and ascend on unpaved Gorge Creek Trail. Left descends, passes Sheep River Falls (worth a look) in 6 km (3.7 mi), soon reaches Bluerock campground and ends shortly beyond.

37.7 km (23.4 mi)
Turn left into the Gorge Creek trailhead parking lot, at 1600 m (5248 ft).

On Foot

Starting near the sign at the SW corner of the parking lot, follow the Gorge Creek trail SSW through forest. It's a former road, broad and smooth. Within five minutes, enter a meadow among aspen. Descend into the creek drainage at 1570 m (5150 ft). Bear right on the trail.

Within 15 minutes, rockhop across shallow **Gorge Creek**. Just beyond is a **map-sign**. The Link Creek / Volcano Ridge trail proceeds straight (WNW). Turn left (S) for Gorge and South Gorge creeks. A minute farther, bear right (SW) at the **fork**. Soon emerge from trees. Bluerock Mtn is visible W.

The Gorge Creek trail, still a former road, continues along the N edge of the gorge, occasionally overlooking the creek. About an hour from the trailhead, enter meadows and a grove of aspen. The road narrows to actual trail here. Watch for a **cascade** flowing through a smooth, rock trough, into deep pools. There's a small, sandy beach here.

About ten minutes farther, reach a **fork**. Left descends to a meadow. Bear right, ascending the main Gorge Creek trail toward an orange blaze. Soon pass through a **gate**, then descend to follow the creek.

At 6.2 km (3.8 mi), 1675 m (5495 ft), about 1½ hours from the trailhead, reach a **signed junction** in a clearing. The Indian Oils trail goes left (SW) through the meadow and crosses Gorge Creek. Bear right (NW) on the Gorge Creek trail. A minute past the junction, immediately before the trail grazes the creek, turn right onto a **game path** and ascend N through forest.

The game path leads between two pines. In 40 m/yd where the path splits, bear right and ascend steeply. About ten minutes above the Gorge Creek trail, reach a small, N-S **gully**. A narrow track parallels the right (E) bank. Pass old flagging as you contour N through lodgepole pine.

This description is detailed, because landmarks are few and discreet. But it's not necessary to follow our route precisely. If you have difficulty doing so, don't worry. You're travelling cross-country now. Just keep ascending generally NNW to the open slopes of Mt. Ware. The grade is only moderately steep. The terrain and vegetation pose little resistance.

Contouring N through lodgepole pine, the narrow track soon vanishes. At flagging, turn right and ascend through open forest. Angle slightly left. About four minutes farther, reach the base of a draw (shallower than the gully). Proceed along its left side to regain a path about 10 m/yd left (W) of the gully.

About half an hour above the Gorge Creek trail, the path curves left and climbs NW. It soon disappears in the tall grass of an open forest. Keep ascending NW, perhaps following traces of path, until you crest the broad, open, **SE ridge of Mt. Ware** at 1884 m (6180 ft). Visible W, across Gorge Creek valley, is 2790-m (9150-ft) Bluerock Mtn. Turn right and follow the ridgecrest NNW toward your goal. Work your way over scree, across rock slabs, through grass and krummholz (stunted trees).

To begin circumambulating the mountain below its summit, gradually curve left (NW). Pick up a game path traversing the SW slope. After cresting the W ridge, contour right (E) across the N slope. The terrain gets rougher and steeper until after you round the mountain's E side. It takes about an hour to return to where you first arrived on the SE ridge.

To summit the mountain, bear right (NNE) above the krummholz. The chunky rocks on the moderate ESE slope afford the easiest ascent route. Clamber upward wherever you're most comfortable. Top out on 2124-m (6969-ft) **Mt. Ware** about 2.5 km (1.6 mi), or 1¼ hours, from the Gorge Creek trail. You've hiked 8.7 km (5.4 mi) from the trailhead.

Calgary is visible NE. Surveyor's Ridge is nearby N, below you. Mt. Rose is NW. 2937-m (9633-ft) Mt. Burns is SW. Gibraltar Mtn is distant SW. The Sheep River Valley is SW and S. Farther S is Junction Creek valley.

On the return, don't drop straight S off the mountain. An angling descent (left / SE) will ensure that you intersect the Gorge Creek trail near where you first departed it.

photos: *1 Roseroot 2 Stonecrop 3 Alpine forget-me-not*

TRIP 53
Grass Pass / Bull Creek Hills

LOCATION	E of Highwood Junction, N of Hwy 541
ROUND TRIP	15 km (9.3 mi) including Boundary Pine
ELEVATION GAIN	719 m (2358 ft)
KEY ELEVATIONS	trailhead 1460 m (4789 ft), Grass Pass 1880 m (6166 ft) highest hill 2180 m (7150 ft)
HIKING TIME	5 to 7 hours
DIFFICULTY	easy round trip, moderate loop
MAP	Gem Trek *Highwood & Cataract Creek*

Opinion

In the Canadian Rockies, fanatic local hikers ache most of the year. Not from hiking, but from the unfulfilled *desire* to hike. Winter lows can plunge to -30° C (-22°F), even in the milder valley bottoms. The snowpack accumulates to 300 cm (118 in) among the peaks. That means hiking season—when it's rock, not ice, crunching beneath your boots on the high passes—is cruelly short. But there are a few special places in the easternmost foothills where snow-free hiking is possible nearly seven months a year. One of them is Grass Pass and the Bull Creek Hills.

This is the edge of the prairie, far from the stirring main range, but you'll see a couple junior peaks nearby and glimpse a more adventurous shoulder-season goal farther south: Mt. Burke (Trip 56). In spring, enough wildflowers flourish on these sun-baked hills to warrant bringing your identification book. Look for red stonecrop, and tiny, mauve cactus. In fall, you might still see lupine and purple harebells before the aspen trees turn brilliant yellow. Either time of year, Grass Pass and the Bull Creek Hills offer you the satisfaction of pounding your energy into the land for a full four to six hours—a veritable marathon for shoulder season. In summer, should a storm dash your alpine plans, retreat to these foothills where the weather is always more genial.

At Grass Pass, before ascending the Bull Creek Hills, take two scenic detours. First, spend a couple minutes proceeding through the pass for a view of Holy Cross Mtn and Mount Head. Then spend 30 minutes on a sidetrip to Boundary Pine peninsula, to overlook the Highwood River Valley and reconnoiter the Bull Creek Hills. Later, atop the hills, you'll have to choose: round trip, or loop? Your surveillance from the peninsula will help you decide. The round trip simply entails turning back at the third and highest hill. The loop, though only a skosh farther than the round trip, adds both challenge and tedium. Loopsters will continue on a rough route over

the fourth hill, descend cross-country, pick up a final spurt of trail to the highway, then endure a 40-minute road-walk to the trailhead unless they hitchhike or pre-arranged a shuttle.

Grass Pass / Bull Creek Hills is just one of several shoulder-season trips near Highwood Junction. The others are Junction Hill (Trip 54) and Mt. Burke (Trip 56). So if you car-camp at nearby Etherington Creek, you can enjoy two hikes on a weekend. Make it your pre-season training-camp jamboree.

Tick attack! All these trails are in sunny, grassy foothills: prime tick habitat. The nasty parasites are active early April to mid-June. Check yourself at lunch and again more thoroughly at day's end. Also bear in mind this isn't pristine wilderness. It's ranch country. Expect to see, and occasionally plod through, muddy, hoof-churned, manure-splotched terrain.

Fact

Before your trip

Be aware that Hwy 40, from Kananaskis Lakes Trail to Highwood Junction, is closed December 1 through June 14, preventing spring access to this trailhead from the north. During that time, drive here only from the east, via Hwy 541 out of Longview. You have two campground options near here: Etherington Creek (open May 15 through October 14) is 6 km (3.6 mi) S on unpaved Hwy 940; Cataract Creek (open May 15 through September 2) is 8 km (5 mi) farther S.

By Vehicle

From **Calgary**, drive S on Hwy 22 to Longview. Turn W onto Hwy 541 and continue 37.6 km (23.3 mi).

From **Trans-Canada Hwy 1**, E of Canmore, drive 105 km (65.2 mi) S on Hwy 40 to Highwood Junction, where Hwys 40, 940 and 541 intersect. Continue 5.4 km (3.3 mi) E on Hwy 541.

From **either approach**, turn S into Sentinel Recreation Area. Park in the first parking lot, at 1460 m (4789 ft).

On Foot

From the trailhead parking lot, return to the highway. Cross to the far (N) side of the pavement. Turn right (ENE). Walk parallel to the highway on a path bootbeaten through the grass. Continue 250 m (273 yd). Pass the culvert and the sign SENTINEL PEAK facing westbound traffic. Turn left (NNW), away from the highway, onto the trail between big boulders. Begin a moderate ascent through mixed forest, on a wide, rocky track that used to be a road. A few big Douglas firs enhance the scenery.

Your general direction of travel will remain NNW all the way to **Grass Pass**, at 3.2 km (2 mi), 1880 m (6166 ft), about 50 minutes from the highway. Here you have four options. (1) A three-track trail ascends left (W), then SW, to a rough-but-hikeable ridge that descends left (SSE) back to the trailhead. (2) Straight through the pass is a track descending NNW into Wileman Creek valley. A couple-minute detour in that direction reveals an impressive sight left (NW). Contour above the trail for the optimal view of Holy Cross Mtn and, just past it, 2782-m (9126-ft) Mt. Head. (3) Right (NE) is the trail ascending the Bull Creek Hills. (4) Sharp right (SE) is a trail contouring to, and soon ending at, a superb vantage point.

Option four, to **Boundary Pine peninsula**, is a 30-minute round-trip digression. Take it. Traverse grassy slopes, proceed among stout, hearty, Limber pines, and within 12 minutes—about 1 km (0.6 mi) from the pass—attain a vista across the Highwood River Valley. The Zephyr Creek drainage is directly S. Its right (W) wall is the long, N ridge of Mt. Burke (Trip 56). The peninsula also grants a fine view of the Bull Creek Hills (N to NE). Take time to study the hills from here, so you'll be oriented when they're underfoot.

photos: *1 Bull Creek Hills 2 Cut-leaf daisies 3 Limber pine, Boundary Pine peninsula*

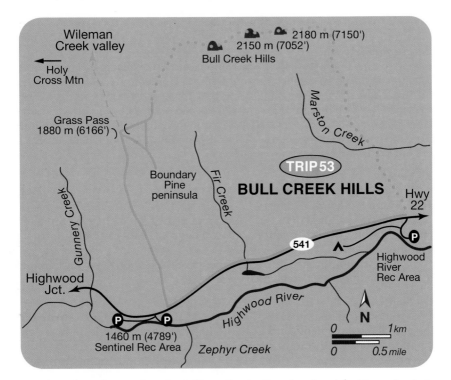

Wileman
Creek valley

Holy
Cross Mtn

2180 m (7150')
2150 m (7052')
Bull Creek Hills

Grass Pass
1880 m (6166')

Marston Creek

Boundary
Pine
peninsula

Fir Creek

TRIP 53
BULL CREEK HILLS

Hwy
22

Gunnery Creek

541

Highwood
River
Rec Area

Highwood
Jct.

Highwood River

N

1460 m (4789')
Sentinel Rec Area

Zephyr Creek

0   1 km
0   0.5 mile

Leaving the peninsula, follow the trail only about halfway back to Grass Pass, then abandon it for the faint shortcut path ascending directly N. It soon intersects the Bull Creek Hills trail, atop the minor hill ahead. If you're uncertain about this, retrace your steps all the way to Grass Pass, where the Bull Creek Hills trail starts.

From Grass Pass, the Bull Creek Hills trail ascends the open, gentle slope NE. Above, dip briefly before continuing over two small bumps atop the **first minor hill**. Then drop 40 m / yd into forest. Stay on the cow-trodden trail until, about 30 minutes from the pass, a swath of **scrubby meadow** opens to the right. Look for a large, blue spruce on the meadow's left side, about 20 m up from the trail. That prominent spruce is your assurance that, yes, you're in the right place. Abandon the trail here. Go right (NE) and begin a short, cross-country ascent through the meadow, among scattered trees, gaining 245 m (804 ft) to the ridge visible ahead.

When you can look right (E) and see no trees, angle in that direction. Just below the outcrop near the ridgecrest, among rock and gravel, pick up a defined route ascending left. Follow it NNE then E to the 2150-m (7052-ft) summit of the **second hill**. The panorama extends to the Great Divide on the SW horizon, and Calgary's office towers NE.

The route continues E, then fades. But the way is obvious, the terrain open, the hiking easy. Descend 30 m (98 ft), then ascend 61 m (200 ft), surmounting the **third and highest hill** at 6.5 km (4 mi), 2180 m (7150 ft), a mere 15 minutes from the second hilltop.

Okay, decision time. From the third hill, you can, of course, turn around and retrace your steps to the trailhead, where your total round-trip distance (including the Boundary Pine peninsula detour) will be 15 km (9.3 mi). But if you're eager and energetic, you can complete a loop by proceeding E along the ridge, then working your way generally SE down to the highway. In that direction, it takes about 2 hours to hike the remaining 3.7 km (2.3 mi) to pavement, where you'll have to walk the highway 3.5 km (2.2 mi) back to your vehicle. The loop entails a 160-m (525-ft) drop—rough, rocky, requiring dexterity and concentration—prior to ascending the **fourth hill**. From there, you'll begin descending. The route becomes a more defined trail just S of where you must rockhop Marston Creek. It intersects **Hwy 541** at **Highwood River Recreation Area**. From there, turn right and follow the highway WSW to the trailhead parking lot at Sentinel Recreation Area, where your total loop distance will be 15.7 km (9.8 mi).

Attracted by the challenge of the loop but turned off by its tedious finale? Capable scramblers who are comfortable routefinding can descend to the highway from atop the second hill, thus reducing the road-walk by half. Begin by working your way S along an escarpment. It gradually relaxes into a mellow ridge; follow it SE. After a nearly level stretch, the descent steepens again. Bear right (S, curving SW). Then scope out the easiest final descent (generally S) to the highway, where you should be within 2 km (1.2 mi) of the trailhead—about a 20-minute walk.

The Great Divide, from Raspberry Ridge lookout (Trip 55), another shoulder-season hike near Highwood Junction

TRIP 54
Junction Hill

LOCATION	Highwood Junction, N of Hwy 541
LOOP	8.5 km (5.3 mi)
ELEVATION GAIN	797 m (2614 ft)
KEY ELEVATIONS	trailhead 1475 m (4838 ft), summit 2233 m (7326 ft)
HIKING TIME	4 to 5½ hours
DIFFICULTY	challenging
MAP	Gem Trek *Highwood & Cataract Creek*

Opinion

A "junction" is a crossroads. An intersection. An opportunity to turn in a new direction. Junction Hill is exactly that. As early as mid-April, you'll find Junction Hill a surprisingly adventurous, robust hike that will spin your attention from "when will winter end?" to "hiking season is here!" Or, if you're interested in but apprehensive about hiking off-trail, Junction Hill is an easy yet intriguing introduction to routefinding. It might widen your scope of what's possible and enjoyable in the mountains.

Junction Hill rises immediately north of Highwood Junction, in southern K-Country. Though visible from the pavement, the hill is unimposing, ignored by hikers, therefore trail-less. But its lacklustre appearance belies the excitement of climbing it, the frequent views it affords, and its commanding summit panorama.

You'll quickly burst through a fringe of trees and stride onto grassy slopes. A sharp ascent leads to a breach in the cliffy southeast ridge, through which you'll attain the crest. Simply follow the rough, treed ridgecrest to the rocky summit. Then drop your pack, break out your Havarti cheese and organic corn chips, and marvel at the Great Divide—a mountainous, peak-studded wall spanning the western horizon.

Descending the south ridge, you'll be in trees only occasionally and briefly. The final descent is wide open, but you'll have to stop to admire the scenery, because the grade is watch-your-step steep. You'll complete the loop by sauntering about 20 minutes along the highway back to your vehicle.

"Hill" doesn't do this little peak justice. Though comparatively small, it is a mountain. If the unrelenting ascent doesn't convince you of that, the severe, final descent will. Wear sturdy hiking boots. Bring trekking poles. Start hydrated. Pack a couple litres of water per person, because you'll find none along the way. And carry a compass. The route will be obvious to

photos: *1 The High Rock Range, from Junction Hill 2 Near summit of Junction Hill 3 Indian paintbrush*

veteran ramblers, but the compass references in our route description will aid less experienced hikers through sections that, to them, might otherwise seem obscure.

Don't worry. You won't be orienteering. You'll simply use the compass to confirm which way is north, south, east or west. Besides, the nearby highways are rarely out of sight. And though we haven't seen cows on top of Junction Hill, there's evidence of bovine summit bids high on both ridgecrests. Surely you can outclimb a cow.

Fact

Before your trip

Be aware that Hwy 40, from Kananaskis Lakes Trail to Highwood Junction, is closed December 1 through June 14, preventing spring access to this trailhead from the N. During that time, drive here only from the E, via Hwy 541 out of Longview. You have two campground options near here: Etherington Creek (open May 15 through October 14) is 6 km (3.7 mi) S on unpaved Hwy 940; Cataract Creek (open May 15 through September 2) is 8 km (5 mi) farther S.

By Vehicle

From **Calgary**, drive S on Hwy 22 to Longview. Turn right (W) onto Hwy 541 and continue 43.2 km (26.8 mi) to Highwood Junction, where

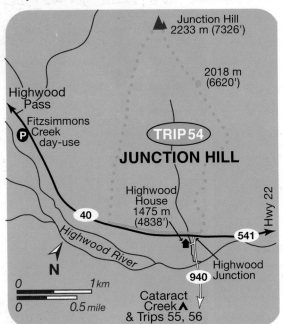

Hwys 40, 940 and 541 intersect. Turn left (S) onto unpaved Hwy 940, then immediately turn right (W) into the Highwood House parking lot, at 1475 m (4838 ft).

From **Trans-Canada Hwy 1**, E of Canmore, drive 105 km (65.2 mi) S on Hwy 40 to Highwood Junction, where Hwys 40, 940 and 541 intersect. Turn right (S) onto unpaved Hwy 940, then immediately turn right (W) into the Highwood House parking lot, at 1475 m (4838 ft).

On Foot

From the Highwood House parking lot, walk out to the intersection of Hwys 40, 940 and 541. Turn right (E) and walk uphill on Hwy 541. About 250 m (273 yd) from the intersection, pass a pullout on the right. Then be looking left for the trail departing the pavement. It's 15 m / yd before (W of) a white **road sign** warning W-bound motorists that Hwys 40 and 940 are ahead.

From the pavement, at 1510 m (4953 ft), head N on the unsigned trail, up the steep slope, into pine forest. You're ascending the left side of a drainage. In about four minutes, follow a faint path curving left (NW).

About ten minutes up, at 1577 m (5174 ft), the Great Divide is visible west. S, below you, is unpaved Hwy 940. The gentle, open slope above is inviting. Angle right (NNW) and ascend cross-country.

Within 20 minutes, you'll be funneled into a narrowing **corridor of trees**. At a worn patch of dirt, where the forested slope ahead falls away steeply into a basin, turn right (NE). Follow a game path through a stand of pines and, in a couple minutes, emerge onto another **open slope**. Ascend NNW. Highwood House is visible below.

After about 40 minutes, reach a **minor ridgecrest** at 1727 m (5665 ft). Its far (E) slope plummets steeply into the upper end of the drainage that you began hiking next to when you departed the highway. Turn left and ascend N, just below the ridgecrest, on its gentler left (W) side.

Pick up a contouring cattle path angling right, around the far (N) end of the minor ridgecrest. When the path disappears, proceed right (NE) onto a gentle **saddle** dividing two drainages. Right is the smaller drainage you began hiking beside and which you overlooked a short way back, from the minor ridgecrest. Left is a much larger drainage beneath Junction Hill (visible N). The larger drainage separates Junction Hill's right (SE) ridge from its left (S) ridge.

Pause on the saddle to orient yourself. You'll ascend the right ridge to the summit, then descend the left ridge to Hwy 40. That means your immediate task is to surmount the right ridge. Though it has the forbidding appearance of a continuous cliff, directly above you is a breach through which even cattle have crested the ridge.

Carry on, NE. The higher you ascend, the more apparent this **breach** will become. After side-hilling to the right, turn left and follow a natural ramp up between boulders. Finally, angle right between more boulders and you'll quickly top out in an open, level patch of grass on Junction Hill's **SE ridge**. Total hiking time: about one hour.

Relax. Enjoy the view. You can now peer NNE into Stony Creek canyon and up at Holy Cross Mtn. The abandoned fire lookout atop Mt. Burke (Trip 56) is visible SE. The mesa beyond it is Plateau Mtn. A continuous wall of peaks—the Great Divide—spans the SW horizon. The Divide comprises sub-ranges. You're primarily looking at the High Rock Range. The Elk Range is WNW.

From here to the top of Junction Hill, your route is the **ridgecrest**. Just keep following it NW. After a few, small (8-m/yd) ups and downs, the ascent is consistently moderate. Expect a pleasantly vigourous hike on rocky terrain, through pine forest, with frequent views. You'll encounter some deadfall that you'll have to clamber over or around, and a couple short, steep, hands-on pitches, but no exposure. Occasionally skirt right or left of the crest, whichever is easiest.

At 2018 m (6620 ft), about 1½ hours after departing the highway, negotiate tilted rock slabs left of the crest. About 2½ hours from the highway, hikers who've maintained a moderate pace will surpass the trees, proceed over a rocky bump, and arrive at the true, cairned summit of 2233-m (7326-ft) **Junction Hill**. Mt. Head is now visible N, in the Highwood Range. The Cat Creek Hills are below you, NW. Much farther NW is Mist Mtn (Trip 34).

Departing the cairned summit, drop to the bump, then descend SW, initially over broken rock. Stay just right of the trees, along the upper edge of the right (NW) slope. Proceed SW as long as the grade remains comfortable. Just before it plunges, bear left (S) to continue descending less steeply.

Briefly work your way down through trees, then across a **boulder field** (large, charcoal-coloured slabs covered with black and green lichen). Below, to the S, is a knoll with a bald top. That's your immediate goal. It will often be in view as you descend.

After the boulder field, re-enter forest. The angle of descent steepens. Drop through trees for about eight minutes. Angle right and emerge onto an open, grassy slope. Keep descending S. At 1845 m (6050 ft), re-enter forest on a **cattle path**. It begins just 5 m/yd below (right of) a treed saddle. Follow it into a stand of aspen. A minute farther, where the path appears to end, proceed over rock slabs; you'll find it resumes, contouring right (W) of a knob. Thank goodness for those enterprising cows, eh?

About 1¼ hours from the summit, reach a small, grassy **saddle**. From here, a three-minute ascent through forest leads to the **bald-topped knoll** you've been aiming for. Keep descending S. Bear right, between stands of trees, where the grade is more gradual.

The terrain is open from here on, and the highway is in view, so you can complete the descent however you please. But this last slope tilts at an

Chocolate lily

alarming angle. To avoid the steepest section, look left for a prominent, standing **snag** at 1768 m (5800 ft). It's on the edge of a 3-m (10-ft) **rock band**. Just below the snag is an easy place to scramble left, through the rock band, to the slightly more gradual slope below.

Proceed S, edging your way down precipitous dirt, rock and grass. After a joint-crunching final descent, step onto **Hwy 40** at 1558 m (5110 ft). Turn left and follow the pavement about 20 minutes E to where the 8.5-km (5.3-mi) loop ends, at Highwood House.

TRIP 55

Raspberry Ridge

LOCATION	Hwy 940, S of Highwood Junction
LOOP	9 km (5.6 mi)
ELEVATION GAIN	653 m (2142 ft)
KEY ELEVATIONS	trailhead 1707 m (5600 ft)
	lookout 2360 m (7741 ft)
HIKING TIME	3 to 4 hours
DIFFICULTY	easy
MAP	Gem Trek *Highwood—South Kananaskis Country*

Opinion

Even into early summer, the peaks in the main range of the Canadian Rockies can remain white as penguin breasts. Though beautiful, it's a frustrating sight for hikers eager to stride.

In the front range, however, snow accumulates less abundantly and melts sooner. Peruse a map of southern Kananaskis Country, and you'll discover several front-range summits crowned by fire lookouts—your assurance of a panoramic vista. Among them is Raspberry Ridge.

On a fine day, the helipad next to the Raspberry Ridge fire lookout invites hikers to sprawl and snooze. The riveting view, however, makes that difficult. A 360° mountainscape, including a huge swath of the peak-studded Great Divide, will likely keep you turning and staring.

You didn't follow your winter exercise regimen with sufficient discipline? You'll still find Raspberry a rational first outing of the season. The hike is relatively short, views are frequent, much of the way is on road reverting to trail, and most of the ascent is gradual. Only the final approach to the alpine ridgecrest is steep.

You've kept fit? Other nearby mountains bearing fire lookouts include Hailstone Butte (Trip 57) and Mt. Burke (Trip 56). You can tag two, possibly three summits on a weekend. So consider staying overnight at Cataract Creek campground. It's a mere 1.7 km (1 mi) south of the Raspberry Ridge trailhead.

Given that a key purpose of fire lookouts is to monitor the effects of lightning strikes, here are a few relevant facts you can use to impress and alarm your hiking companions while en route to Raspberry Ridge:

- The thunder resulting from a lightning strike is audible up to about 19 km (12 mi). The average lightning bolt is 10 to 13 km (6 to 8 mi) long. Lightning bolts commonly travel 40 to 64 km (25 to 40 mi) horizontally before turning earthward. One lightning bolt in Texas traveled 177 km (110 mi): from Waco, over Fort Worth, to Dallas. In other words, if you see lightning, forget about counting "one-thousand one, one-thousand two..." between flash and bang. Lightning you hear can conceivably strike you.

- At any given moment, about 2,000 thunderstorms are active worldwide. Each generates an average of 100 lightning strikes per second. During a five-year study, 20,000,000 lightning strikes were recorded in Canada. In a single 24-hour period, 5,000 lightning strikes were recorded in Alberta. The Alberta foothills are among the four places in Canada where lightning is most common. Lightning is 33% more likely here than elsewhere in the country.

- The temperature of a lightning bolt is 30,538° C (55,000°F), which is five times hotter than the surface of the sun. That's why lightning instantly turns water or water vapor into super hot, high-pressure steam. Even cement containing a tiny amount of moisture will explode when struck by lightning. An adult human body is 55 to 60% water.

Obviously you should check the weather forecast before hiking to Raspberry Ridge. Wait for a shatterproof blue sky.

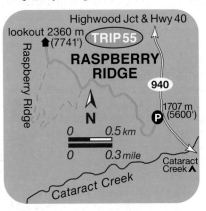

Fact

Before your trip

Be aware that Hwy 40—between Kananaskis Lakes Trail and Highwood Junction—is closed December 1 through June 15. So, spring access to Raspberry Ridge is via Hwy 22, SW of Calgary.

By Vehicle

From **Highwood Junction**, drive 11.4 km (7.1 mi) S on Hwy 940. (Highwood Junction is where Hwys 40, 541 and 940 intersect. It's 43 km / 26.7 mi SW of Longview; 105 km / 65.1 mi SE of Trans-Canada Hwy 1.)

From **Hwy 532**, drive N on Hwy 940. Pass the entrance to Cataract Creek campground at 18.8 km (11.7 mi). Proceed N another 1.7 km (1.1 mi).

From **either approach**, look for the unmarked, gated, dirt spur on the W side of Hwy 940. Park in the pullout before the gate, at 1707 m (5600 ft).

On Foot

Follow the spur past the gate. In 40 m/yd, overgrown Raspberry Ridge road forks right. Follow it, ascending SSW. In a few minutes, at a **Y-junction**, bear right and ascend. The wider left track descends into Cataract Creek valley.

Above the Y-junction, the old road is rehabilitating to trail. It curves W, then N, through pines. At 1738 m (5700 ft), about 15 minutes from the trailhead, Raspberry Ridge is visible left (NW). Drop into a **stream gully**, then ascend more steeply. After a gentle southward stretch, the trail bends NNW.

At 1939 m (6360 ft), about 50 minutes from the trailhead, you're approaching the SE end of Raspberry Ridge. Visible SE is Plateau Mountain.

On Raspberry Ridge

Mt. Burke is E, its abandoned, dilapidated fire lookout barely discernable. The Mt. Burke trail ascends through forest, then follows the open, rocky ridgeline left to the summit.

Reach a **cairned fork** at 1950 m (6396 ft) after hiking about one hour. Ignore the left fork—an old road descending W. Turn right (NNW) and ascend. Raspberry Ridge fire lookout is visible ahead, on the skyline. Continued upward progress soon grants you an overview of Cataract Creek valley.

After hiking about 1 hour and 15 minutes, the trail steepens at 2134 m (7000 ft). Strong striders will crest **Raspberry Ridge** in another 20 minutes. Turn right (N) for the final five-minute ascent to the **fire lookout** crowning the 2360-m (7741-ft) summit. Total hiking time: about 1⅔ hours.

Ascending Raspberry Ridge

Numerous clearcuts mar the scenery below. Above and beyond, however, is an engaging Rocky Mountain panorama. Mt. Head, at the S end of the Highwood Range, is N. The prominent, lone massif of Mist Mountain is far NNW. Mist Ridge is below it, NW.

Nearby NW and W are peaks of the High Rock Range. Fording River Pass is NW. Mt. Armstrong (NW) is the highest peak N of the pass. Baril Peak is directly W. Etherington is WSW. Multi-peaked Scrimger Ridge is S of Etherington. 2896-m (9500-ft) Mt. Farguhar is SW. Crowsnest Mountain is way S. Calgary is NNE.

TRIP 56
Mt. Burke

LOCATION	Hwy 940, S of Highwood Junction
ROUND TRIP	16 km (10 mi)
ELEVATION GAIN	935 m (3067 ft)
KEY ELEVATIONS	trailhead 1605 m (5264 ft), summit 2541 m (8333 ft)
HIKING TIME	5 to 7 hours
DIFFICULTY	moderate
MAP	Gem Trek *Highwood—South Kananaskis Country*

Opinion

Mt. Burke is the most exciting K-Country peak mere hikers can fling themselves at in shoulder-season and expect to summit. Its front-range location, sun blasted, west-facing trail, and barren, wind-ravaged upper reaches ensure you'll encounter a minimal snowpack.

It's startling how early you can get up here. Without gradually easing into the mountains on several lower-elevation rambles, a springtime ascent of Burke is like entering a theater mid-movie and being assaulted by explosions, celebrations, chase scenes: totally out of context, but sensational.

The derelict, ramshackle, fire-lookout cabin teetering atop Burke attests to the panorama awaiting you. You'll see much of southern K-Country: from Calgary and the prairie, to the Great Divide. It's just a long way up. This would be a lot to ask of indolent muscles if not for a most compassionate trail. The switchbacks are actually so languorous they might try your patience. That's why you're sure to at least achieve the vantage above treeline. From there on, the slope is tantalizingly open and will re-ignite your resolve to prevail.

Need more inspiration? Last time we were hiking up, we met a 76-year-old bounding down. Regular exercise should enable most of us to remain summiteers into our 80's. Anyone under 50 better have a doctor's note if unable to surmount Burke. Even declining middle-agers can reclaim their natural vitality and stamina. That's what our hero said he did after retiring early from his career.

While you're clacking across scree on the slim summit ridge, imagine the bug-eyed, heart-racing terror of the hapless pack horses forced to carry supplies to the fire-lookout attendant. Cliff bands plunge into Salter Creek canyon 854 m (2800 ft) below. The lookout was manned every summer from 1929 until 1953, then superseded by Raspberry Ridge lookout (Trip 55) to the west.

photos: *1 Mt. Burke summit ridge 2 Mt. Burke, from Raspberry Ridge (Trip 55)
3 Cinquefoil*

1

2

3

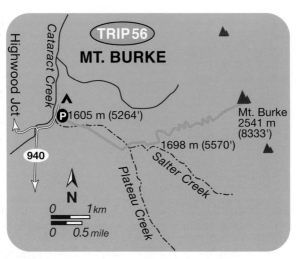

TRIP 56
MT. BURKE

Highwood Jct

Cataract Creek

P 1605 m (5264')

940

Mt. Burke
2541 m
(8333')

1698 m (5570')

Salter Creek

Plateau Creek

N

0   1 km

0   0.5 mile

Fact

Before your trip

Be aware that Hwy 40—between Kananaskis Lakes Trail and Highwood Junction—is closed December 1 through June 15. So, spring access to Mt. Burke is via Hwy 22, SW of Calgary.

By Vehicle

From **Highwood Junction**, drive 14 km (8.7 mi) S on unpaved Hwy 940. (Highwood Junction is where Hwys 40, 541 and 940 intersect. It's 43 km / 26.7 mi SW of Longview; 105 km / 65.1 mi SE of Trans-Canada Hwy 1.)

From the **junction of Hwys 940 and 532**, drive 19.5 km (11.8 mi) N on unpaved Hwy 940.

From **either approach**, upon reaching Cataract Creek day-use area, turn E onto the Cataract Creek campground access road. Cross Salter Creek bridge in 0.7 km (0.4 mi). Just 100 m (110 yd) farther, turn right into the trailhead parking lot, at 1605 m (5264 ft). From here, Mt. Burke is in full view E, from its forested lower slopes to the scree-covered summit.

On Foot

Make sure you've packed plenty of water for the dry ascent. Then follow the road back to **Salter Creek bridge**. On the N side of the bridge, turn left (E) onto the grass-covered imprint of an old road paralleling the creekbed. In several minutes, cross the rubbly, usually dry creekbed and continue generally SE. Proceed briefly through a stand of aspen and pine. Where the trail vanishes, follow a faint cattle track between berms. Then pick up an old two-track road and go left (E) toward Mt. Burke.

Within 20 minutes, cross a creekbed. Follow another scrap of trail, then a cobbly stretch. At 2.7 km (1.7 mi), 1704 m (5590 ft), about 25 minutes from the trailhead, reach the **confluence of Salter and Plateau creeks**—both probably dry. Plateau Creek enters via the narrow, steep-walled gorge immediately ahead. Don't go that way. Turn left (E) and cross Salter Creek's main channel. On the far side, ascend an old road NE into forest. In a minute, ignore the cairned route forking left (NNW) upslope. Keep following snippets of trail and eroded road along the boulder-strewn bed of Salter creek. The old road favours the left side of the drainage.

At 1698 m (5570 ft), about ten minutes above the Salter/Plateau confluence, arrive at a **yellow sign**. Just beyond is a **metal pipe** protruding from the ground, perhaps creatively adorned by previous hikers. Turn left (N) here onto the **steep trail ascending the W-facing slope**, initially through Engelmann spruce, and lodgepole pine. You've begun the switchbacking ascent of Mt. Burke.

Near 1980 m (6495 ft), about 1¼ hours from the trailhead, attain views through the forest. Raspberry Ridge is visible WNW, beyond Cataract Creek valley. Alpine fir now beautify the forest. A bootbeaten path rockets directly up the fall line, shortcutting the switchbacks. But it's easier to keep to the main trail and cruise briskly. On the descent, zooming down the direct route does save time.

Swift hikers will emerge above the 2186-m (7170-ft) **treeline** about 1¾ hours after departing the trailhead. The Highwood Range is visible NW. Mist Mtn (Trip 34) is just beyond. The Great Divide runs the length of the W horizon. Plateau Creek canyon is SW. Plateau Mtn is the oddly flat expanse S, beyond Salter Creek Canyon. Yellow, shrubby cinquefoil brighten the grey rock underfoot. Surprisingly, purple monkeypod also survives in this desolation.

The trail zigzags upward through chunky rock. At 2287 m (7500 ft), you can see your destination ENE: the Mt. Burke fire-lookout cabin. The trail gets more exciting as it switchbacks up the north side of the SW-jutting summit ridge. A short stretch is just 4 m wide. The final ascent is just below the crest of the **narrow summit ridge**, on the right (S) side, 550 m (1800 ft) above Salter Creek canyon.

Speedy hikers drop their packs on the 2541-m (8333-ft) **summit of Mt. Burke** 2¾ hours after departing the trailhead. Total distance: 8 km (5.1 mi). Stay out of the abandoned, rickety, fire-lookout cabin. It's unsafe. The High Rock Range is W to NW. The Livingstone Range is NNE. Sentinel Peak is nearby SE, just left of Plateau Mtn.

It's possible to be back at the trailhead within 1¾ hours, if you gallop.

Penstemon

TRIP 57
Hailstone Butte

LOCATION	Hwy 532, SE edge of K-Country
ROUND TRIP	4 km (2.5 mi)
ELEVATION GAIN	327 m (1073 ft)
KEY ELEVATIONS	trailhead 2037 m (6680 ft), summit 2364 m (7753 ft)
HIKING TIME	2 to 3 hours
DIFFICULTY	easy
MAPS	page 284; Langford Creek 82 J / 1

Opinion

The serendipitous combination of a high-elevation trailhead, alpine slopes, and exposure to the snow-melting warmth of our sacred star, distinguishes Hailstone Butte as a premier, early-season destination. The fire lookout garnishing the summit affords a panoramic vista capable of resuscitating a keen hiker's winter-dormant enthusiasm.

Available as early as May or as late as November, Hailstone's prime time is spring, when the grass is verdant and the frequently ferocious winds are less frigid. Whenever you come, pack your toque, gloves, and windproof shell. Gusts up to 150 kph (93 mph) have been clocked at the fire lookout. Imagine hunkering down all night with a gale like *that* battering your door.

Enhance your exploration of southern K-Country by reading the description of Windy Peak Hills (Trip 58), which shares the same trailhead as

Plumed aven

Hailstone Butte. You should hike both, perhaps in a single day, while you're here. Also read Raspberry Ridge (Trip 55) and Mt. Burke (Trip 56). They're in Hailstone's neighbourhood, are likewise crowned with fire lookouts, and will reward you with grand views. You can bag two, possibly three lookouts on a weekend.

Coming from Calgary? Be sure to drive unpaved Hwy 532 (off Hwy 22) at least one way. It rolls through beautiful, lush foothills blanketed with aspen. Lightly traveled, mostly by those working the land, the area has a soothing, pre-bustle atmosphere. And don't worry, the road's maintained. You won't hurt the Audi.

Something else you need not be concerned about is the word *scramble* in the *On Foot* description. Attaining Hailstone Butte entails a quick, easy, no-exposure scramble near the top. Anyone who can hang on while lifting knees to chin for a couple steps will slither up, no problem.

Fact

Before your trip

Be aware that Hwy 40—between Kananaskis Lakes Trail and Highwood Junction—is closed December 1 through June 15. So, spring access to Hailstone Butte is via Hwy 22, SW of Calgary.

By Vehicle

Following directions for Windy Peak Hills (Trip 58), drive Hwy 532 to a pass called *The Hump*. A roadside pullout here affords trailhead parking: south of the Texas gate, beside the small pond, at 2037 m (6680 ft).

On Foot

From the S side of the Texas gate, head SW, cross the road, and walk up the short slope. Then go NW through a grassy gully. You'll see two trails. The upper one soon ends. Follow the lower one around the low, grassy ridge, into the upper drainage. The fire lookout atop Hailstone Butte is visible NW. You'll be ascending just left of it. Keep that in mind, because you'll be unable to see the lookout when you're below it, farther up the **drainage**.

When the lower trail fades in willows and along the creeklet, proceed NW. Ascend the **grassy slope** just left of where the lookout is perched atop the butte. Above this slope, the rock band is thin and broken, granting an easy scramble onto the crest.

Nearing the **rock band**, there's a gully between grassy ribs. Ascend NW between them. Surmounting the first 3 m/yd of the rock band requires athleticism. Above that you'll find easier stairstep ledges. Strong hikers will top out on **Hailstone Butte** within 30 minutes of leaving the road.

Turn right (N) and follow the path just below the left (W) side of the crest to reach the now visible **fire lookout** in a couple minutes, at 2364 m (7753 ft). The butte extends farther NW. A fire road descends the W side. Calgary is visible NE. Sentinel Peak is nearby N. Mt. Burke is NW. Plateau Mtn is WNW. Windy Peak is SE, and beyond it is Mt. Livingston.

Time permitting, enjoy striding S about 1.5 km (0.9 mi) along the open butte before returning the way you came.

Ascending Windy Peak Hills (Trip 58). Upper left ridge is Hailstone Butte.

TRIP 58
Windy Peak Hills

LOCATION	Hwy 532, SE edge of K-Country
LOOP	9 km (5.6 mi)
ELEVATION GAIN	500 m (1640 ft)
KEY ELEVATIONS	trailhead 2037 m (6680 ft)
	Windy Peak 2250 m (7380 ft)
HIKING TIME	3½ to 5 hours
DIFFICULTY	easy
MAP	Langford Creek 82 J / 1

Opinion

Hiking is a conversation with the earth. The greening-up of the land in spring indicates that it's ready to talk again and is inviting you to listen. The Windy Peak Hills is a fine place to respond.

These front-range hills green-up early and can be hikeable by May. Granted, they're merely hills, not mountains—not by the Canadian Rockies standard anyway—but they're beautiful and offer a varied, vigourous loop hike with constant views. If you're lucky, you'll witness the pre-summer burst of wildflowers featuring lavender harebells and brown-eyed susan.

Further burnishing the hills' appeal is another premier hike, Hailstone Butte (Trip 57), sharing the same trailhead. Plus, you'll find officially sanctioned, free camping nearby. So this is an ideal destination for your first hiking / camping weekend of the season. Or your last. The Windy Peak Hills are attractive in autumn too, when snowfall dampens your more vigourous dialogue with the main range alps.

You'll swoop up and down the emerald hills by following a faint, bootbeaten trail that occasionally vanishes. It sometimes reappears as a cattle track or barely distinguishable route. Easy navigation is briefly necessary in a few places. But no worries. You're frequently on or near a crest, so the whole area is often in view, and the way forward is usually obvious. You'll also have our precise directions.

The loop is a tour of five hills (ridgeline bumps, really), plus Windy Peak—the last and highest promontory in this compact group and the only one with a name. From Windy, you'll descend a forested slope, cross a clearcut-cum-pasture, then intersect a dirt highway. The final 1.8 km (1.1 mi) is a road-walk back to your vehicle. Don't let this deter you from completing the loop. You'll likely encounter little or no traffic on this remote road, so the home stretch is pleasant enough. If a vehicle does appear, hitch a ride.

About those cattle tracks. Expect to see the lumbering beasts and their splatterings. It's a minor blemish on an otherwise superlative hike during shoulder-season—the time of year when you feel fortunate to be hiking at all.

TRIP 57 HAILSTONE BUTTE
🏔 lookout → Hwy 22
2364 m
(7753')

The Hump
Ⓟ 2037 m (6680')

1

2

3

532   TRIP 58
WINDY PEAK
HILLS
4

N

0   0.5 km
0   0.3 mile

Windy   5
Peak 🏔
2250 m (7380')

In summer, however, you want to be much higher in the Rockies, stepping over grizzly-bear scat, not cow pies.

Fact

Before your trip

Be aware that Hwy 40—between Kananaskis Lakes Trail and Highwood Junction—is closed December 1 through June 15. So, spring access to Windy Peak Hills is via Hwy 22, SW of Calgary.

By Vehicle

From **Highwood Junction**, drive SE 31.8 km (19.7 mi) on Hwy 940. (Highwood Junction is where Hwys 40, 541 and 940 intersect. It's 43 km / 26.7 mi SW of Longview; 105 km / 65.1 mi SE of Trans-Canada Hwy 1.) Upon reaching Hwy 532, go left (NE) another 4 km (2.5 mi) to a pass called *The Hump*, where a roadside pullout affords trailhead parking: S of the Texas gate, beside the small pond, at 2037 m (6680 ft).

Or, from **SW Calgary**, drive S on Hwy 22 to Longview. Proceed another 28.5 km (17.8 mi) to the junction with Johnson Creek Trail (Hwy 532). Reset your trip odometer to 0 and go SW on Hwy 532. Enter K-Country in 8.2 km (5.1 mi). Just after crossing Johnson Creek, pass Indian Creek campground on the right at 13.3 km (8.2 mi). At 18.5 km (11.5 mi) the Windy Peak Hills are visible left (S). Ahead you can also see Hailstone Butte (Trip 57) above and beyond the road you're about to traverse. At 22 km (13.6 mi) reach a pass called *The Hump*, where a roadside pullout affords trailhead parking: S of the Texas gate, beside the small pond, at 2037 m (6680 ft).

On Foot

From the N side of the Texas gate, ascend SE on the remains of an old road. In 20 m/yd it dwindles to trail. Soon climb over a barbed-wire fence. Proceed where the trail disappears. It resumes on the S side of the first bump. Where it fades again, stay left. About 30 minutes from the trailhead, surmount the 2174-m (7130-ft) **first bump**. You can now see that lichen-adorned rock covers much of these slopes, though from a distance they appeared grassy. Dwarf lupine and other colourful wildflowers are abundant here in spring and early summer.

Faint trail resumes just below the first bump's summit. Continue SE about ten minutes along the obvious ridge to the 2146-m (7040-ft) **second bump**. Trail resumes below, to the right. Descend through krummholz five minutes to a junction in Timber Creek Pass. Left (NE) leads to Johnson Creek. Keep following the ridgeline SE. The route crosses small, rock slabs, skirting the **third bump** on its right (SW) side. Hailstone Butte is visible NW.

Drop to the **second pass**, at 2030 m (7040 ft). You're now 3 km (2 mi) from the trailhead, having hiked about 50 minutes. A cattle track descends right (SW) across meadow into the forest of South Twin Creek. It offers a shortcut exit, intersecting Hwy 532 just 1.8 km (1.1 mi) below (S of) The Hump. But if you want to resume the loop, ascend the trail SE along a fence.

Swift hikers will surmount the 2125-m (6970-ft) **fourth bump** about ten minutes above the col. Visible SSW is rounded Windy Peak. Behind it is Mt. Livingston. Way beyond, the prominent, lone peak is 2787-m (9140-ft) Crowsnest Mtn. Saddle Mtn is SE. Chain Lakes Reservoir is partially visible E.

The trail now rounds the head of the draw down which you can see the two-track trail on the right side of the meadow. Curve briefly SE, then SSW toward Windy Peak. About 1½ hours from the trailhead, descend a bit to reach the bottom of a **third pass**, at 2085 m (6840 ft). Ascend a bit more, passing below and just W of the **fifth bump** (two bumps close together). Do not follow the road-trail descending between the fourth and fifth bumps to a meadow between forested slopes.

Where the trail disappears, aim for the far end of the fifth bump. Within minutes, pick up a well-defined rock-and-dirt trail through trees. It soon veers NW, ascending through more trees. The trail traverses a slope, then pops out onto Windy Peak's open, gentle, summit ridge. Turn left (S) and stride uphill across grass and heather to quickly surmount 2250-m (7380-ft) **Windy Peak**. You're now 4.8 km (3 mi) from the trailhead, having hiked nearly two hours.

From the summit, retrace your steps down the generally NW-trending ridge. Pick up a faint trail as you descend, initially curving N. Then bear NNW over rock and grass, on the left (W) side of the ridge. If you're experienced at cross-country navigation, skip the detailed directions below and sniff out your own route down to the tussocky meadow, then NW to Hwy 532.

Re-enter trees about 15 minutes below the summit of Windy Peak. Look left (rather than down the center of the ridge) for the easiest descent route: a one m/yd-wide **swath cut through the trees** long ago. Follow it W. About five minutes below treeline, drop through a meadow and angle right. Pick up traces of cattle track. Continue down NW through forest broken by grassy clearings. The going is easy so far.

About ten minutes below treeline, reach the edge of the willowy, **South Timber Creek drainage** at 1951 m (6400 ft). Go right (NW) to take advantage of a broad cattle-track. Tiptoe through a bog and hop a creeklet. On the low slope just above the bog, follow a trail NW through the cutblock. Progress is briefly impeded in the tussocky, willowy, muddy bog of North Twin Creek. Stretches of cattle track are helpful. Cross a creeklet twice before finally intersecting **Hwy 532** at 1907 m (6255 ft). Total hiking time: about three hours. Turn right and walk the road 1.8 km (1.1 mi) N back to your vehicle parked at The Hump.

Upper Ribbon Lakes basin, from below Guinn's Pass (Trip 18)

INFORMATION SOURCES

For EMERGENCY 24-hour response, including Mountain Rescue assistance, call 9-1-1. To phone provincial park offices toll-free within Alberta, first dial 310-0000. To report bear or cougar sightings, phone (403) 591-7755.

Hiking

Barrier Lake
Visitor Information Centre
(403) 673-3985

Bow Valley Wildland Prov. Park
(403) 678-5500

Elbow Valley
Visitor Information Centre
(403) 949-4261

Friends of Kananaskis
Suite 201, 800 Railway Avenue
Canmore, AB T1W 1P1
(403) 678-5593
www.kananaskis.org
friends@kananaskis.org
trails@kananaskis.org
   for trail maintenance

Peter Lougheed and Spray Valley
Provincial Parks
Visitor Information Centre
(403) 591-6322
www.Kananaskis-Country.ca

Sheep River Information Centre
(403) 933-7172

Camping

Backcountry Permit Desk
Kananaskis Country
(403) 678-3136

Bow Valley Provincial Park
(403) 673-2163
www.bowvalleycampgrounds.com

Mount Kidd RV Park
(403) 591-7700
www.mountkiddrv.com

Mt. Kidd, from Hwy 40

Kananaskis Country
Peter Lougheed and Spray Valley provincial parks, Elbow and Sheep river valleys, southern Kananaskis Country
(403) 591-7226, or 1-877-537-2757
www.kananaskiscountrycampgrounds.com

Lodging

Alpine Club of Canada
P.O. Box 8040, Indian Flats Road
Canmore, AB T1W 2T8
(403) 678-3200
www.alpineclubofcanada.ca
info@alpineclubofcanada.ca

Canmore Bed & Breakfast Assoc.
P.O. Box 8005, Canmore, AB T1W 2T8
www.bbcanmore.com

Kananaskis Wilderness Hostel /
Ribbon Creek
(403) 591-7333, or 1-866-762-4122
www.hihostels.ca

Weather

www.weatheroffice.gc.ca

Your Guides

Kathy and Craig are dedicated to each other and to hiking, in that order. Their second date was a 20-mi (32-km) dayhike in Arizona. Since then they haven't stopped for long.

They've trekked through much of the world's vertical topography, including the Nepalese Himalaya, Patagonian Andes, and New Zealand Alps. In Europe, they've hiked the Scottish Highlands, Spain's Costa Blanca and Els Ports mountains, Mallorca's Serra de Tramuntana, the Alpes Maritimes, the French, Swiss, and Italian Alps, and Italy's Dolomiti. In North America, they've explored the B.C. Coast, Selkirk and Purcell ranges, Montana's Beartooth Wilderness, Wyoming's Grand Tetons, the Colorado Rockies, the California Sierra, and Arizona's Superstition Wilderness and Grand Canyon.

Visit Kathy and Craig's website: www. hikingcamping.com. You'll find their blog posts are often mini-guidebooks, and their photo gallery is constantly growing.

In 1989, they moved from the U.S. to Canada, so they could live near the range that inspired the first of their refreshingly unconventional books: *Don't Waste Your Time in the Canadian Rockies, The Opinionated Hiking Guide*. Its popularity encouraged them to abandon their careers—Kathy as an ESL teacher, Craig as an ad-agency creative director—and start their own guidebook publishing company: hikingcamping.com. They now migrate annually to southern Utah, where they wrote *Hiking From Here To Wow: Utah Canyon Country*. Their most recent book, *Heading Outdoors Eventually Leads Within*, explores the interior dimension of hiking.

Though the distances they hike are epic, Kathy and Craig agree that hiking, no matter how far, is the easiest of the many tasks necessary to create a guidebook. What they find most challenging is the need to spend twice as much time at their computers—writing, organizing, editing, checking facts—as they do on the trail.

The result is worth it. Kathy and Craig's colorful writing, opinionated commentary, and enthusiasm for the joys of hiking make their guidebooks uniquely helpful and compelling.

nomads@hikingcamping.com   hiking camping.com

photos: **1** *Bow Peak, Canadian Rockies* **2** *Aravaipa Canyon, Arizona* **3** *Le Mejie, Parc National des Ecrins, French Alps* **4** *Gertrude Saddle, Fiordland, New Zealand* **5** *Cedar Mesa, Utah* **6** *Snow Canyon, Utah* **7** *Beauty Creek headwaters, Jasper NP, Canadian Rockies* **8** *Angels Landing, Zion NP, Utah* **9** *Tonto Trail & Colorado River, Grand Canyon NP, Arizona* **10** *Tasman Sea, North Island, New Zealand* **11** *The Iceline, Yoho NP, Canadian Rockies* **12** *Mallorca, Spain* **13** *Craig & Kathy*

Other Titles from hikingcamping.com

The following titles—boot-tested and written by the Opinionated Hikers, Kathy & Craig Copeland—are widely available at outdoor shops and book-stores. Visit www.hikingcamping.com to read excerpts and purchase online.

Don't Waste Your Time®
in the Canadian Rockies
The Opinionated Hiking Guide

ISBN 978-0978342753 Even here, in a mountain range designated a UNESCO World Heritage Site for its "superlative natural phenomena" and "exceptional natural beauty and aesthetic importance," not all scenery is equal. Some destinations are simply more striking, more intriguing, more inspiring than others. Now you can be certain you're choosing a rewarding hike for your weekend or vacation. This uniquely helpful, visually captivating guidebook covers Banff, Jasper, Kootenay, Yoho and Waterton Lakes national parks, plus Mt. Robson and Mt. Assiniboine provincial parks. It rates each trail *Premier, Outstanding, Worthwhile,* or *Don't Do*, explains why, and provides comprehensive route descriptions. 138 dayhikes and backpack trips. Trail maps for each hike. 544 pages, 270 photos, full colour throughout. 6th edition January 2011.

Where Locals Hike
in the West Kootenay
The Premier Trails in Southeast B.C.
near Kaslo & Nelson

ISBN 978-1-927462003 See the peaks, glaciers and cascades that make locals passionate about these mountains. The 50 most rewarding dayhikes and backpack trips in the Selkirk and west Purcell ranges of southeast British Columbia. Includes Valhalla, Kokanee Glacier, and Goat Range parks, as well as hikes near Arrow, Slocan, and Kootenay lakes. Discerning trail reviews help you choose your trip. Detailed route descriptions keep you on the path. 304 pages, 130 photos, trail locator maps, full colour throughout. Updated 3rd edition July 2012.

Hiking from Here to WOW:
Utah Canyon Country
90 Trails to the Wonder of Wilderness

ISBN 978-0-89997-452-1 The authors hiked more than 1,600 miles through Zion, Bryce, Escalante-Grand Staircase, Glen Canyon, Grand Gulch, Cedar Mesa, Canyonlands, Moab, Arches, Capitol Reef, and the San Rafael Swell. They took more than 2,500 photos and hundreds of pages of field notes. Then they culled their list of favourite hikes down to 90 trips—each selected for its power to incite awe. Their 480-page book describes where to find the redrock cliffs, slickrock domes, soaring arches, and ancient ruins that make southern Utah unique in all the world. And it does so in refreshing style: honest, literate, entertaining, inspiring.

Like all *WOW Guides*, this one is full colour throughout, with 220 photos and a trail map for each dayhike and backpack trip. Updated 1st edition May 2012.

Bears Beware!
Warning Calls You Can Make
to Avoid an Encounter

Here's the 30-minute MP3 that could save your life. Download it from hikingcamping.com to your computer. Go to Guidebooks > Bear Safety. Listen to it at home, or on your iPod while driving to the trailhead.

You'll find out why pepper spray, talking, and bells are insufficient protection. You'll realize that using your voice is the only reliable method of preventing a bear encounter. You'll discover why warning calls are the key to defensive hiking. You'll understand how, where and when to make warning calls. You'll learn specific strategies for worry-free hiking and camping in bear country.

Bears Beware! was endorsed by the wardens at Jasper National Park, which has the biggest grizzly-bear population in the Canadian Rockies. It was also approved by the wardens at Waterton National Park, which has the highest concentration of grizzly bears in the Rockies.

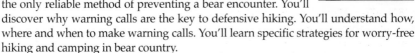

HEADING OUTDOORS EVENTUALLY LEADS WITHIN

Thoughts inspired by
30,000 miles on the Trail
by Kathy and Craig Copeland

The wisdom we glean from the wilds is a match lit in the rain. That's why we created this book: to cup our hands around the flame. These journal entries are the mental waypoints we recorded while hiking 30,000 miles (more than the circumference of the Earth) through wildlands worldwide. Accompanying them are photos of the places (primarily the Canadian Rockies, Utah canyon country, and New Zealand) where we conceived and noted the initial ideas. We hope our words and images compel you to recognize, voice, own and honour the thoughts arising from within while heading outdoors. Doing so will deepen your fulfillment. A truly adventurous life is contemplative as well as vigourous. Hardcover, 96 pages, 72 full-colour photos. First edition January 2011. Available at hikingcamping.com, or your local bookstore. ISBN 978-0-9783427-6-0.

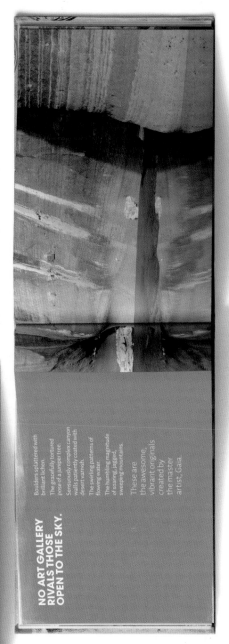

Everyone walks.
What distinguishes hikers is that walking does more than transport us. It transforms us.

NO ART GALLERY RIVALS THOSE OPEN TO THE SKY.

Boulders splattered with brilliant lichen.

The gracefully tortured pose of a juniper tree.

Sensuously complex canyon walls patiently coated with desert varnish.

The swirling patterns of flowing water.

The humbling magnitude of soaring, jagged, sweeping mountains.

These are the awesome, vibrant originals created by the master artist, Gaia.

Superstition Mountains, Arizona, February 5

Never Winter
Hiking Arizona November to April
Your guide to 45 premier desert trails

ISBN 978-1-927462-03-4 For hikers who want to keep hiking, the Copelands will soon offer a superior guidebook to the region that enthralls them during the "off season." These are the trails Kathy first hiked as a native Arizonan, and that she and Craig first hiked together. This is the backcountry that spawned their lifelong commitment to hiking and still inspires them to return every year when northern mountains whiten.

Never Winter will feature the premier hikes in Arizona's vast, Tonto and Coronado national forests, including the parks, wilderness areas and protected regions near these cities:

Flagstaff and Sedona

Grand Canyon National Park, South Rim, Red Rock-Secret Mountain Wilderness, Sycamore Canyon Wilderness

Phoenix and Mesa

Superstition Wilderness, Mazatzal Wilderness, Spur Cross Ranch, Cave Creek Park, Phoenix Mountains Park, Sierra Estrella Wilderness

Tucson

Pusch Ridge Wilderness, Santa Catalina Mountains, Saguaro National Monument, Rincon Mountain Wilderness, Aravaipa Canyon Wilderness, Chiricahua National Monument, Cochise Stronghold

Don't dream it. Plan it.
...with the help of your personal,
hiking/travel counselor.

Hi, I'm Kathy, co-owner of hikingcamping.com, and co-author of this guidebook plus a dozen others. If you're dreaming about a hiking-focused vacation, I'll help you plan it.

I love planning trips. I learned long ago that smart, thorough planning is trip insurance. Knowing what you want and don't want to do, and knowing how best to organize each day, allows you to pack more in and create a fulfilling journey. That's true whether you're roughing it on a long-distance trek, or dayhiking while staying at B&Bs.

Cinque Terre, Italia,
Sentiero 4B

Publishing *Don't Waste Your Time in the Canadian Rockies, The Opinionated Guidebook,* was my first effort to help others plan their hiking adventures. I recognized that most "guidebooks" offer facts but rarely venture an opinion, so they fail to truly guide. I wanted to arm people with much more than just the facts, so they could make optimal use of their precious, free time.

We frequently receive notes from avid hikers all over the world. Some ask us to tailor the detailed advice in our books for them. Others seek my counsel on hiking destinations elsewhere in the world. They've read the mini-guidebooks Craig and I have posted in our blog, and they want my help planning a similar trip.

I now formally offer my services as a hiking/travel counselor. I'm available to do for you what I'm constantly doing for myself and Craig.

I have a lifetime of experience planning trips devoted to hiking. I'm intimately familiar with far more destinations than we've written books about. For a complete list, see the *Your Trip* and *Photos/Videos* pages of our website.

I'm confident I can help you make the most of the time, energy and money you invest in your next hiking-focused vacation. I will, of course, charge for my service (see the *Your Trip* page of our website). In return, you'll receive (1) a phone consultation with me, (2) about 1½ hours of my research and planning, and (3) a detailed, trip plan customized for you. If you've considered splurging on a guided trip, you'll find my customized trip plan will save you big money and give you confidence to travel independently.

If you want to hire me as your personal, hiking/travel counselor, sign up at our website. Or email me <nomads@hikingcamping.com>, and I'll suggest how to proceed.

Let's plan a wondrous trip for you.

Smiles,

Kathy

Little and Middle Sisters, from Bow River, Canmore

Final ascent to Petain Basin (Trip 26)

Index

Arethusa Cirque 172
Aster Lake 130
Banff National Park 2, 64
bears 20
Beatty Lake 120, 124
Big Sister 24, 33
bighorn sheep 102, 106, 171
Birdwood Lake 62
Birdwood Pass 58
Birdwood Traverse 58
Bow Valley 24, 31, 226
Bull Creek Hills 263
Buller Passes 47
Burstall Creek valley 58, 66
Burstall Pass 13, 58, 64

Calgary 2, 254, 276
Canmore 2, 24, 31, 225, 230
Centennial Trail 88
Chester Lake 71, 75
Commonwealth Creek 58
Cougar Creek canyon 226
cougars 22
Cox Hill 243
dogs 18

Elbow Lake 14, 148, 154, 160
Elbow River 251, 254
Elbow River Valley 23, 148, 154, 160
elk 19
Elk Lakes Prov. Park 142
Elk Range 164, 172, 181
Elpoca Mtn 148, 160, 168
Evan-Thomas Pass 195

Fairholme Range 31, 206, 226
Forgetmenot Ridge 13, 249
Forks campground 126
Fortress, The 75, 81, 98
French Glacier 67
Frozen Lake 142

Galatea Creek 97
Galatea Lakes 97
Gibraltar Mtn
Goat Creek 31, 224
Goat Range 36, 51, 224
Gorge Creek 258
Grass Pass 263
Grassi Lakes 216
Great Divide 48, 53, 76, 84, 114, 183, 268, 273, 276

Grizzly Col 166
Grizzly Ridge 165
Grotto Canyon 208
Guinn's Pass 13, 17, 23, 47, 97

Ha Ling Peak 31, 217, 223
Haig Glacier 118
Hailstone Butte 280
Headwall Lakes 76, 81
Hidden Lake 130
Highwood Junction 264, 268
Highwood Pass 164, 169, 172
Highwood Range 181, 184
Highwood River Valley 263
hypothermia 22

Invincible Lake 12, 114, 119
James Walker Creek 9, 23, 84
Jumpingpound Mtn 243
Jumpingpound Ridge 13, 207, 240
Junction Hill 268
Kananaskis Lake, Lower 108, 110, 164
Kananaskis Lake, Upper 110, 114, 124, 133, 138, 245
Kananaskis River 2, 93, 97
King Creek gorge 107
King Creek Ridge 105

Lawrence Grassi 216
Lawson Lake 120
LeRoy Creek 120
lightning 22, 273
Lillian Lake 97
Little Arethusa 172

marmots 153, 170
Maude Lake 120
Memorial Lakes 92
Middle Sister 24,
Mist Creek valley 182
Mist Mtn 8, 175, 178, 182
Mist Ridge 8, 13, 182
moose 19
Moose Mtn 243
Mt. Allan 88
Mt. Arethusa 169, 174
Mt. Beatty 121
Mt. Birdwood 58
Mt. Blane 108
Mt. Bogart 12, 39, 91, 95, 98
Mt. Burke 263, 276
Mt. Castelneau 147
Mt. Chester 53, 75
Mt. Foch 147

Mt. Fox 142
Mt. French 70
Mt. Galatea 75, 98
Mt. Indefatigable 110, 114
Mt. Inflexible 86
Mt. Invincible 114
Mt. James Walker 86
Mt. Jellicoe 123
Mt. Jerram 153, 206
Mt. Joffre 133
Mt. Kidd 2, 91, 97
Mt. Lady Macdonald 226
Mt. Lipsett 175
Mt. Lorette 232
Mt. Lougheed 37, 89
Mt. Lyautey 115, 246
Mt. McDougall 231
Mt. Maude 122
Mt. Smith-Dorrien 7
Mt. Packenham 108, 197
Mt. Putnik 121
Mt. Rae 148, 157, 160, 164, 169
Mt. Robertson 70
Mt. Romulus 190
Mt. Rundle 217, 220, 227
Mt. Sarrail 112, 115, 122, 136, 138, 246
Mt. Sir Douglas 63, 64
Mt. Sparrowhawk 39, 43, 91
Mt. Ware 258
Mt. Warspite 114
Mt. Wintour 108
Mt. Worthington 127
Mt. Yamnuska 23, 211
mountain goats 19, 75, 106

Nihahi Ridge 193, 254
North Kananaskis Pass 118
Northover Ridge 1, 124, 130

Old Baldy Mtn 237
Old Baldy Ridge 13, 207, 235
Old Goat Glacier & Mtn 28
Olympic Summit 88
Opal Range 103, 105, 112, 199, 200

Palliser River Valley 122
Paradise Pass 13, 190, 195
Petain Basin 10, 142
Petain Creek 142
Picklejar Lakes 187
Piper Creek canyon 149, 158, 202
Piper Pass 148, 200
Pocaterra Cirque 164

Pocaterra Ridge 164
porcupine 119
Porcupine Creek canyon 231
Powderface Trail 242
Ptarmigan Cirque 13, 169

Rae Lake 154, 160
Raspberry Ridge 267, 273
Rawson Lake 138
Read's Tower 39, 43
Ribbon Creek 92, 104
Ribbon Lake 17, 47, 97
Ribbon Peak 95
Rickert's Pass 184
Rimwall 38
Robertson Glacier 67
Romulus campground 149, 190, 202
Royal Group 132
Rummel Lake and Pass 71

Salter Creek canyon 276
Sheep River Valley 154, 161, 258
Smuts Creek and Pass 58
Snow Peak 58
South Kananaskis Pass 120, 124
Sparrowhawk tarns 13, 39
Spray Lakes Reservoir 28, 31, 35, 44, 48, 53
Spray Mountains 115
Stewart Creek 24
Storm Mtn 172, 182
Sundance Range 73

Talus Lake 190, 202
Tent Ridge 53
Three Isle Lake 15, 124, 130
Three Lakes valley 75
Three Sisters Pass 31
ticks 22
Tombstone Lakes 23, 154
Tombstone Mtn 148, 154, 164, 206
Tombstone Pass 154
Turbine Canyon 118

Warrior Mtn 133
Wasootch Creek & Ridge 207, 231
West Fork Little Elbow River 149, 190, 200
West Wind Pass 35
Whiteman's Pond 221, 224
wildflowers 13, 169, 183, 240, 249, 283
Windtower 35
Windy Peak Hills 13, 283